HEMINGWAY'S DAUGHTER

A Novel

Christine M. Whitehead

Christine Whitehead© Copyright Hadley Press 2020

ISBN: 9798723557581

To Bo.

You know why.

1

June 17, 1961

A mi hija hermosa, to my beautiful Daughter:

Well, Flea! Despite being in prison, also known as a forced hospital stay courtesy of my present wife, I've finished the book, the one for your mother. Finito! I never forgot what you said 13 years ago—that it broke her heart that I never put her in my books; wrote her out of my life, you said. Well, she's in this one, all the way. It's about us and Paris and the way it was then.

And if I live that long—ha! at least another couple weeks!—the dedication will read, "To Finley Hemingway, My Daughter and My Muse."

You still there, Flea, or have I bored you into oblivion already? You knew it was always you, right? Without you, do you think I could have written a page of the finest book that ever came out of this much-battered Midwestern boy's head? "A Single Drop of Red Wine" never would exist without you dancing across each page, hija mia. You were the engine. It's that simple. And that's the one that should have won the Noblitzer Prize (Nobel and Pulitzer together!), if it existed. Should we create one?

And sure, I might have had some vigor injected at times by some of the "others" who shall remain nameless so as not to bitch the fine mood I have going here (I know you hated them, so let's not talk about that). But the unvarnished truth is, I needed you, only you, to be proud of the old man, that you were Hemingway's Daughter with a capital "D." Not embarrassed or ashamed. Made me try for more each time I sat down to write, one sentence, then another. Sometimes flowing, sometimes drilling.

I'm calling the new one "A Moveable Feast." And it will make her immortal. Love can do that.

I love you, kid. Forever. No way around it. See you in your dreams.

Con todo mi amor siempre, Papa.

With all my love always. That was the last letter I got from him and while a bit garbled, it was him, like he always was. A bit of Spanish thrown in and some of his own odd phrasing. If I didn't know better, I wouldn't have guessed how ill he was.

He was gone two weeks later. The highs and lows of living with him were over and the loss of both was as excruciating as a finger bent to the breaking point, then twisted off to be sure you appreciated the pain the first time around. Still, without knowing it, he'd thrown me a lifeline. I now knew. Finally, after thirty-six years, I knew.

2

You can't get away from yourself by moving from one place to another.

~ Ernest Hemingway, *The Sun Also Rises*

I had four Finn Hemingway Family Reality Rules, four immutable truths about my family that in one way or another bled into every aspect of my life.

Family Reality Rule #1: My mother always got her way. My father's guilt about leaving my mother shortly after I was born to marry her good friend, Pauline Pfeiffer, meant he always agreed to whatever she wanted as to us kids. He might commiserate with me, but he felt he'd forfeited the right to wrangle with Mother about raising my older brother, Jack, and me. Her decisions were final, based on her occupation of the moral high ground.

Consequently, despite my father being opposed to girls' boarding schools, which stressed smiling pretty to snare an accomplished husband instead of being accomplished yourself, I was shipped to The Ellsworth School for Girls in Greenwich, Connecticut, when I was fourteen. I'd lived happily in Chicago with my brother, my mother, and her new husband since I was nine, and was horrified at the prospect of leaving. We lived in Paris before the move to Chicago and it was hard enough making that move, but now another move that I had no voice in? It felt unfair.

"It will be grand, Flea," Papa said unconvincingly in our Sunday night phone call the week before my departure. "Your mother said they're letting you skip a grade, and the riding program is first-rate. And they have a debating club. Great for a budding trial lawyer, honey. I'll be up to visit you to see how it's going."

"But I love Chicago," I said, "and it's your hometown! Your roots and family are here, Papa." I hoped to draw on some vestigial sentimental pull with this manipulative comment.

"Nice hustle, Flea," he chuckled, "but I haven't been to Chicago in over twenty years, and they didn't like me all that much when I was there—*especially* my family. But I'll see you in a few weeks in Connecticut, honey."

Family Reality Rule #2: My father was 100 percent reliable 60 percent of the time, and that was when he was sober. I knew he would never visit me in Connecticut. He was too busy. He meant what he said as he was saying it, but between trips to Spain in support of the anti-Franco forces, his social life, and his writing, he seldom came through. When you tossed in his drinking days, his 60 percent reliability rating dove to 25 percent, and his drinking days were often. In fact, his drinking deserves a stand-alone rule, but I'll wrap it into this one.

Family Reality Rule #3: My father was a maverick force who loomed large, famous for all the right and wrong reasons, all of which got reflected onto me, and I had to live with that. Sometimes I made up a fake name to stroll through life anonymously, without associations being tagged to me, and sometimes I enjoyed being on the periphery of his fame. He was either an acclaimed literary icon or a denounced communist degenerate, depending on the audience. I just never knew what territory I was in as I waited for the guilt by association/gut punch, or the jolly arm around the shoulder with whispers of, "Wow, you've got his dark eyes. You look just like him. Do you write too?" or, "I heard he always wanted a daughter. You must have been his favorite. So what's he *really* like, Flea?" They used his nickname for me like they *really* knew me.

My father was Papa to the world, and every woman he took a liking to even slightly—and they were legion—was called "daughter" by him. I resented the heck out of it. It wasn't that I wondered if he loved me. He did. But I spent much of my life wondering if I would ever be as necessary to him as he was to me. And the only way to be necessary to him was to play a part in his writing, the part of him he believed to be the only thing that justified his existence. It was all that truly mattered to him. If I didn't impact that part of him, I was his pleasant and loved, but not essential, biological, sidekick.

Finally, Finn Hemingway's Family Reality Rule #4, and this is the really important one: Love always ends for us, and usually, it ends badly. From my father, I learned well the lesson that love can turn on you like a black mamba, and lasting love is a mirage. Joy and bonhomie with your beloved at 10:00 a.m. could be a mere preface to depression and drunken hostility roaring in at 6:00 p.m. You dote on me today, you dote on me not tomorrow.

We Hemingways did not excel at blissful eternal love. We lacked the skills, and maybe the familial destiny, for forever love. I didn't want to believe this fact, but it was what I saw from the time I was a kid and watched my mother regularly dabbing red eyes and holding *The Sun Also Rises* open to its dedication to her and my brother. She'd swipe a tear, then smile, hoping I wouldn't see, but I saw. I saw that being left behind by someone you adored left a wound that lingered, partially exposed, forever. That was the Hemingway love doom at its most toxic. My mother, Hadley Richardson Hemingway Mowrer, had remarried, but she never got over my father. Tears in the dark years after a divorce and remarriage were hardly the happy-ever-after I dreamed of.

And as to my father and his various women and wives—well, nothing lasted. I would become fond of a new woman only to have her gone the next time I visited. The wives stayed longer, but the decline in each relationship—and each one began with epic passion—was obvious each summer and Christmas when I visited my father. There was a blaze, then a sputter, then an end.

From my observation, it was far better never to have loved at all than to be left crying in the dark. Even Shakespeare got it wrong sometimes.

Dragging all of my Reality Rules with me, I headed to Ellsworth School for Girls hoping it was the start of my route to becoming a female Clarence Darrow as I had no interest in being Mrs. Darrow. And above all, I intended to defy and eradicate Reality Rule # 4, at least as to me. It was too dire to be countenanced.

3

"The bulls are my best friends."

I translated to Brett.

"You kill your friends?" she asked.

"Always," he said in English, and laughed. "So they don't kill me."

~ Ernest Hemingway, *The Sun Also Rises*

September 1939

It was ironic that the least-liked and most-feared girl in the sophomore class at the Ellsworth School was also the most popular. Ellsworth had a quasi-feudal system with old money at the top, new money was next, smart girls whose families could pay their way followed (this is where I fell), and at rock-bottom were bright scholarship girls who worked in the kitchens and were identifiable by their gray uniforms as they ran from class to scullery. The top-tier girls came from elite private schools in Manhattan or Boston, and they were the rulers.

I had a single room on the third floor of an old, four-story brick building. My room was just about the same as every other room on the floor: cream walls, wide-board floors, and a small-paned window. I was one of the lucky ones, though, with a working fireplace. Mother and I had arrived in a Pontiac stuffed with things I couldn't live without. As we dragged the seemingly endless boxes up the three flights, I dreamed of all the doors that would open to me over the next few years here.

Mother made up the bed with fresh, white linens as I threw down the two red oriental rugs we'd hauled from Chicago. Then I tacked up photos of my Jack Russell terrier, Harriet, my horse, Sassafras, and two of my father and me. After four hours of folding, stacking, and hanging clothes, Mother said with a break in her voice, "Shall I get on the road, Finn? Will you be all right here, darling?"

I bounced a little on the bed, then stood. I didn't want her to worry. "I'll be fine. Thank you for your help, Mother. I know you have a long drive back to Chicago."

Mother nodded, an uncertain look in her eyes, then she stepped in and wrapped me in a tight, almost desperate hug. I held her hard. Then we both relaxed, a little embarrassed. She straightened and smiled.

"Your horse will arrive tomorrow, Finn. Just remember, when things get rough—if they do—that you're the best of your father and me: strong, and resilient, and so kind. Those things will always get you through." She paused, then held me at arm's length. She was tall, but I was already taller. She shook me a little. "And yes, that fool Zelda Fitzgerald was right. You *do* look like your father, but in a remarkable way all your own. Ernest Hemingway was always the handsomest man I'd ever met, and those looks translate gorgeously to a young woman. I love you, Finn."

My mother was rarely demonstrative, and I was touched by her unexpected and heartfelt words. Usually, she was more, "Buck up. Life is like that sometimes, so stop feeling sorry for yourself." She smiled, quickly turned, skirt swirling, and was gone. I felt very alone as I glanced around my room and at the photos of home and family.

Still, the next morning I woke with a smile mortared to my face, ready to make the best of it. I flung open my dormitory door only to find a flurry of newspaper clippings tacked to the door detailing my father's exploits. ***BANNED IN BOSTON, IRELAND! THE SUN ALSO RISES (AND SETS!) ON HEMINGWAY; TO HAVE OR HAVE NOT: WE WON'T HAVE IT HERE! BURN THAT BOOK: HEMINGWAY ON FIRE! COMMUNISM, SEX, AND FILTH? NO THANK YOU, MR. HEMINGWAY!***

I gritted my teeth. *Well, isn't this a nice welcome.* I was accustomed to whispers in my wake about the degenerate Hemingway but not to in-my-face insults. I seethed as I scurried to tear down the wreckage before the other girls spied it. Guilt by association: Reality Rule #3.

Gertie, a girl I'd met the day before at the barn, opened her door and stared as I finished the last of the removal. She pulled one of the articles from the trash, scanned it, then crumpled it and threw it back. She shook her head, curly brown hair swinging, and sighed.

Already dressed in the school uniform of a navy skirt, white blouse, and saddle shoes, she said, "Oh, Finn. I'm so sorry. Most of the girls are nice, but one—Prill Lamont—isn't. She's a sophomore like us, and the prettiest girl in the school. She runs everything, and knows all the cutest boys at the prep schools. You can't miss her: blonde, tiny, stuck-up. She has a pack of three girls, and I saw her moving in yesterday. We all got the school newsletter this summer telling us who the new girls would be. You know, those stupid things." Gertie put on a voice as if reading from a wedding announcement. "*Finley Hemingway, of Chicago and Cuba, daughter of Ernest Hemingway and Hadley Hemingway Mowrer.*"

Then she continued in her normal voice. "We all know who your father is—I mean, we read *TIME* magazine's People section—and Prill said some things." Gertie looked down. "Not nice things. Just ignore her. Last year, she picked on some scholarship girl to the point of her dropping out of school. Don't let it get to you."

"I won't," I said, crossing my arms over my chest, but still chagrined that I'd made an enemy before my first breakfast here.

The remaining slice of my designs for an easy first day flew skyward when the initial thing my English teacher said when I answered her question about Shakespearean tragedies was, "Finley, lose that Midwestern flat twang and French inflection as soon as possible. They do you no favors." She turned away, and the class tittered. I'd lived in Paris for the first nine years of my life and spoke French almost before I spoke English. I did sometimes, when nervous, say words with a French accent or phrasing. I flushed and looked down.

A girl in the front row with white-blonde hair and a gorgeous face turned around. "Or maybe you can speak Spanish for us if your English isn't good enough, Señorita Hemingway! But no Spanish obscenities, please—given your family history and all."

The teacher cut in, "I don't recall inviting you to comment, Miss Lamont."

The girl turned away with a smirk: Prill Lamont. Old-money girl meets pays-her-way girl.

I didn't complain about the dead mouse in my bed, the short-sheeting, or the peanut butter in my riding boot. I had three brothers and was used to much worse. Prill's next attack, though, was painful. I was at the barn putting away my horse, Sassafras, when Prill and Joannie Janssen, one of Prill's group, strolled down the aisle. Joannie's horse was next to mine, and Prill, as usual, was braying about her weekend.

"God, Joannie! You would love Danny Delano. He's the president's nephew, or cousin—or something. Next time, come with us! Nick couldn't make it, but we had a terrific time."

Joannie moaned, "I miss everything good! My parents won't let me go off campus, ever!"

I took a breath. So far, I hadn't found a good friend at Ellsworth. Although Gertie was lovely, she'd made her friends her first year, and the position of confidante was definitely taken by Helen Vandersen. But Joannie Janssen loved her horse like I loved Sassafras. Maybe Joannie wasn't that bad.

As both girls leaned against Birthday Boy's stall door, laughing and whispering, I stuck my hands deep into my jacket pockets and decided to take a chance. I stepped into the aisle and smiled broadly.

"Hey, Prill, Joannie," I said. "Great day for riding, right? I wondered if you'd like to listen to some records in my room tonight. I just got Glenn Miller's 'Moonlight Serenade.'"

Prill frowned like a bad smell had wafted by. She then flipped her hair over her shoulder, eyed me up and down, and said in a voice that could be heard in Vermont, "Wow! You really *are* freakishly tall, Finn. Not much chance of getting a boyfriend, being so gigantic." She tilted her head and pointed. "And it seems, unfortunately, you ended up with a boy's nose and brows by mistake. Tragic when that happens." She shook her head three quick shakes as if it were all too incredible before turning away, laughing. "Come on. Let's go, Joannie."

Joannie looked like she might cry, but then spun and followed Prill out of the barn. I reddened and looked around to see how many of the girls heard. Most had resumed their chores, but one girl I didn't know yet said from across the aisle, "She's mean. Ignore her, Finn."

"I will. Thanks," I said more nonchalantly than I felt as I fumbled with Sassafras's halter, then quietly shut his stall door.

4

I don't know. There isn't always an explanation for everything.

~ Ernest Hemingway, *The Sun Also Rises*

Prill's words were not a surprise. I'd known since I was eight that I wasn't pretty when no less a beauty than Zelda Fitzgerald, a long-time family friend, told me so. The look of the day was petite, pert nose and, thin, penciled brows, like Claudette Colbert or Jean Arthur. I was far from that ideal.

Mother, my brother Jack, and I, were still living in Paris at the time Zelda made her pronouncement. On that spring afternoon, as I sat cross-legged on the red Heriz rug, dressing a doll, Zelda was perched on the couch behind me in a shiny, green flapper dress, slim legs crossed at the knee. She took a drag of her cigarette, sucking in the air hard. When I held up my doll for her to see, she stared off as the tip of her cigarette glowed, then faltered. She twisted and blew a perfect smoke ring over her right shoulder.

Suddenly, as quick as a king cobra, her hand shot out. Sharp fingers locked into my bony shoulder hollow and jerked me up. Surprised, I regarded her with my dark eyes and she gazed back with her own hard, blue ones. With my chin in her hand, she said to her husband, Scott, as if I weren't there, "What a shame she takes so strongly after Ernest. Yes, the red hair is Hadley's and it's lovely. But her jaw is too strong, her nose too straight, her brows too heavy, and her gaze too direct with those . . . oh, Hemingway eyes. No fineness. Too tall, not pretty. She'll never inspire poetry." She said it with disgust, dropped her hand from my face, and turned away. "Pity."

My mother's mouth opened, then shut, shocked into speechlessness. I blinked, eyes burning as I still stood facing Zelda, unable to move.

Scott, always kind, reached over and touched my arm. He looked beautiful and golden in his three-piece suit. He said quickly, "Don't mind her, Finn. She's a tease. You're lovely, sweetheart." Then he added in a voice with some menace, "Zelda, you are such a joker. But remember, dear, children don't always see the humor."

She looked at him and sniffed. She was the only person I knew with no verbal filter. She was also the only woman I knew who was not only *not* attracted to my father, but who truly hated him. The feeling was mutual.

After Prill's insult at the barn, I felt the same torrent of despair that swamped me the day Zelda pronounced me fatally lacking. *No fineness; will never inspire poetry.*

When I got back to my room, I stared out the window for a few minutes as the sky darkened. I was bewildered by Prill's clearly intentional cruelty, and wondered how she could so dislike someone she didn't know. I wanted badly to be the girl who didn't care what anyone said, but I also wanted friends to laugh with, like I had in Chicago. I wanted to be a lawyer to find fairness for others, but didn't yet know how to push back at unfairness aimed at me.

I glanced at the calendar and desperately wanted to go home. I wanted to see my wild but loyal little dog, and to sit on the banks of Lake Michigan laughing with my best friend, Susan, and teasing my brother as we all ate Chicago pizza around the kitchen table. Only the thought of being with my father at Christmas in two months made being here feel even close to tolerable. With him, everything was fun, even making a routine breakfast. He'd say, "Flea, you cover the right flank with those three eggs and don't let your brothers get near that slab of bread or the *leche* (milk) over there. Old Cat is going behind enemy lines with lifesaving intelligence for our boys in the trenches." One of his many cats would sit calmly blinking and looking noble.

Then there were all of his friends. On any given evening, Humphrey Bogart and Lauren Bacall might be mixing martinis on the back patio while Gary Cooper, Papa, and Ava Gardner manned the grill as Marlene Dietrich critiqued their technique from the sidelines: *Papa, mein bärchen, zat one is under done. And Ava, mein liebling, enough flipping.* It was like having the preeminent seat at an improvisational theater of the absurd.

It wasn't their fame that was so alluring—although it was—but their familiarity with my father, the inside jokes. And when I was with him, I was inside the circle. They'd smoke, drink, laugh, name-drop, pound the table, and tell wild stories as I sat on the floor laughing along with them. When I held up Papa's beloved, small, good-natured mongrel, Negrita, and danced around with her to big band music, waving her paw energetically at them, they hooted and clapped like it was hilarious. They laughed not because it was that cute, but because they liked me, and because I was Hemingway's daughter, and because we were all enjoying the thick, Cuban night air and the pleasure of being alive here together. When I had to go back home at the end of each summer, it was like going from Technicolor to gray. He was that good.

I stared at my calendar again. Prill had hit my greatest vulnerabilities in a grand, lucky, exploding bull's-eye. Actually, she'd hit all of the Family Rules that made my situation inescapable. Rule #1: My mother wanted me here and she always won, so I was stuck with no choices. Rule #2: My father couldn't give me a reprieve because he was inconsistent (and see Rule #1). Rule #3: Prill unearthed the baggage that came with being a Hemingway and blew it up as big as she could in this tiny fiefdom. I was the daughter of a libertine whose books were banned routinely and who was declared by some to be a communist writer of deviant themes. And Rule #4: While Prill harped on my looks, what I heard above all else was, "You are cursed, and all of your family is cursed, giant girl. You are the spawn of evil, of someone worshipped as a false god, and who never has had lasting love himself and you never will either. You're incapable of it." *Love always ends, and usually badly for us Hemingways.*

I despised Prill's viciousness and sense of superiority, preying on those she felt were weaker than she was. But her accusations crawled into the corners of my mind, where they found purchase. Still, I vowed never to be shamed the next time I had a showdown with Prill Lamont.

I knew it would be soon.

5

Brett was damned good-looking. She wore a slipover jersey sweater and a tweed skirt, and her hair was brushed back like a boy's. She started all that. She was built with curves like the hull of a racing yacht and you missed none of it with that wool jersey.

~ Ernest Hemingway, *The Sun Also Rises*

October 10, 1939

Hola Flea:

Sorry I couldn't get up to Connecticut. I know I promised, but I just got back from Spain and things went badly for our side. Taking stock of our options is taking more time than I thought it would. And then, at home with Pauline and the boys, well, if I hired someone to run my life badly, he couldn't have done a more complete job of it than I have. Pauline is hanging in. Gig and Mouse are ok. Can't wait for Christmas to see you, hija mia!

Your mother mentioned a girl is picking on you at the school. I wish I could make it all go away, querida, but I can't. The first and final thing you have to do in this world is last it, and not be smashed by it or by small people like this Prill. I'm sorry, Flea. There are idiots everywhere, and you have to endure them until *they tire of their petty games or when all else is exhausted, knock them out—figuratively I mean, or your mother will kill me. Let them know you're a fighter and won't ever be broken. Not ever. Se fuerte! Be strong.*

Working hard on "Bell Tolls." Should come out next year. Max thinks it's swell and could be something fine. Jaysus! You never know where your personas are going to end up! Pilar started out as a minor character, and then she just grabbed the plot by the horns and took off with it. Not much I could do about it, since she couldn't be argued out of it.

I'm heading back to Spain soon. Worried about a few friends left there. I'll be up in a couple months to see you ride. Seguro! For sure!

Con amor (or is it chile con carne?) And don't change ever, Flea. Don't forget our talk way back when re: Zeldommage! Papa

I smiled, pleased that Max Perkins, Papa's editor at Scribner's, liked the book, and I laughed at the comment about Pilar, the secondary heroine in his book. I could see Papa shrugging as he paced in his study as if his literary creations sprang forth determining their own plot points. I frowned too. He would be in Connecticut in a couple of months to see me ride? *Seguro* my foot! I knew he wouldn't be, but I couldn't help hoping. I pictured me taking scary jumps higher than he expected of me, and him being bowled over by my courage, proud of me.

He never did see me ride until I rode in Madison Square Garden when I was seventeen, some three years later. See Finn Hemingway Family Rule #2: 100 percent reliable 25–60 percent of the time.

Still, he took with one hand but gave with the other. I told him about Zelda's "you'll never inspire poetry" speech the summer after it happened. I spied the photo of him and Marlene Dietrich on the bookshelf as we read in his study as we did every afternoon, and I slumped in my chair. "I'm never going to be pretty, like Mrs. Dietrich, am I, Papa?"

Papa was in his khakis and a rumpled, blue shirt, sleeves rolled up, his back to me as he hunted through the bookshelves for his battered copy of *Anna Karenina*. He twisted around and peered at me over his shoulder. Then he stared out the window, hand rubbing his forehead with a blank expression on his face as if to say, "A mere world-famous writer can't be expected to deal with this question from his eight-year-old daughter." Then he gamely suspended his search, walked slowly over to his favorite chair, and lowered himself into it. "Flea, take a seat, would you, please?"

He gestured to the straight-backed chair across from him and I shuffled over to it. I was a little nervous to hear his next words, and was painfully aware of a big ketchup stain on my lavender t-shirt from lunch.

Papa gazed out the window for so long I thought he'd forgotten me. Then he fixed his chestnut-colored eyes onto my own, took a deep breath, and blew it out slowly.

"Where in the *hell* did that come from, Flea?"

I looked at my hands, then blurted, "Mrs. Fitzgerald said my jaw is too strong. And my nose is too straight, and that I have your eyes—and that's bad. And I'm not pretty. And I'll never inspire poetry." I was out of breath when I finished.

Papa colored, a high crimson on his cheekbones, a sure sign of anger. His fists flexed and I heard him mutter, "That goddamned infernal lunatic!"

He took a sip of his drink, slapped it down, and leaned closer. "Okay, Flea, listen up. Zelda wouldn't know true beauty from a vaudeville clown. Zeldommage!"

I'd lived in France my whole life up to then and I knew he was playing on the phrase *"Quel dommage"*—meaning "What a shame." I smiled a little.

He leaned forward again. "For starters, you *are* in fact going to be a beauty. And, honestly, in some ways, I wish you weren't, because it's a lazy way some women have of making their splash in the world without really knowing what they're capable of. However, second, and more importantly, you are more than pretty because you are unique, not cookie-cutter, where everything is even. It's the unusual that's beautiful, Flea. Remember that. Pretty, pff..." He waved his hand dismissively. "Pretty isn't something that lasts or has value, Flea. It's what you add to it, the work, the discipline to skip easy things to accomplish the harder ones. Like you being a lawyer. That's not for the ordinary. It's going to be hard, at times impossible, and you'll want to quit, but you won't, because you're made of stronger stuff. Pretty? That's nothing."

I was not convinced. "But Mrs. Mason and Mrs. Dietrich are so pretty that even you want to be around them all the time. All the men do." Jane Mason was a gorgeous socialite who lived in Cuba but was in Key West often. She was a favorite of my father's.

Papa threw back his head and laughed so loudly that Pauline poked her head into the room. She said, "What's so funny?"

"Flea. She's amusing me beyond reason."

Pauline smiled and held up a hand as if to say, "Fine you two! Whatever it is!" She backed out and closed the door. Papa walked over to me and stooped to my level, balanced on his haunches.

"Here's the thing, Flea—and this is a little grown-up. Yes, both of those women are easy on the eyes, but I wouldn't have either of them around here for more than a minute if they didn't have the rest. Jane is an expert sailor, a great storyteller, and a swell artist. The Kraut is brilliant. She's worked hard, and no one gave her a free ride even though she is beautiful. She has substance and honor, and the pretty face is way beside the point. Way beside the point. Do you understand?"

I kind of did. Papa touched my face gently.

"Flea, you'll have the beauty, and dammit to Hell, you *will* inspire poetry. But don't put any stock in it. It's quicksilver, and nothing to count on. Develop the rest, and you'll be a winner no matter what life throws at you. Never forget that."

I'd nodded, but Zelda's words still felt like a death sentence that even my father's comments couldn't commute. I was his daughter, after all, and Zelda was an uncensored albeit crazy truthteller.

Still, I needed to find a reason to stay here at Ellsworth or invent a reason to get out—one or the other—and soon.

6

You'll lose it if you talk about it.

~ Ernest Hemingway, *The Sun Also Rises*

All grim things seemed to attach to me at Ellsworth. While my grades were fine and the riding was superb, all else was bleak. No friends, family distant, my disobedient but loyal Jack Russell terrier was home in Chicago, and me, an object of ridicule here, a Mongrel out of my depth in Greenwich, Connecticut. Now, on top of all else, I was sick.

I'd had an aching throat for a week. It felt like I was consuming knives with each swallow—never once had this sort of pain in Paris or Chicago—and I'd delayed going to the infirmary because it looked like the picture of despair: a low cement building at the edge of campus with no grace or charm. But when I could barely croak out a few words in my weekly call with my father, he bellowed, "Flea! Get the hell to a doctor, or I'll come up there on the next plane."

The infirmary was as expected, a sad, pea-green little place with tiny, square rooms spoking off a central nursing station. A frowning nurse pointed, and within two minutes, I was in a room with two cots, a cabinet between the beds, and one window looking out at treetops and sky. Venetian blinds were drawn up and the place smelled like Comet cleanser.

Another second-year student was in the bed next to me. I didn't know her, but I knew who she was. She'd starred in the fall concert and was now hospitalized for a broken arm she'd earned acting on a dare to jump off a second-floor balcony while drunk. The school was about to expel her, but a hefty donation from her father encouraged the school to give her a second chance. When she told me that part she wore an apologetic, crooked smile, half making fun of the school and half making fun of herself.

"That's kind of neat, though," I said. "Maybe they'll use the donation for one of those mattresses for the next girl who jumps."

I was secretly thrilled by her boldness in breaking the school rules, as well as her arm in one grand gesture, but I'd hate incurring Papa's wrath and possible appearance here. The last time I got in trouble was in Chicago a year ago, when I'd been caught smoking under the bleachers with my best friend as we loudly sang "God Bless America" until the girls' softball coach stuck her head under the planks and yelled, "To the principal's office. Now!"

I was confined to my room except for classes for two weeks. Papa got me on the phone and simply said, "Don't smoke, Flea. I did during the war, but don't even smoke the Cuban cigars as much as I used to. Just stog on special occasions. Bad for you, and it stinks." Papa made up words sometimes. *Stog?* Somehow, you always knew what he meant. He also threw in Spanish if he thought it fit. Even though he didn't yell at me that day, I was embarrassed that he was seeing me in a bad light.

The girl in the other cot now smiled a sweet smile. "You're funny." She held out her unbroken arm, the left one, and we shook across the space between our cots.

She said, "I'm Jeddrah James."

"And I'm Finn Hemingway."

"Hemingway's daughter, right? I read the newsletter about your enrollment. And Finn, like Huck?"

"Yes and yes. And your name's Jeddrah? I've never heard that before."

"I know," she said, miserably. "No one has. I sound like an outlaw. I wish I were named Sally."

"Oh no. I love Jeddrah. It sounds like the wind blowing across the desert." I was thinking we all want what we don't have.

Jeddrah's face lit up. I looked at her more closely. She was tiny, only five foot one or so, and not more than a hundred pounds. She had straight, yellow-blonde hair halfway down her back, blueberry eyes and a large, full mouth that smiled without looking happy. And she had those Greta Garbo eyes, lots of upper lid even when her eyes were open. A Gatsby Girl: new money and lovely.

"I'll tell you my story, and then you tell me yours," she said.

Jeddrah lived in New York City. Her parents were divorced and unfriendly. One lived on the East Side and the other on the West Side. Jeddrah's father was a banker and her mother, a famous socialite. A car came for her on vacations, and she never knew if she'd be seeing her mother or her father until she saw on which side of Central Park the car ended up. They never visited here.

"If I want to know what my father is up to, I read the financial pages. If I want to see my mother, I look on the society page," Jeddrah said. "That's how I know who her new lover is and if she's in London or Buenos Aires. I'm happy they stay away. More time for me to party, not that they'd notice."

I didn't say anything, but I wondered if that's why Jeddrah drank. She looked away, her blonde hair swinging, then she spoke brightly. "How do you like The Ellsworth School for Girls so far, or as I like to think of it, The Ellsworth School for Effete Girls?"

I laughed, then thought about that for a moment. "I miss my mother, my dog, and some of my friends, but I like the riding here and the classes. I don't like Prill Lamont."

Jeddrah laughed. "Join the group. She's a bully, but runs the social life here, so there's that. And she did that mean thing to you, right? Took your clothes in gym or something?"

I winced, just remembering it. "Yeah, she did."

Jeddrah paused. "So, what's it like having the great Ernest Hemingway as your father?"

I thought about that. What *was* it like? I took in a breath, then blew out the air. "It's kind of like having this big spotlight all around, but it's never on you. We have the same birthday, but he gets three thousand cards from around the world, and I get five from my family. And people are interested in you only because of him. They'll ask, do you like to go fishing *with your father*? Are you spending Christmas *with your father*? Sometimes, they'll call me 'Flea'—his nickname for me—like they actually know me. They've read about our family, you know, from the articles written about him. They all want to know what he's *really* like. And I can't answer that. He's so many things and he's different at home than in public, so I never can answer." I shrugged. "But it's OK. I'm not the star. No one really sees me."

Jeddrah was silent, then said, "But does he? See you, I mean."

I picked at my blanket. "Sometimes." I lifted my head to see Jeddrah nodding. Just thinking about him made me feel excited, but then I thought about the rest. "But then he has meetings, and his friends, and his interviews, and his writing. He's on his second marriage. Pauline's nice, but he's losing interest in her, and I sometimes wonder if he'll lose interest in me, kind of like he did with my mother and some of his friends, and now in Pauline . . . and then he may never visit me at all, or maybe replace me." I was kneading the blanket now like a nervous cat.

Jeddrah was shaking her head. What I'd wanted to say was: *Yes, he sees clear to my soul when he makes the time to look.*

Then Jeddrah, hands clasped hard, said, "No, he won't do that. You have the same birthday. You are bound by love and destiny for life."

I laughed, wanting to believe her.

Jeddrah laughed too. "Yeah. Well, at least it's interesting, right? I mean, he's always doing stuff, fishing, traveling, movie stars hanging around, by the looks of the magazines."

I paused, recalling that just a week ago, Dean Byrne had asked me if my father would consider being the Guest of Honor at our Art Week in April at the school. I'd been caught off guard. I knew my father was famous in his writing world. A movie had been made of *A Farewell to Arms*; his African safari resulted in *Green Hills of Africa* and *The Snows of Kilimanjaro*, both of which were well-received and created more publicity.

Still, to me he was just Papa: a man who hated to wear ties and almost never did, who loved his cats and dogs like family members, who flipped trout on our grill like a short-order chef, who read *Anna Karenina* at least once a year, who made all of us laugh with his funny jokes and mimicking of voices, and who made being in his shadow feel better than sharing the limelight with anyone else.

I shook my head, then looked back at Jeddrah, who looked expectant. "I'm not usually doing any of it with him." I took a sip of water. "I get my hopes up, and sometimes it happens, but mostly, it doesn't. But you know what's weird? When it *does* happen, I forgive him for all the times he missed."

"It's not weird. Love is forgiving, and then when he does include you, it's like you matter."

I nodded. "I feel bad though, because my mother's the one who makes time, but he's the one I want. Is that terrible to say?" I stared at my hands, a little embarrassed. Jeddrah was so honest about her family flaws and disappointments that I felt able to talk about my own.

Jeddrah shook her head. "No, it's just real. It's your heart." She took her good hand and patted her heart. "Do you write too? In the blood, so to speak?"

I hesitated, not wanting to seem too ambitious or just too weird. Then I plunged in. "No. I'm going to be a trial lawyer. It's all I've ever wanted."

Jeddrah's blue eyes went wide. "Really? When did you know that was what you wanted to do?"

"I knew when I saw men dying after the hurricane a few years ago on Key West. I was helping my father get aid and food to them. They were vets who had no help, no money for their families, no one rescuing them even though they were working for the government and fought in the war for this country. I want to do something to try to make things better. Help people." I shrugged, feeling a little grandiose, but she bobbed her head.

I changed the subject and pointed at her cast. "So, is that thing itchy?"

Jeddrah stuck her finger into the cast as far as she could, then sighed in frustration. "Yeah. I need a chopstick or a pipe cleaner or something. Hey, when we get out of here, and I get this thing off, we can do stuff together. You ride, right?"

"Yeah. Do you?" My riding attire gave me away.

"No, but I'm trainable. I love animals of any kind." Jeddrah looked eager as she pushed herself upright, not an easy task with one arm totally useless. "You can show me what to do and I'll do it. Deal?"

She held out her good hand again, this time vertical in the air, and we gently touched palms.

"Deal," I said.

"And I think you being a lawyer is wonderful. You'll be a humdinger!"

I felt understood in that moment. I lowered my head and looked at my hands. "Thank you, Jeddrah. I'll try my best."

Jeddrah nodded, and it felt like the first line of a long, exquisite poem had just been written in the air between us. I had a friend, and I felt braver.

7

Everyone behaves badly—given the chance.

~ Ernest Hemingway, *The Sun Also Rises*

By Christmas, Jeddrah and I were inseparable. Together, we plotted against Prillie and how I would beat Joannie Janssen in the Southampton Classic. After that, look out Madison Square Garden. I wasn't sure I could beat the reigning champion, Jacqueline Bouvier, who was bogarting all the ribbons on the East Coast, but I'd try.

I called Papa to ask if I could bring Jeddrah home with me for Christmas.

"Sure, Flea. Love to meet your friends. The more the merrier."

When he and Pauline separated, he apparently decided that Key West was not a big enough island for both of them so he found a fresh island: Cuba. He had a "fresh" lady too. I felt terrible for Pauline, even when Jack reported that in addition to being beautiful, this new one, Martha, was a real peach.

"What is she like?" I reluctantly asked when Jack told me about it over the phone. I wanted to know, and I didn't. It was odd and not particularly comfortable to have a father who was dating.

"She's gorgeous, with legs that go on forever and wavy, blonde hair. Can't believe someone like that is with Papa. And young!" Jack gushed.

I sighed at the unsatisfying description, realizing it was the best that could be expected from an eighteen-year-old boy. Jack was in his last year at The Storm King School, a boarding school north of New York City, and he recently met up with Papa in Manhattan, and Martha was there.

"Get a grip, Jack. I didn't ask what she looked like. I asked what she's like."

"Oh." He paused, as if stumped. "Well, she's friendly and nice, just came right up to me and said, 'You must be Bumby. I'm Marty.'"

That made me pause, thinking about Pauline and her kindness to Jack and me, of the sadness Patrick and Gregory must feel. I'd never really lived with my father, but they had, so were bound to miss his daily presence as I never had.

As it turned out, my father was already divorced and had married Martha shortly thereafter. None of us kids were at the wedding or even knew about it until after. By the time Christmas came, Papa had been married for a month.

I felt hurt that Papa hadn't included us or at least told me about it before I read it in the newspaper. When I asked him why he hadn't told us, he rubbed his head. "Geez, Flea, didn't think of it. I just wanted to pin it all down. Got married in Cheyenne, Wyoming. A wedding is nothing. Just a formality. Don't worry. You'll have lots of time to get to know Marty."

Papa missed my point. I knew I would meet Martha. What I wanted was to be *part* of it. I wanted to know before the world knew. I wanted to put on a yellow, flowered dress that floated around my ankles, and to carry a nosegay down the aisle as a bridesmaid while Pachelbel's *Canon* played, and to help Martha with her hair, and to stand up as Papa's family when he vowed to love and stay with this woman forever—again—whoever she was. Instead, Jack and I congregated that Christmas in Cuba after he was already married and met the new Mrs. Hemingway.

Jeddrah was thrilled to be in Cuba with me and enjoyed the lively chats we all had with Papa around the dinner table. Jedd bloomed like one of the sunflowers in the garden, always tilting her head toward the sun and smiling.

"You mean he stops working when you're here?" Jeddrah asked.

"Well, not completely, but he writes in the morning and takes the afternoon off to be with us."

"That's really nice."

The farm was outside Havana, and very run-down when Marty and Papa took it over. However, it boasted ten acres of restorable gardens, cow fields, a ramshackle tennis court, and a pool. The house was limestone, long and low, and enjoyed a stunning view of Havana, which shone like a twinkling jewel at night.

When I arrived, I took in its well-worn, deep leather sofas, simple, polished wooden tables, unadorned beds, and African tribal rugs on tiled floors. The Key West house was sophisticated and stylish, but in Cuba, everything was soft, squishy, and comfortable. Most of the time, we all were in bathing suits with bare feet tucked up on sofas and chairs and a cat or dog in our laps. Or for a change, I'd sit on the front limestone steps, pillow cushioning my back, book in hand, and breathe in the thick air and feel the hot breezes on bare arms and legs. I loved it.

Papa was at his best on that visit, teasing us, taking us fishing, swimming with us, and entertaining us at the best little seafood dive in Havana. He drank, but it was controlled, and he was always relaxed on his boat, *Pilar*, where we all enjoyed the afternoon sunsets.

Martha actually was lovely. She was tall, blonde, and easygoing. She had her own work, and often ducked into her bedroom to write or edit. Initially, I had mixed feelings about her. On the one hand, my father seemed happy whenever she joined us on the boat or at a jai alai game and she was solicitous of Jack, Jedd, and me. On the other hand, I felt disloyal to Pauline. Martha was, after all, the temptress who'd pulled Papa away from Pauline, according to Patrick. I felt that way about most of Papa's lady friends: drawn to them and repelled by them.

As I sat by the pool sunning, Martha's presence brought back memories of Jane Mason, one of Papa's other women to whom I became quite attached when Papa lived in Key West. Jane was a strawberry blonde with violet eyes—and a husband. I studied her like an exotic species of butterfly. She was funny and breath-catchingly beautiful, and didn't make trite comments about my height or red hair as so many of my father's other women did. Instead, the day I met her, she said, "So, Finn, do you want to get on the back of my motorcycle and feel the wind in your hair?"

She called over to my father, who was holding court around a bocce game. "Papa, can Finn come with me for an hour or so?"

My father looked up. "Ask Flea. She can speak for herself."

I nodded vigorously, and he gave Jane a thumbs-up, then said, "Take good care of my girl."

Jane saluted like the first mate. My father saluted back, then winked at me. I blushed, then I trotted off with Jane.

We careened around beach paths on her motorbike, skinny-dipped in secluded coves, and danced on hot, soft sand that squished between our toes while she held my hand and I went under her arm in a turn. We ducked into bars, too, where Jane knew everyone.

"Hey, this is Papa's girl! Isn't she something? See you around midnight!" She waved, held my hand, and lifted it in the air like I'd just won the welterweight championship, and we headed back to the house.

As a kid, I didn't know anything about sex, but I knew that there was some chemistry between Jane and my father, and I knew that Pauline knew. When Jane was around, Pauline's face hardened and her smile was forced. I felt sorry for her. I sure wouldn't want to compete with Jane when it came to winning my father's attention.

I don't know what happened to Jane. After a few summers, she was not around anymore, and I missed her. Still, I felt I should have resented her for Pauline's sake, but instead I loved being with her. Then, because my connection to her was piggybacked onto my father's own, when he snapped it off, I too lost Jane, with no say in the matter.

I sighed recalling it all. And here I was, older, but still back in that loyalty bind, feeling drawn to Martha's accomplishments, beauty, and charm, but sad for Pauline and the boys. Papa never made me feel that he'd forget about Jack and me with each new marriage, but my insecurities were such that I wondered if he had enough room for all of us to share his inner sanctum. I shook away the cobwebs and snapped back to the present.

While Jeddrah and I enjoyed the beaches most mornings, in the late afternoons, we would sneak into the liquor cabinet and take little sips from the many bottles. While I'd take a slurp, she really drank the stuff. By bedtime, she would be pretty tipsy. Still, we thought we were urbane, and I felt full of myself until the day before we were to leave. Papa tapped me on the shoulder as I sunbathed around the pool.

"Flea, come into my study, please," he said. "I need to talk to you."

From the way he said it, I knew it wasn't good. I walked slowly down the hall, leaving Jeddrah at the pool with a few of the cats. Once in the study, I perched on the edge of a chair, apprehensive and ready to run.

Papa was already in his swivel desk chair, wielding a nail file, looking down and cleaning his nails. He finished the nail effort, closed the file with a crack, and slapped it on his desk with a thud. He pivoted back to me. "Flea, how old are you?"

"You know how old I am, Papa. I'll turn fifteen in July."

"Exactly. July twenty-first. And I'll turn forty-one. Did you think I wouldn't notice?"

I tried to look innocent. "Notice what?"

"Don't," he snapped, looking right at me. "The most essential gift for a good writer is a built-in, shock-proof shit detector. And I have it in spades."

I had the grace to blush. "We were just having some fun."

Papa looked out the window for a few seconds, then turned back to me. "Fun? Drinking at your age is not fun. It's a detour down a road to hell. You stop. You stop now. And if you ever touch my liquor again before you're twenty-one, you'll wish you'd never been born to me."

I swallowed. Papa was the fun parent, not the enforcer.

"I . . . but you drink. You drink a lot." I trembled, fearing his wrath at criticism from me.

Papa slammed his fist down on his desk, mouth set in a grim, straight line, eyes narrowed and glaring. He leaned forward so his face was two inches from mine.

"Don't you *ever* use me as an excuse or an example. I'm forty years old, and you're fourteen. We are not equals. You are too young to drink, and too young to think you can get away with it. You are my job, and I take it as seriously as death."

Papa's temples were throbbing and his face was red. I swallowed hard and asked, "Do you take it as seriously as your writing?" I trembled a little. It was the crux of the matter—

how much I mattered compared to his work—and I had never had the nerve to give it voice before.

Papa sat back, cocked his head, and to my surprise, laughed. "Some days. Some days I do. Now git, and I don't ever want to discuss this again. Are we clear, and can I trust you?"

I squirmed in the chair, but the answer was easy. It would kill me to lose Papa's confidence. "You can trust me, and we are clear."

Papa swiveled in his chair. His face relaxed, and he looked out the window, quiet. "Flea, you're responsible for anyone you bring into this house. You decide if they're someone you'll stand up for, and if not, don't bring them here, because I hold you accountable."

He got up and looked at me with softness in his eyes. My own eyes were moist, and I was ashamed that I'd tried to pull one over on him. I wanted to be sophisticated and cool like Jedd, and thought this small act of rebellion would go unnoticed.

He continued, his voice lower now, and kind. "I like your friend Jeddrah very much. I really do. But she is in a world of pain, and you're too young to know how to help her. Just be as good a friend as you can to help her survive it. The job of living is surviving."

I was still stricken, and the tears started to roll down.

"Don't cry, Flea. I love you and always will. But you have to decide who you're going to be. Are you going to run down your own road or follow someone else's path whether it's a good route or off a cliff? You have to decide what you stand for, what you'll fight for, and who you are. Either way, I love you, Flea, but you don't get a free pass."

8

It is awfully easy to be hard-boiled about everything in the daytime, but at night it is another thing.

~ Ernest Hemingway, *The Sun Also Rises*

Back at Ellsworth after Christmas break, Prillie and company renewed their attacks, but I had an ally now and that made all the difference. I looked straight back at Prill instead of skittering into the shadows.

As Jeddrah and I shambled through the buffet line in the dining hall, a high-ceilinged room that resembled a Gothic church hall without the pews, a girl ahead of us turned. "I hear you girls spent Christmas together. Isn't that sweet?"

Prillie stepped into line behind us and threw an arm over Jeddrah's shoulder. "I hope you two will be very happy."

I glared at Prillie, and Jedd shook her arm off. "I guess you'd know, Prillie. It takes one to know one." I uttered this sophomoric cliché in my snottiest tone.

One of her cronies said, "You are so ignorant, Finn. Prill has the dreamiest boyfriend ever. Someone should teach you a lesson for being so rude."

I just walked away. "It will get old fast," I said to Jedd, hoping.

But it didn't. The next day when I went to ride, I found Sassafras's back legs tied together so tightly with rope that he had to hop to me when I opened his stall door. He hung his head when I rushed toward him. I groaned as I knelt, but I couldn't undo the knots.

I raced into the aisle. "Gertie! Bring a knife. Please. Quick. Sassafras is hurt!"

Within seconds, Gertie and another rider were there. Gertie shoved the knife at me and grabbed a halter and lead rope, latching both deftly. As she tried to calm Sassafras, who was panicking at his confinement, I sawed through the ropes.

It took some strength, but in a few minutes, I'd freed him. He had bruises on his lower legs, as well as burns from where the hair had rubbed off.

"Hey, boy. We're OK now. Right as rain," I crooned as I rubbed his legs with liniment. He still held his head low, and I knew there would be no shows for a few weeks. I began a slow broil and slid his stall shut.

"Did anyone see who went into Sassafras's stall?" I asked. No reply. Heads were bowed, but I knew the answer. I just couldn't prove it.

A few nights later, Prillie and her three friends pushed into my room and Jeddrah's room at 2:00 a.m.—no one had locks on their doors—and tried to drag us out to the front lawn where hazed girls were traditionally duct-taped to trees in their underwear for the other girls to find as they headed to breakfast. I recognized Joannie Janssen, Rachel Warner, and Cheryl McAdams. Quickly shaking off Rachel, who was ineptly attached to me, I dashed down the hall to rescue Jeddrah, tiny elf that she was. Jedd was being hefted down the staircase, kicking and screaming. Prillie was directing Joannie and Cheryl to hurry. I grabbed Prillie's arm and slammed her against the wall. The two who were hauling Jedd stopped.

"No!" I roared, raising a fist at Prillie. I'd had my share of slam-downs with my brothers and wasn't afraid to fight. "Tell them to let her go, or I swear I *will* twist your arm until it breaks."

Heads popped out of doorways. Murmurs started. Someone said, "Call house mother!"

The four girls taunted us. "What are you going to do, Finley? Have your stupid horse kick us? Tell our mommies? Make us listen to your stupid Chicago accent?"

Still, Prill peered at the witnesses now lining the hall. Finally, she said, "You're not worth the trouble. Can't even take a joke. You're both pathetic." She turned to Cheryl and Joannie. "Dump her."

Her cohorts dropped their hold on Jedd, whose eyes were wild. She flopped onto the floor like a beached baby flounder, looking tiny and scared. I stood over Jedd until they walked away. Jedd was quivering, and her legs were shaky as she stood. She took a step and stumbled, then leaned on me as we hobbled together into her room.

That night lying in bed, I thought of asking Mother to send me to another school, but I didn't want to leave Jeddrah, and I didn't want to complain to Papa. It sounded so weak. And I loved the riding program. Still, the jibes continued.

"Finley, I hear the communists lost the war in Spain. Wasn't that the side your father was on? Lost again! And his new book, the one about the bells. I hear that's been banned too. What a proud moment for you! Isn't he on his third wife?" Prill said loudly enough to be heard throughout western New England.

What I heard was, "You and your father are losers and unworthy of love."

9

Never fall in love?

Always, said the count. I am always in love.

~ Ernest Hemingway, *The Sun Also Rises*

Despite the fact that love always ends, and usually badly, for us Hemingways, I wanted it. I was almost fifteen and had never had so much as a date to see a movie. Prillie, on the other hand, apparently had a super boyfriend. They'd known each other since the womb, or so she said, and the two families vacationed every summer on Nantucket. His name was Nicholas Armstrong, "of the Newport Armstrongs." Prillie said it as if it were part of his name.

I had romantic dreams, and at school socials, I would identify a few kindred souls among the boys attending from Choate and St. Paul's—but only in my head. In reality, I sat alone, optimistic and smiling for a half-hour, the hope and smile fading as the minutes ticked by. No one asked the now five-foot-ten stooped girl with thick, red hair and strong brows to dance. No one handed me a corsage and asked me to attend a football game. Still, there smoldered faith that, against all odds, it *could* happen that a less-than-average-looking girl like me—like Jane Eyre, who was kind, but plain—could find her soul mate.

"Your time will come, Flea," Papa always said, as he fed scraps to the dogs. "Be patient. It takes some time for boys to find the pearl among the tawdry rhinestones."

Mother said, "Just as well, Finn. Boys at that age are such scamps."

Jack said, "Hell, Finn, you're just not very attractive, so there it is. Maybe you can be one of those homely spinsters living in an attic somewhere with a hunchback and a million cats." He began to lurch around the kitchen, hobbled over and bending to pet imaginary cats, all while stuffing his mouth with Mother's chocolate chip cookies.

I threw a magazine at him. "You're disgusting, Jack!"

Still, my spirits plummeted. He was kidding, kind of, but he never lacked for girlfriends.

"You could introduce me to some of your buddies," I said. "That would be a nice thing to do."

"Hell no. Why would I want one of my friends hanging around with you? Then you'd know everything I'm up to and report to Papa and Mother."

"No I wouldn't, and don't expect me to introduce you to any of my friends, then." I squinted at him with pursed lips.

"Don't ever make that face in public, Finn. It's hideous, just so you know. And you only have one friend—Jeddrah—and while she is very pretty, she's weird, so no thanks."

All of this flashed through my mind, including the Zelda "you will never be pretty or inspire poetry" incident, as I sat in the Ellsworth Library on a Saturday afternoon in February, daydreaming of just having a date someday. I sighed and flipped open my book to study for my English exam on Thomas Hardy's *Tess of the D'Urbervilles*. I wondered once again why we always read such tragic books. Their message was likely true—love is doomed—but I would have liked some positivity.

The library was large, with a wall of windows at one end and ten round tables in the center for studying. I was the only one there, and its spartan atmosphere felt in tune with the themes of *Tess*: drudgery begets drudgery, and love is always fatal.

I heard a rustle and looked up to see a boy of about seventeen or eighteen shrugging off a tan trench coat and sitting down across from me with his own book. That alone was a showstopper. We had no boys at Ellsworth. He was dressed in gray slacks and a blue argyle sweater-vest. He had sky-blue eyes and a few freckles. When he put on a pair of horn-rimmed glasses, my enchantment was complete. I stared, then quickly looked down when he smiled at me. He flicked open his own book and began making notes in a loose-leaf notebook.

The book was—oh gosh—*The Sun Also Rises*. I cast my eyes back to the hapless Hardy, but as time passed, I barely turned a page. After a half-hour of creating a whole tragic biography for him—his mother was a recently deceased Ellsworth alumna, and his father long dead of cholera after a dangerous trip to India, this dutiful son had stopped by to make a donation to the school's scholarship fund in his dead mother's name—my reverie was interrupted when he spoke.

"Hey, psst," he said in a stage whisper. "What are you doing? It's Saturday afternoon."

Flustered, I pushed my hair behind my ears, then whispered back, "I have an exam on Monday, and I try to ride most of Sunday." I straightened in my seat, then immediately slumped down, fearing he would notice how tall I was. "I want to be a lawyer, and my father says I need top grades because they only take a few women."

"Law school? Sounds good. But I always try to leave Saturday afternoon open for some fun." He shrugged and slid over one chair so he was next to me. He picked up my book and twisted it to see the spine. "Ah, Thomas Hardy and his cheerful tale of loss and loss . . . and loss."

I smiled. My soul mate! "Exactly."

"You should try mine. It's swell. I read it in a few hours. Couldn't put it down." He shoved *The Sun Also Rises* over to me. "Take it."

"I . . . I couldn't. It's yours."

"I'll be back in a couple weeks. You can return it to me then. I promised to watch some tennis thing here later this month."

I should have said, "Gee, I've read this a hundred times, and played the part of Lady Brett in a dramatic recitation a few months ago." But that might have led to an awkward silence. I wanted this conversation to go on. So, I nodded. "Thanks. I'll take good care of it."

The librarian rushed over and glared at us (mostly me). I looked at my dreamboat. He was far from chastened and smiled even wider.

"Sorry," he said to her, holding his palms up in conciliation. "It was not this young lady's fault. All me. Tess here is trying to study, and I've been a total distraction. I promise to mend my wretched ways." *Oh, brother*, I thought. *Putting it on a little thick.*

To my surprise, the librarian smiled, saving the end of her sour look for me as she turned back to her perch at the checkout counter.

Then he whispered for real, "Let's get out of here, Tess. How about a walk? You can show me the lovely campus of Ellsworth before I head back north."

I hesitated, then nodded. "OK." *The heck with Thomas Hardy!* I grabbed my books and slowly rose, unfurling to my height. He then stood to a height of at least six two, and I smiled in relief. He stuck his glasses in his pocket.

"You look a bit smudgy, Tess, without my glasses. Can't read at all without them, and one eye is hopeless on its own. You won't lead me astray, will you?" he teased.

"Hmm. We'll see. Let's go."

We strolled out the library's double doors and he waved to the librarian like she was his best friend instead of an old crab. She waved back with a closed-mouth smile. I looked sideways at this guy as he ambled along. I so wished I had that kind of confidence.

I asked, "So are you always this charming?"

"What do you mean?" he asked innocently.

"Oh, Madam Librarian, it's all me, just me. May I beg your most generous indulgence, my sweet flower," I mimicked in a simpering voice.

He laughed for real. "OK, OK, but I didn't want any trouble for you, and yes, the smile and 'Aw shucks, ma'am' usually works."

I smiled. "So, what would you like to see?"

"Truthfully, Tess, I've been here a few times. I'd like to see what you think is important."

I snatched his arm. "OK, this way." I turned toward the stables. "Why *are* you here?"

"Came to return something to a friend, but she's away for a few hours with her mother."

"Oh. And what's your name?"

"Won't tell you mine until I know yours."

"Finley Richardson," I said without hesitation. It was only a lie of omission; my mother's maiden name was Elizabeth Hadley Richardson and my full name was Finley Richardson Hemingway. I just left off the last third.

"Nick Armstrong. Nice to meet you, Finley. But to me, you'll always be Tess."

I froze. "Of the Newport Armstrongs?" I asked without thinking.

He stopped, turned toward me, and laughed. "That is too funny, Tess. Where on Earth did you hear that? And yes, as luck would have it, I am of the 'Newport Armstrongs.'"

My stomach spun and dropped, and my delight in taking him to the barn was flattened. He was Prillie's boyfriend. Not only was he taken, but he was taken by *her*. My next thought was, *Of course he is*. She was beautiful, accomplished, and socially connected.

I turned to him slowly. "You're Prillie Lamont's friend."

It was a statement, not a question. Nicholas kept walking, taking my arm and pulling me along gently. "Ah, has she mentioned me? I've known Prill forever."

"Yes, she has mentioned you. A lot," I said, my legs now feeling leaden.

"Hmm."

Hmm? That's all I get? Do you like her the way she likes you, Nicholas? But I couldn't ask anything. I was nobody but a way of passing time for him.

However, when we got to the stables, Nicholas was all interest and questions. He put on his glasses and stepped into Sassafras's stall. Clearly, he was used to being around horses. He reached in his pocket and pulled out a peppermint. Sassafras nuzzled his hand, took the mint, and munched rhythmically. Nicholas stroked his nose and lifted each hoof to examine his feet.

"Good feet. Horses are my greatest passion," he said quietly, not looking at me. "I can't live without them." He was now running his hands down Sassafras's legs, then his neck. "He's lovely." He continued petting the horse, measuring his conformation. "How big is he? Sixteen two?"

"Exactly. And even though I'm tall, most of my length is in the legs, so I look balanced on him." He cocked his head and gave me the once over. I blushed, wondering what possessed me to mention my proportions. I quickly added, "I mean, he suits me, even though I'm tall."

Nicholas patted my back. "Yes, I agree that he suits you, Tess." He was now putting a halter on Sassafras and leading him out of his stall into the small indoor arena. He put his glasses back in his pocket, but I worried about Nicholas's leather shoes, shiny and fresh.

"It's dusty in there. You don't want to get your shoes messy," I said, reaching to take the lead rope from him. He held onto it and kept walking.

"I've ruined more than a few pairs in my day. Don't worry. I'd like to see you on him." He looked at me and my heart leapt.

I said, "I can't. I'm in my skirt and saddle shoes, Nicholas."

"I'll help you on. Don't worry, I won't look," he said, raising an eyebrow. "I'll lead him, just in case he's frisky."

I hesitated. It sounded like a daring plan. Me in a skirt, riding alone with this boy, my legs bare. My heart sped up again, and I always felt most myself when in the saddle.

"OK, but just for a moment," I said.

We entered the arena, and I looked for the mounting block. It was shoved into the far corner of the arena with the jumps piled on top of it. I sighed.

"Leg up?" Nicholas asked.

Hardly appropriate in my skirt, I thought. "OK."

I stood, left leg bent, and Nicholas linked his two hands under my shin. I felt a thrill as I bounced, and he lifted as I sprang up. I landed softly on my horse's back, and it was glorious. It was the nearest thing to heaven on earth, I thought, as I nestled into the center of his back, a slight hollow, with high withers and mane to grab onto. My legs dangled and my skirt settled around me in swirly, navy-blue folds. My ankle socks slumped, but I was on my horse, and for the moment, I had the full attention of the most dashing boy I'd ever seen.

"You good?"

I nodded, and Nicholas started walking slowly around the arena, lead rope loose on his right. I seized a handful of mane for extra balance. We were quiet as Nicholas walked slowly around the arena, both of us taking in the scent of oiled leather, fresh hay, sweet horse sweat, and fresh, late-winter air. He began singing, quietly at first, a hum that became a phrase, then a verse. *When the deep purple falls, over sleepy garden walls, and the stars begin to twinkle in the sky* . . . He had a lovely tenor voice.

"That's nice," I said. His back was to me as he led Sassafras. "You have a great voice."

He looked up at me over his shoulder and smiled, but kept walking. "Thanks. My second passion is my music group. 'Deep Purple' is a swell song, don't you think?"

I nodded. "I do. It's very romantic. What's your favorite dance tune? Do you dance?"

Nicholas answered quickly, "Glenn Miller's 'In the Mood.' I could dance to that all night."

"Oh, me too. My friend Jeddrah and I dance to it whenever it's on the radio." He laughed. I felt silly; the picture I'd conveyed of two girls dancing in a dorm room felt pathetic. I quieted.

After once more around, Nicholas began to jog, and Sassafras moved with him into a gentle trot. I followed the rhythm. After two more times around, I felt uneasy and a little sad that I was here with Nicholas when there was no chance of anything more. He was Prillie's boyfriend, and I could never compete with her. She would always win. I said, "I should get down now."

Nicholas slowed and looked up at me. "Had enough?"

I nodded. Nicholas stopped and turned to face me as he held Sassafras still. "He's beautiful."

I swung a leg over and slid down my horse's side, thumping when I hit ground. I turned and Nicholas was right in front of me. We stood awkwardly, face-to-face. He wrapped one arm around my waist. My left arm, as if by memory, went to his shoulder. He dropped the rope and Sassafras, an unruffled soul, just stood. Our hands met and he sang a few bars of "Deep Purple." We took a few dance steps, then I let go, embarrassed but happy. We both looked down, smiling.

"Thank you," I said as I backed up, color rising to my cheeks. "I'm not sure what for, but . . . it felt kind of neat just then."

Nicholas picked up the lead rope. "It felt nice to me too. Thank you." We passed the stall of my rival Joannie Janssen's horse, Birthday Boy, Sassafras ambling between us. Nicholas led the horse into his stall and unlatched the rope.

"Where do you go to school?" I asked, although I knew. I lifted Sassafras's halter over his head and hung it on its holder outside his stall. Nicholas slid the door shut behind me.

"Phillips Exeter up in New Hampshire."

"I know where it is."

"Oh, have you been there?" Nicholas asked as we left the stable.

"Um, no. I meant I know of it."

"Ah."

We walked comfortably back to the main campus, chatting about classes, teachers, and my dream of being a female Clarence Darrow, righting wrongs, helping people. I rushed on. "I know it sounds impossible, but President Roosevelt appointed Florence Ellinwood Allen to the U.S. Court of Appeals. It can happen! She went to NYU. It's all I ever wanted to do."

Nicholas grinned. "That sounds swell. And I think you'd be great!" He looked like he believed what he was saying.

I nodded eagerly. It turned out Nicholas was a junior, and hoping to go to Yale.

"But with the war, I may enlist after Phillips Exeter. My mother will be devastated and my eyesight is probably poor enough to get me out, but I wouldn't want that." He shrugged and seemed to decide to go back to the lighter mood. "But until Uncle Sam puts a gun in my hand, I'll devour Fitzgerald and this Hemingway fellow, and play as much polo as I can. You should play!"

"Oh, I'd like to try, but my mother thinks it's not for girls. Too rough."

Nicholas laughed. "Hmm. A girl with attitude on a thousand-pound horse pretty much equalizes the playing field, I suspect. I think you would be amazing at it."

I blushed. We had reached my dorm, and I wished I could think of something witty to say, but all I could do was grin and hold out a hand. He took off his glove and grasped my hand. "Very nice to meet you, Tess. Or Finley Richardson, if I must; but you'll always be Tess to me. I hope I see you again."

"I do, too. Thank you for some fun, Nicky. I mean Nicholas." *Why did I call him Nicky?*

He was still holding my hand. It felt cool and dry. He tilted his head. "Nicky? Hmm. I like it. You're the only one who ever called me Nicky."

He let go of my hand, and I turned to run up my dorm steps. At the top, I spun around. "How many horses do you have?"

"I have twenty-three." He turned and was gone.

10

I can't stand it to think my life is going so fast and I'm not really living it.

~ Ernest Hemingway, *The Sun Also Rises*

I flew up the stairs to my room, tossed down my books, and ran to Jeddrah's room. I rapped at her door.

"Come in," she called. "But make sure you're interrupting my nap for something interesting, or better yet, scandalous."

I pushed the door open, and the afternoon's events tumbled out. Jeddrah turned on the radio, which warbled a big band sound. Then she sank back onto her bed and listened to my tale of the afternoon doings with rapt attention.

"So, am I to understand that you just had a date with Prillie's boyfriend, whom you've totally fallen for, and who loves your father's writing, but doesn't know he's your father, because you told him your name was Finley Richardson, but he calls you Tess? Is that about it, Finn?"

I nodded. "Yup, that's about it."

Jeddrah sat back on her bed, leaning her head against the headboard. She smiled broadly and rubbed her hands together. "I love it! This is too rich!"

"No, no! This is terrible. And I have not fallen for him; I just think he's very nice. I have in no way fallen for him." I began to pace.

"Just keep telling yourself that, and maybe it will be true," she said smugly.

"Oh, God. Seriously, Jeddrah, this is really terrible. He's Prillie's . . . boyfriend, which means he can't even be my friend. Add to it that I just lied to him about who I am, and nothing good can ever come from something that starts with a lie." I was now wringing my hands. "But the way he petted Sassafras, and walked me back, and smiled, and knew exactly what it was like to love horses like they're an extension of yourself, like without them you think maybe nothing makes sense. I don't know. Maybe we can stay in touch about our horses." I looked at Jedd, hoping she would affirm this possibility.

"No chance," she said. She pointed. "There it is again! That look in your eyes. Shining and hopeful." She began to sing loudly, "It Had to Be You."

Jeddrah's slightly raspy, alto voice was surprising coming from such a sprite. I was at first horrified that I was so transparent, then I laughed and she did too until we were both gasping. It was too preposterous.

"You are gone on him, Finn," she said. "Admit it. You can't wait to see him again. Oh, gosh. Can't wait for the taunting now! You're in for it, Finn Hemingway. If Prillie finds out, Sassafras will be wearing that jockstrap as a headdress, not just dragging it around his neck! And you and I will be taped out front naked—forget our underwear—with honey and feathers."

"Nothing happened. There is nothing to find out," I said, a little panicked.

"Doesn't matter. Something *could* happen now that Nicholas has met you." She stopped, and her face became serious. "I've been meaning to tell you this, but the time was never right. It is now. You sell yourself short, Finn Hemingway. You are smart, funny, and interesting. But you are also beautiful. I know you won't believe it, but you are. You are far more beautiful than Prillie, with her flat, white hair and disappearing eyebrows." Jeddrah wrinkled her nose at the thought. "*You* look downright stunning sometimes. Strong. Just lovely."

I reddened. Jedd said it matter-of-factly, like it was a truth, in the same no-room-to-argue-about-this tone that Zelda had used to tell me I would never be pretty or desired. "Thank you, Jeddrah," I said softly, staring at the floor. "But Prillie will never know, because he has no interest in me."

Jeddrah said simply, "Oh really? Then why did he want you to show him around when he's already been to Ellsworth?"

***

Through most of March, Jeddrah was away weekends dealing with "family things," she said, and I was frantic preparing for the East Hampton Horse Show. If I did well there, I'd have enough points to qualify for Madison Square Garden in November. The girl to beat that year was Jacqueline Bouvier, the undisputed champion of the Long Island circuit. She and her horse, Danseuse, had style and confidence. My pulse sped up just seeing Jackie's dark hair peeking out from under her riding hat and Danseuse's silky tail streaming out behind her. I always held my breath when they took the highest gates in the arena, and I let it out only when they were over safely with no faults. I could almost stand losing to them.

As busy as I was, I could not forget Nicholas. In the few weeks since the Saturday we met, I'd awakened each morning feeling the touch of his hands as he lifted me onto Sassafras's bare back and the cool feel of his skin when we danced.

One day as I groomed Sassafras absentmindedly in the crossties, picking out his feet and polishing his hooves, I heard Prillie approach with Joannie Janssen. As Joannie tacked up, Prillie prattled on.

"He stopped by, but I missed him. He promised to return this Saturday. I know he's going to ask me to the Junior Dance at Exeter in May. I bought a dress for it, just in case. Mother says his family is just like ours, and that Nick and I will stay in touch when he goes to Yale and I go to Vassar. She's sure of it."

"That's so romantic," said Joannie, sighing as she straightened from wrapping her horse's leg. "And he is the cutest. I'm sure he'll ask you."

"I'm sure, too. I mean, he missed me enough that he's coming back, right?"

"For sure."

I felt dizzy, but finished tacking up Sassafras and led him past Prill into the arena. As I passed, Prill said, "I'm sure you're going to the Exeter spring dance, right, Finn?" She and Joannie dissolved into peels of snorting ridicule.

I schooled Sassafras for an hour, but it was not a good workout. I was sloppy and distracted, which led him to be confused and clumsy. At one point, he started refusing jumps—something he never did. I decided I'd tortured him enough for one day. By the time I got back to the dorm, I was tired and disheartened. Nicholas would be visiting this weekend, but not for me.

I sat down and wrote a long letter to my mother and a shorter one to Papa. He was in China with Marty, and I wondered when and if it would ever reach him. I also wrote a reply letter to my grandmother, Papa's mother. After over a decade and a half, she was still heaving and moaning over *The Sun Also Rises,* the filthiest book of its time, she declared. Every letter seemed intent on mentioning it. It was difficult to like Grandmother when she talked like that, and I knew—heck, we all knew—that Papa hated his mother.

I also had vowed to stay in the barn all day on Saturday so there would be no chance of running into Nicholas. I didn't want to see him with Prillie, arm draped around her shoulder. I wasn't jealous, as I had no rights; I was despondent because I had no rights.

After classes ended on Saturday, I put on my oldest pair of riding breeches, pulled my hair back into a low ponytail, and threw on a wool riding jacket. I jogged down to the barn, determined to keep my mind off of Nicholas.

I spent a few minutes with my favorite barn cat, a gray tabby I'd named Baby. She'd appeared one day last fall as a motherless, seven-week-old kitten and just stayed. I started hand-feeding her daily, had her spayed, and she'd become sort of my cat. I adored her sweet meows, her tail curving over her back, her gentle head butts and rubs on my legs, and her slowly blinking amber eyes.

After giving Baby a few treats, I hopped onto Sassafras to take a trail ride in four inches of fresh snow. I lifted my face to the March sun. There would be a spring after all, I thought, feeling a spark of joy despite no Nicholas.

Sassafras and I rode for over an hour on the wooded trails, crossing icy streams with quick-running water and trotting on level meadows. Heading back to the barn and feeling a little better about my prospects of survival, I spied another rider in the distance. I stopped, curious. As the figure drew closer, my mouth went dry, and I almost turned to canter in the other direction.

Straight ahead was Nicholas Armstrong, trotting toward me on an Ellsworth school horse. He waved tentatively when he spotted me, then full out when certain it was me.

"Hey there!" he called.

I waved back, an unenthusiastic slow mitt in the air. When we were close, he pulled back on his reins. "Well good afternoon, Tess. How are you on this great day?"

"Hello, Nicholas." I composed myself as much as I could. He looked beautiful on a horse in his riding boots, a casual jacket, and no hat. He was smiling, and the corners of his blue eyes turned up. I couldn't help smiling back. "Um, what are you doing out here? Aren't you supposed to be at a tennis event or something?"

"Tennis is not really my thing, so I ducked out. Thought I might find you at the barn." He stood up in his stirrups and stretched his legs. "When I saw your horse was gone, I tacked up a school horse and followed the tracks in the snow." He paused, shielding his eyes from the sun. "So! What are you up to?"

"You tacked up your own horse? You don't just have a groom to do the dirty work?" *There's nothing like pushing someone away before they push you away.*

Nicholas looked startled, but recovered. "Actually, I do most of the dirty work. You know, not all of the Armstrongs of Newport are rich."

I studied him, and noticed some freckles on his right cheek that disappeared into his hairline. "I didn't know that."

He nodded. "Yeah, my father lost almost everything in the Depression, but he's been rebuilding the family fortune in the last ten years." He said "family fortune" mockingly. "But as a kid, I had just one old horse that I took care of by myself until, well, you know, we became rich again. Surprised?"

I liked his self-deprecating tone. "Yes. I thought maybe you were one of those guys who had horses handed to him by a valet and wouldn't know how to tighten a girth if your life depended on it, which sometimes it does. I am upgrading your rating, Armstrong."

He looked relieved as his brow smoothed. "I have a rating?"

I smiled at him, but wondered where my comment had come from. I not only didn't flirt; I didn't know how.

"You do. Do I have one?"

He cocked his head first, then shook it. "No, ma'am. I couldn't possibly rate you. It would humiliate all the other competitors."

"Ha! Now I may have to downgrade you for overshooting with your flattery."

He smiled. "Aw shucks. And I thought I was getting somewhere." He moved his horse forward two steps so he and I were across from each other. He leaned over and gave me a feathery kiss on my cheek.

I felt fluttery and my skin tingled where he kissed me as I tried to act like that happened to me all the time. He straightened and added, "But as for me, it was riches to rags and back again."

This was so much fun I wanted to keep it going. "I love a guy who lost it all and made a comeback. Sort of a Scarlet O'Hara tale of scraping to reach the top again. Let me hear you say, 'As God is my witness, I will never go hungry again.'"

Now he laughed, raised a fist to the sky, and howled, "As God is my witness, I will never go hungry again!"

The horses looked worried, and his started to dance. Almost as if relieved I was playing along, he said, "But don't feel too sorry for us. Grandfather passed in 1935. He had not lost it all in the Depression, so that funneled in, and we never have had to go hungry again."

I got quiet, recalling why he was really here.

He asked, "Are you OK? Did I do something?"

Yes. Yes, you did. You came here to see Prillie, not me. "I'm just a little tired. Sorry."

He looked at me, nodded, then smiled. "I'm glad to hear that, because the real reason I was trying to find you, other than just wanting to see you again, is that there's this dance every spring at Exeter. I wondered if you might consider going with me. I wanted to give you enough notice."

I'd been studying my gloved hands and playing with my reins as he talked. When he finished, I lifted my head to stare at him. Nicholas's cheek muscle was twitching and his fingers were playing with his own reins. My God, I thought, he's nervous. He's nervous about asking me to the dance.

I blurted out, "I . . . I thought you were here to ask Prill to the dance."

Nicholas's face looked blank, then his eyes widened. "You thought that? Why would you think that, Tess? I've known Prill since we were kids. She's OK, but not my type of girl. I was here before to return a bracelet to her she'd left at our house, but that was it."

All of a sudden, the world flipped back to wonderful, superb, perfect. I grinned and straightened, tilting my face again to the sun. His horse was still dancing around, but he steadied her. He continued, "I'm sorry if I did anything to lead her to think there was anything more to my visit, but honestly, that wasn't my intent. And if you are able to come up to Exeter, I can show you a few of my horses."

I settled back into my saddle, feeling a lightness I had not felt just a few minutes before. "I would love that."

He grinned. "Phew. I was worried you might have a boyfriend or . . . well, you know." He spun his horse around so we were both facing the barn. "Race you to the barn. Last one there is a demented barbarian!"

"You're on!" I pressed Sassafras's sides, and he took off like a Roman candle. The snow gave us great footing as long as we didn't need to stop fast. We both tore toward the barn, neck and neck.

11

Despite the fact that he's been tied to certain women, Jake suspects that Cohn has never really been in love with them—Cohn doesn't have an understanding of what love really is, beyond obligation.

~ Ernest Hemingway, *The Sun Also Rises*

July 1934

In the law, we call it an attractive nuisance: something you can't resist even when you know it's unsafe. Its flash and sparkle draw you close, and then it breaks your leg. That was my father. His joie de vivre and charisma lured you in and then wham! You were left alone to quiver in the tundra without a coat. In our case, he broke hearts, the hearts of everyone dear to me—my mother, my brothers, my three stepmothers—and me.

The first time I saw it up close—that destruction—was when he shattered my stepmother, Pauline, with a quick pinch and a turn of the back. I was eight, and visiting for the summer. That pinch and pivot was breathtaking in its quiet power.

It was late afternoon, and the family was all out back on the patio. From my slumped position on a rattan chair, I looked up from reading *Anne of Green Gables* and knew trouble was coming as soon as I saw Pauline's face. Jack was playing a few yards away with his new fishing pole while my half-brother, Patrick, age five, watched the bobbing end with rapt attention. Approaching with too careful steps, Pauline, who was usually smiling with one brow cynically raised, now had narrowed eyes, and her mouth strained into a tense circle. She carried a tray full of glasses: iced tea for me and my brothers, and a martini in a frosted glass for Papa, who was leaning forward on a lawn chair, oblivious to the Vesuvius heading his way.

Pauline handed me my tea, then swung around to slam Papa's martini down so hard on his side table I thought the stem would shatter. The gin sloshed from side to side like a mini-tsunami, with some liquid lapping over the rim.

Papa's head snapped up. A look crossed his face like a mental Rolodex had begun flipping as he tried frantically to grasp which transgression had been exposed. Pauline stood over him, the rare time she had that advantage. She was tiny, and Papa was not.

Hands on hips, Pauline gathered steam as we kids froze, not wanting to bear witness, but unable to flee the disaster movie about to roll. And we'd all seen this show before. Jack backed away, trying to hide the fishing pole as if it were an offending party. Patrick, known in the family as Mouse, stepped behind Jack to disappear. Gregory, my other half-brother, who was just two, pulled his blanket over his head. I bit my lip. Even at eight, I was pretty sure it had to do with another woman.

Papa cleared his throat, then his jaw set rigidly. "Fife, the kids . . ." He jerked his head in my direction, but meant all of us.

She exploded. "Oh, so now you care about what the kids will see? It's a little late for that, isn't it?" She took a breath, then hissed. "What was she doing in *my* house?"

Papa tilted his head and tried a small smile. "Fife, come on. She was just passing through. I couldn't be rude to her. She's just a fan." When sober, Papa's tone when confronted about other women was mild and conciliatory, sometimes even jovial. But when drinking, which was more common, it was bombastic, defensive, and accusatory. That day was a drinking day. He said, "Oh, so this is *your* house now? You rich think everything is *all* yours."

Pauline, an heiress in her own right, attacked back in disgust. "Oh, don't start that. You like my money well enough when it suits you. I couldn't believe she practically sat in your lap."

The problem was that all my father had to do was smile like a pirate and scratch his beard and the women flocked like crows to a sequin. He was just starting to become famous when this particular confrontation occurred, but even without the fame, he had the magnetism, plus the looks and charm, that made women swoon. Suddenly, there would be a new woman at the dinner table whom Papa said he met downtown, a woman who took my usual seat to his left, who leaned in a little too close, who laughed a little too loud, and whom he called 'daughter,' all followed by overheard sniping that night between Pauline and Papa. The next morning, I pretended all was normal despite the Siberian chill around the breakfast table.

The day of Pauline's outburst my father went silent, making no effort to calm Pauline beyond a feeble deflection.

He usually tried to assuage her but he didn't that day. Pauline looked stricken as she nervously ran her fingers through her dark, cropped hair, then got up to uncover baby Gregory with shaking hands and swiped at her eyes. My own eyes slid from my father, back to her. He looked unmoved; she looked like she was melting. That day, instead of affirmations of love, my father merely parried and thrust, a faker's ploy. A writer can do better than that with words if he wants to, but he didn't want to. He no longer cared enough to deny her accusations.

My stomach fluttered unpleasantly at the ease with which Pauline was about to be shoved to the perimeter just as my mother had been. Those mornings after the "other women" explosions, my father usually looked contrite. He'd read the paper at the kitchen table, head down. Those mornings, I got only a nod instead of a grin and snippets of funny articles between his gulps of coffee. Pauline may have been right—was right—to be angry, but I was always on his side. The cost was too high not to be. I wasn't afraid of him; I was afraid of losing the little I had of him.

At the age of eight, I absorbed my first and most haunting lesson in love: *it always ended, and usually badly,* at least in the Hemingway family. I saw it; I hated it; I absorbed it. It's what I knew to be my destiny.

However, now that I had just the tiniest morsel of a snippet of hope of maybe distant romance with Nicholas, the reminder of the Hemingway deficits in lasting love rushed in, guffawing scornfully at my optimism that love could be different for me. And that reminder reared up like a gargoyle, poised and sneering, eager to slaughter my dream of love before it could begin.

12

"Oh Jake," Brett said, *"We could have had such a damned good time together."*

Ahead was a mounted policeman in khaki directing traffic. He raised his baton. The car slowed suddenly, pressing Brett against me.

"Yes," I said. "Isn't it pretty to think so?"

~ Ernest Hemingway, *The Sun Also Rises*

I rushed up to Jedd's room after Nicholas left, taking the stairs two at a time and flushed with the amazement. When I told her about Nicholas, Jeddrah was as excited as I was. "Serves her right, snotty bitch."

"She'll now be even meaner to us," I said, dropping to the floor and crossing my legs.

"Oh, who cares?" I looked at Jeddrah closely. She was the one who most feared the taunts, the foot trippings, the smelly mouse in a drawer, the short sheets on the bed. She seemed brave all of a sudden. I'd been preoccupied with my riding and daydreaming about Nicholas for the past several weeks, but not too preoccupied to notice that Jeddrah had not seemed right since our December break. She wasn't getting to all of her classes, and now she sounded a little loopy. I stopped my story.

"Jedds, are you OK?"

"Me? Of course, I'm OK." She looked down, guilty, then back at me, innocent.

"You seem like maybe you've been drinking."

She giggled and wagged a finger at me. "You are a sly one. You found me out." She began to laugh, but not like anything was funny. "A little nip helps me through the day, Finn. Shhhh. Don't be a tattletale goody-goody."

She stood up and began to twirl around to "In the Mood" on the radio, grabbing me and pulling me to my feet. "I love Glenn Miller! I just want to dance and dance and dance. I want to go back to New York and out of this stupid school."

I couldn't help laughing and did a few jitterbug steps with her, then tightened my grip on both of her arms to make her stop. She stumbled, and I shook her. Her head bobbled a little. I steadied her and grew serious.

"Jeddrah, no, you can't do this. You'll flunk out of school, and if they catch you drinking, you'll be expelled. Come on. You can't drink and get your work done."

I sat down on her bed. She started to spin again alone in the middle of the room, stopped and flopped down on the bed, her head on her pillow.

"Well you see, my darling Finn, it doesn't really matter." She caught her breath for a few seconds, and sat up propped on her elbows. "I, too, have a little itty bitty secret."

I turned to face her, expectant, perched on the bed's edge. I smiled because she seemed so pleased. "What secret? Tell me."

Her face took on a dreamy look, a softer look. She flipped her blonde hair over one shoulder and whispered, "I have a boyfriend, too!"

I got excited, happy for her. Neither of us had ever had a real boyfriend. We'd made a million plans in this room and in my room and on walks to classes and on Saturday nights as we dreamed about a boyfriend. A million unreal, imaginary plans.

"He has to love animals," I would say. "Otherwise, it's doomed."

"And he has to dance and be happy," Jeddrah would add. "I want a guy who smiles all the time! And who smells good and is smart! No chuckleheads allowed!"

"Yes! Must smell really good! And he has to be smart, really smart, so we can talk about everything: theater, politics, religion, and s-e-x!" I'd giggle and so would she. We'd never even kissed a boy, but we had hopes. Now, at this moment, Jeddrah and I both—maybe—had boyfriends, and we would be able to yammer endlessly about some real guys, not our imaginary, someday-in-the-future guys.

I exploded. "Why didn't you tell me? Who is he? Where does he go to school? How long has this been going on? Jedds! Why haven't you told me about him?"

She smiled her best Mona Lisa smile. "Because he's my secret. But I will tell you because soon, when I turn sixteen, he's going to take me away and marry me." She held her breath and exhaled. "It's Walter Chandler, our English teacher—and if I were Prillie, I'd add 'of the Boston Chandlers.' He's twenty-eight and adores me." She fell back onto the pillows in peals of giggles. "He says I look like an angel, and he wants his friend to paint me."

My delight plunged to horror. "Mr. Chandler? The one who reads poetry and always wears a bow tie? That Mr. Chandler? Jeddrah, he's a grown-up, and our teacher. You can't be dating a grown man. Why would he want to date a girl in high school?"

Jeddrah sat upright, and at first, I thought she was mad. Then I realized she was hurt. "Because he thinks I'm smart and interesting and pretty," she said, and hiccuped. "And he has a car, and we go to clubs on weekends, and we drink and dance. But I have to pretend I barely know him during the week. It's so tedious, darling Finn." She sounded not just loopy, but quite drunk now. *Darling Finn* again?

"I thought you were going home on weekends. You lied to me?"

"Just a little," she said quietly. "That was part of my secret. He thought we should keep it hush-hush because of my age."

My face felt hot, and I was furious. "I'll bet he thought you should keep it secret! He'd lose his job, and maybe more. I'll just bet he wanted to keep it 'hush-hush.'"

Jedd went pale, and her hands were shaking as she tried to button her sweater. I was unable to say anything else for a moment. I could not imagine spending time with a man thirteen years older than we were and who was one of our teachers. It seemed creepy, vile.

Jeddrah lay on the bed, staring at the ceiling. I grabbed her arm and shook it a little. She shrugged it off. "Stop it. You're getting hysterical, Finn, and it's quite unattractive."

I ignored her comment. "Jeddrah! Look at me." She turned her head toward me, but her eyes were bleary and unfocused. "Hey, you aren't, you know . . . sleeping with him, are you?" Her silence was my answer. "Oh, no. You're too good for that."

She sat up and looked at her hands. "No, I'm not," she said.

"Oh God. He's using you. And how much are you drinking?" This close to her, I could smell liquor. Her eyelids were droopy and her speech was slurred.

She lay back down on her pillow, closing her eyes as if trying to remember, then opening them. "Oh, maybe a bottle of wine or two most days, and something for a nightcap, maybe a jigger of whiskey—to sleep. I need to sleep."

I was stunned. *How had I missed this?* Me, the one who wants to help people, defend rights? I hadn't paid enough attention to my best friend to see what trouble she was in. I felt sick inside, and so disappointed in myself.

I recalled Papa's words from our vacation in Cuba when he'd caught Jeddrah and me invading his liquor stock. *Your friend is in a world of pain, and you're too young to know how to help her. Just be as good a friend as you can to help her survive it. The job of living is surviving.* Horses and Nicky had taken too much of me. I'd let her down, but had no clue what to do.

"Jeddrah, give me whatever you have, and we'll get rid of it." I began scanning her room, wondering where she kept her booze.

I walked over to her closet and flung the door open. In front of me were at least two cases of wine and five or six bottles of something that looked like scotch or whiskey. I gasped and reached for one. Jeddrah came to life. She leapt over, shoved me aside hard, and planted herself in front of the door. "You can't take it. It's mine."

"Sure I can. We'll dump it and mix the bottles in with the trash. No one will know. And then end it with Mr. Chandler. He's bad for you."

"And how would you know what's bad for me, Miss Goody-Goody?" Jeddrah wheeled on me, spitting out words. "You have your horses. You have two parents who love you. Your father may not show up much, but you're important to him, and you don't even know it." She gazed off, and her eyelashes fluttered. "And your mother is like some perfect dream of a mother. Letters, cookies in the mail, going to your horse stuff. And you know what? I don't think you need me at all. I think if all you had were your horse and ten percent of your father, it would be enough. Nobody cares about me except Walter. And I need the booze to get through the day."

I slid to the floor, stricken. She did too, sitting cross-legged opposite me. "That's not true," I said, but I wondered if it was. "How long have you been drinking like this?"

She shrugged. "Two, maybe three years. I can't get along without it. I get shaky. One drink sets me right." She was nodding, as if to reassure me. "I'll stop at the end of the school year. I promise. I just need to get through this year."

I shook my head. "No. You can die from this stuff. We need to tell someone and get some help. Maybe the school or your parents?"

A wild look came into Jeddrah's eyes and she gripped my arm. "No! Not my parents and not the school. Walter will be in trouble. I can try to stop. I can stop. I can cut down. No, I'll stop."

I hesitated. "You have to stop seeing Mr. Chandler. I feel funny not telling someone. I leave here on Saturday for a week to compete, and I'm really worried about you."

"I'm fine. We all drink. Except you. Maybe I drink a little bit more. Hey, I have some homework to do. See you in the morning."

I got up slowly. "I don't want to leave you. Are you all right?"

"Right as rain," she said brightly. "Good as new. Perfect in the morning."

I went back to my room reluctantly and packed for my trip to Long Island, where I'd be riding. Mother was driving out from Chicago. Papa was still in China, but had sent a best-of-luck message. I thought about how I'd let Jeddrah down but vowed to make up for it when I returned.

***

When I returned, Jeddrah was gone. The day after I left, she was found by the morning maid—maids knocked on our doors at six each day to be sure we didn't develop lazy habits—unconscious on the floor in her room. She'd made a good dent in the booze in her closet. An ambulance was called and as they wheeled her out on a gurney, the dorm hallway lined with girls and red-and-blue lights of police cars flickering on the wall, Jedd barely moved.

Gertie told me all, adding, "I thought she was dead."

As soon as I found out, I got a cab to Greenwich Hospital and flew up to her room. Jedd looked fragile in her white johnny that billowed around her neck like some Elizabethan collar, like she had the wrong part in the wrong play. Her blueberry eyes were red-rimmed, sunken, and without spark.

I stepped into the room quietly, my saddle shoes large and clumsy. I sat on the edge of her bed and gazed around the private room. There were no cards or flowers on display, and I felt a shiver as I gazed at Jeddrah. I pulled my white cardigan closer.

"I brought you some books in case you want to do a little work. There will be less to catch up on when you're back." I placed a pile of books on her side table. Jeddrah looked at them but said nothing. I straightened her sheet. "Fluff your pillow?"

"No, it's OK."

"When do you get out?"

Jeddrah shrugged. "I don't know. No one said." She reached for her glass of water, and I handed it to her. Her hand shook as she grasped it, and it slid through her fingers, crashing to the floor, water and fragments exploding everywhere.

I leapt up, scooting back with paper towels and the trash bin.

"You don't have to do that, Finn."

"I know, but I want to."

Once done, I asked again, "When are you coming back, Jedd? I am dying without you." I had a few friends now among the other riders and girls in my class, but no one like Jeddrah.

She hesitated, looked out the one window, and shook her head. "I'm not sure I'm coming back, Finn. They're saying I have to go to a hospital for girls with 'my problem.' That's what my father called it. And my mother is in London and said she has no interest in returning to address 'the mayhem,' as she put it, that I created."

I ached for her. If Papa heard I'd been hospitalized for something this serious, he'd be on the first plane out of China. He might be mad as hell when I got better, but he'd be there to be sure I *got* better. My own mother would have gotten here if she had to crawl every mile from Chicago with one hand duct-taped to her head.

"You have to come back, Jedds. Please, let's figure this out."

She stared at me, blinked, then looked away. "You have Nicholas now."

Isn't it pretty to think so, I thought.

13

Oh darling. I've been so miserable.

~ Ernest Hemingway, *The Sun Also Rises*

"My real name is Finley Richardson Hemingway," I said as I got off the train from Boston in Exeter, New Hampshire. I'd decided I had to come clean. I handed Nicholas his copy of *The Sun Also Rises*. "I've read this book at least thirty times, and I'm related to the author. I don't want to start our friendship with a lie. If you hate me, I understand, and I'll take the train back. I'm so sorry, and I hate to leave you in the lurch for the dance tomorrow."

I was so nervous, and it felt like I was ending something that had hardly started, like I'd reached for something I'd longed for and that was within my grasp, but was suddenly jerked out of range. I gripped my luggage in one hand, certain I was headed back to Ellsworth. Nicholas had looked so happy and expectant on the landing, poised to give me a hug as I stepped off the train. Now his smile drooped. He reached out slowly for the book and looked up at me with a confused expression. He started to tuck the book under his arm, then flipped it over to read the back cover. "It says the author lives in Paris. You don't live in Paris."

"That was when he was younger. That was his first book, published in 1926. He lives in Cuba now."

"The dedication is only to a wife and son."

"I was born the day he started writing the book, and then my parents split up. He said my turn for a dedication will come. Of course, it never has yet."

Nick sagged a little. "You're not making this up?" I shook my head. Nick's mouth made a funny shape. "You're related to *the* Ernest Hemingway?"

I nodded.

"So, Tess, how closely *are* you related to him?" he said, a tease in his voice.

I hesitated, but played along. "As close as you can get."

He deadpanned, "You're his wife, and didn't want to tell me you're married?"

I made a face as if to say, *very funny,* and said, "I didn't want to tell you that the writer you were praising so much was my father because . . . I don't know, it sounded pretentious or something. You're saying all this great stuff like you're telling me something new, and for me to say, 'I know all that. That's my father's book,' felt like a put-down. I just wanted to keep talking to you. I'm really sorry." I was standing, feet shuffling.

Suddenly, Nicholas wrapped me in a hug. His glasses slipped down and he took them off. I dropped my suitcase and returned the hug, holding tight. Nicholas whispered in my ear, "So you could probably get Hemingway to autograph my copy for me?"

I laughed into the shoulder of his coat. "I think I could manage that. Just have to catch him at a still moment."

He loosened his grip and stepped back to look at me. "Tessa Hemingway it is, then. Sounds very literary, doesn't it? Give me that bag. We've cleared out a dorm completely for you girls."

Once at Exeter, I hurried to my room, so relieved by Nicky's reaction that I sank into the bed for a few seconds and took some deep breaths. He was as kind as I had hoped he might be. Instead of anger, he'd turned my lie into a light joke that we could—in my dreamiest of daydreams—tell our grandchildren.

Thirty minutes later, I was standing on a curb, trees bare but reaching high into blue sky, brick buildings everywhere, and expanses of lawn for breathing room. Nicholas pulled up in a shiny maroon Packard with a cream convertible top.

"Wow, nice car, rich boy!" It was jazzy.

"I think so. Get in, and let's fly this chicken coop."

Nicholas pulled out with a screech of tires and we headed to the barn where he kept three of his horses. It felt grown-up to be with a boy away from parents, doing what we wanted. Nicholas pulled up to the barn and we tumbled out, me in my navy skirt, white shirt, and a pale-blue cardigan. Nicky wore navy-blue slacks with a lighter blue pullover sweater and white shirt.

"We're practically twins!" I was giddy standing beside him and pointing to our getups.

"Practically, but not exactly," he said with a wink, and I flushed pink. He grabbed my hand, pulling me into the barn. I saw his ponies immediately. In a row on the right were three stalls with mahogany nameplates and gold lettering—Perfect Arc, Owner: Nicholas Armstrong. Dancing Girl, Owner: Nicholas Armstrong. Sara's Silence, Owner: Nicholas Armstrong.

I'm not a squealer, but I squealed with delight. "Oh, Nicky. My God, they are simply gorgeous. Can I go in?"

Nicky's face lit up. "Of course. I want you to."

I visited each horse for a few minutes, lingering with Dancing Girl. She was a dark bay with four white socks, elegant and sassy. She tried to muscle her way into my pocket for the gumdrop there, and when I turned to leave, she nudged my back as if to say, "Go ahead. See the others, but you'll always come back to me."

I said, "Oh, Nicky, they're so wonderful. Which one is your favorite?"

He beamed at me, one hand in his pocket and the other grasping mine. "Dancing Girl has my heart. She's killer-diller. When you find a special one, you never let them go, no matter what."

I took off my glove and began patting her neck. "I know what you mean," I said. Nicky watched me for a minute as I spoke to her, and she played with my fingers.

"Most girls would be afraid to do that," Nick said. "They think she'll bite."

I looked at Dancing Girl, who blinked her soft, brown eyes. "She and I are *simpatico*. We understand each other."

Nicky nodded and took my hand. I stepped away from the horse and we walked out together. He said, "I'll be playing polo all summer in Newport. Maybe you can come?"

I was flooded by the thrill of holding his hand and tried to focus on answering a simple question. "I'm in Cuba for most of the summer, but maybe I can get to Newport at the end."

For the dance the next night, I wore my first long dress—dark-green satin—and Nicky was in a charcoal-gray suit. When he danced with me for the first time, not counting the little dance in the barn, he held me close.

"We fit perfectly," I said. I was atwitter and felt bold and glowing.

He leaned back to look at me, then pulled me closer and my pulse quickened. He whispered in my ear, "Exactly my thought, Tess. And you never let go once you've found the one that fits."

***

The second I stepped into the Ellsworth dining hall on Sunday night, I knew Prill knew. A shiver of tension combined with anticipation hung like a shroud in the air. Her sources must have reported back. Me, the loser girl, got something Prill not only wanted, but thought she was entitled to. Instead of exultation, however, I felt tired. I certainly didn't *have* Nicholas, and I didn't like this game. It took too much energy to maintain this hostility.

I moved to the buffet line and quietly spooned out meatloaf and green beans, sensing two hundred pairs of eyes on my back. I took a deep breath and tugged on the hem of the white shirt over my blue plaid skirt. I missed Jeddrah's steady presence like a lost thumb. My eyes reached Prillie's table. She, Joannie, Cheryl, and Rachel, were all sitting tightly, forming a wall of enmity. My eyes moved from one to the next, stopping on Prill. The hatred radiating from her was so palpable that I felt its heat. Our eyes locked, and I stared back. All motion in the room stopped like a collective intake of breath.

I put my tray down and walked slowly to Prill's table. I stood rigidly. "Prill, I'm sorry. I'm sorry about all of it: my ignorance, my effort to fit in, and . . . Nicholas. I swear I had no idea who he was when I met him. I don't want to do this anymore."

Prill's words reverberated like a death rattle. "You think you won so it's over? Not ever. I *will* break you, Finn Hemingway. You are a liar and unworthy, and can never win against me."

I said nothing for a few seconds. Then, looking straight at Prill, I said in a quiet voice, "If you so much as come near me or Jedd, you will regret that you ever heard my name. Whatever you do to me, I will do to you ten times harder and ten times worse." I pivoted away and then back. "You will *never* break me. Hemingways don't break."

The room was motionless, and my words could be heard in every corner. Prill opened her mouth and closed it without saying anything else. I spun away and sat down alone. I knew this would never be over.

14

My life used to be full of everything. Now if you aren't with me I haven't a thing in the world.

~ Ernest Hemingway, *A Farewell to Arms*

Jeddrah didn't return to school that semester. She went to a hospital in the Berkshires. We wrote twice a week and spoke on the phone every Sunday. She had good days and bad days, but by May, her good days were more frequent. Her letters had become funny, and there was a gaiety in her voice some days.

One Sunday, as I huddled on the floor in the dorm hallway, knees drawn up, clutching the phone, I listened to Jeddrah's recap of the week. "Finn, you won't believe how crazy some of the girls here are. One girl won't eat—I mean, at all. Then another one steals anything that isn't locked down. She stole my barrette the other day. And there's this other girl who tries to have sex with any man who passes through here. I'm sort of normal here. Kids look to me for advice! Can you believe it?"

I smiled. "Yes, I can believe that! And how are you doing with the drinking?" I was apprehensive, as I'd seen Papa try to cut down on occasion. He'd grump around, and sometimes even seem sick. And the more anyone pointed it out, the more depressed or nasty he became, sometimes staying in his room all day.

"Well, I'm not drinking at all since I can't, but I think I'll be OK for junior year in September. And I take a riding class every day so I can ride with you at least a little bit. I was going to surprise you, but I cantered today for the first time. I loved it!"

"Oh, Jedd! I'll put you up on Sassafras and you'll think you are on a cloud. Did your parents promise you can come back in the fall?"

"They did. My father was a little mad that Ellsworth hadn't noticed anything sooner, but I told him I wanted to return. He said, 'OK then,' in that solemn voice of his." She mimicked his tone, and we both laughed. "And my mother said that one school is as good as another, so I have a counselor lined up. How is it all going for you?"

"Really well!" I hesitated. "What about . . . you know, Mr. Chandler?"

"Ha! Get this. I got a Dear Jeddrah letter saying, 'You're a dish of a girl, but you deserve more, blah blah.'" She paused. "You're still the only one who knows about him. I don't want him to get in trouble. I think he really did care for me, but still! What a drip!"

I laughed with relief. "I'll say."

I told Papa, and only Papa, about all of this, except for the Walter Chandler part. I felt that wasn't my confidence to share. After listening quietly on his end of the phone, Papa said, "Jeddrah is brave. She fell, but she's pulling herself up. I admire the hell out of her. And I'm so proud of you, Flea. A real friend shows up when everyone else is running for the exits. Me siento orgulloso de ti, querida hija."

I feel proud of you, beloved Daughter. I held onto those words tightly.

15

God knows I had not wanted to fall in love with her. I had not wanted to fall in love with any one. But God knows I had and I lay on the bed in the room of the hospital in Milan and all sorts of things went through my head but I felt wonderful.

~ Ernest Hemingway, *A Farewell to Arms*

Nicky and I wrote a few times a week that spring, scheming on how to soften up our parents for our desired visit that summer. Nick was starting his last year at Phillips Exeter that fall, and I would be a junior at Ellsworth. My mother was on the phone repeatedly with Nicky's mother and endlessly with my father. I was on the extension as often as I could manage when home, slinking upstairs in socks to avoid detection.

"I don't know about this visit, Tatie. Isn't Finn too young to stay for a week at a boy's house without either of us being there?" Tatie was one of the many nicknames they had for each other. We were a family overrun by nicknames.

"There are parents in the house, right? And she'll have her own room," my father said.

"Yes, and the Armstrongs seem very proper, but . . . oh, you surely remember what it's like to be sixteen and in love. I don't think we need to make it easy. Finn is so young and impressionable, and she thinks she's in love."

"And being in love is the greatest antidote to feeling alone in the world. Not a bad thing for our daughter, is it?" my father said.

"Oh, Tatie, this is serious, not just an idea. She has a reputation to uphold."

"So, are we talking about sex here, Cat? Because if we are, I want to go on record as being for it." Cat: another nickname.

Mother sighed. "Fine, kid around all you want, but if they . . . you know. Do you trust her?"

"Flea has a good head on her shoulders. The only way to find out if you can trust her is to trust her, and let her have her moment. Every girl deserves her moment to be full-blown loco in love and loved back by her guy like there's no tomorrow. Whether it lasts or it dies, she'll keep that memory for the rest of her life. We should let her have that. We should let her go."

I silently blessed Papa as I hung on anxiously for Mother's reply. He did always defer to her ultimately. Finley Hemingway Reality Rule #1.

Mother sighed more heavily. "Yeah, well, let's hope the ramifications don't last the rest of her life. I need to talk to her about boys and that stuff before she leaves."

"I suspect you don't. I suspect she knows that 'stuff.'"

I quietly hung up the phone, but not before Mother bellowed, "Finn, are you on this line? Hang up right now."

I was excited and nervous at the same time to be going to Nicky's house. I loved being alone with Nicky so much that it scared me a little, and Newport gave us lots of chances for it. On the other hand, I was anxious that his family might feel I wasn't good enough for their son, or an able Grable, girl of low morals. My father was a mixed blessing. Brilliant literary icon or reckless banned in Boston communist?

I received Mother's sex talk with respect and silence. The only point that caught my attention was the birth control part. The thought of Nicky being forced to marry me due to a baby made me shudder with horror. I only wanted him if he wanted me freely and for love.

Mother didn't have to worry much about sex, at least not that summer. We hovered around first base, tentative and thrilled. The reality is that it took all of my willpower to put the brakes on our explorings, and it was usually Nicky who insisted—in his newly acquired Spanish—that we halt by whispering in my ear, which made it worse, "Peligroso, querida niña, peligroso." Dangerous, darling girl, dangerous. I would move away, flushed, breathless, and exhilarated.

***

At the end of July, I left Newport for Cuba after my week with Nicky's family. The Finca was in better shape each time I saw it: fresh paint, repaired windows, and rediscovered gardens. Most of the rooms opened to lawns or patios, letting the ripe, Cuban air waft in.

The Finca Vigía was fast becoming a second home, much as Key West had become a refuge when Papa was married to Pauline. However, I could tell something had shifted for Papa and Marty that summer. Although Papa still praised her and wanted her around, he also made sly comments and delivered pointed put-downs.

"Marty, could you bring me my glasses? That is, if it's not too much trouble, or you're not packing for Singapore," or, "Yes, Marty is quite the writer now. She'll be supporting all of us in a few years," or, "Geez, Marty, how cheap could you be with the Christmas bonuses to the help? God help me if I ever need your charity."

Marty generally remained unfazed. To me, she was a goddess as elegant as a fashion model, plus a top-notch journalist who knew Eleanor Roosevelt well enough to sometimes stay at the White House. She was fun and athletic, and would jump up on a horse and ride with me many an afternoon in Cuba, and even more often when we were in Idaho.

I decided to take up the matter of Papa's marriage one rainy day as we sat reading in his study. Marty was in Havana entertaining friends from out of town. I slouched in a lounger, reading, trying to pick my moment as Papa sat straight in his. Now that I was in love, I yearned to know how love could just go away. That was frightening to me.

"Papa, you don't seem like yourself," I began. "You've been sleeping more than usual."

He didn't look up from *Anna Karenina*. "I like to sleep. My life has a tendency to fall apart when I'm awake."

I laughed. "But, Papa, you and Marty aren't going to get divorced, are you?"

Papa looked up, owlish eyes wide, surprised. He took off his glasses. "Now, Flea, why would you ask a crazy question like that?"

I shrugged. "I don't know. You just seem to yell at her a lot more now than at Christmas."

He sighed and rubbed his eyes. "Married people don't always have the smoothest of times, chiquita."

"I know, but we all love her, and it's hard for us to be starting over again—you know, if you get a divorce again." I looked down at my book, nervous about the mood of the room.

"Well, it's hard for me too, but we're in a rough spot."

"Why? What's so hard about loving someone?"

Papa sighed. "I don't know, Flea. Your mother is the only woman who seemed to be able to cope with my peaks and valleys and still laugh at the end of it. Except for that time she lost my manuscripts." He growled a little at that memory, which was still a sore point some eighteen years later. On a Paris train in 1923, my mother lost a valise with all of Papa's drafts to date—just about everything. Papa shook his head. "But for that, I can't say a bad word about her. I don't know. It all seemed so easy then." He looked at me, closed his book, and smiled almost apologetically. "I love to be in love, Flea, but I can't ever seem to repeat what your mother and I had. I keep trying, but I'm not an easy fit. When day-to-day life starts to encroach, I'm not so good. I know that. Marty has her own dreams, and so she should. But she's decided I'm an obstacle, and that I'm trying to crush her ambitions."

I didn't know what to say. "Are you?"

Papa shook his head. "Hell no. I want her to get credit for the work she does. She's a damned fine writer and a brave person."

"But isn't she happy here with you? With us?"

"Well, Flea, happiness in intelligent people is the rarest thing I know. Marty needs what I have—recognition for her work—and I can't give it to her. So she's always leaving to find it on her own. I've offered a hand up, but she wants none of it," he said.

"I don't get it." The fact that love could rush in so strongly and then recede just as fast terrified me. I hated considering that this crash of love I felt for Nicky might vanish next week, or worse, his for me could evaporate tomorrow. Papa's romantic calamities made love feel like something slippery, something you couldn't build a future on, nice as it might be for a few moments. I persisted. "But, when you're in love, don't you just always want to be together and do stuff for each other?"

Papa paused and thought. "Well, ideally, yes. But, in day-to-day life? Yes and no. And this is just me. When I have all of the balls in the air and they're twirling just right, love rises to a place of primo importance. When the rest is not so great, all I want to do is spend every morsel of gray matter on the writing. Then I crave writing a novel greater than . . . than that asshole Faulkner. Geez, what the hell? Does he think I don't know his ten-dollar words? I know 'em, all right. I just choose to use older, simpler, and better words. Anyway, when I'm writing, love falls from the top five list, Flea." He put his glasses back on and peered at me over the tops. "The top four, by the way, are the book. But for what it's worth, you, Flea, are number five, querida mia."

I smiled, as I always wondered where I fell on his list. I didn't necessarily believe him, but it was nice to hear. "But, Papa, please, will you try to make it work with Marty?"

Papa sat back. "I'll try, but no matter how it comes out, being in love is sure worth it all while it's going on. It's the *only* thing worth a damn, Flea. Remember that. I still love Marty, and I think she still loves me. That can cover a shitload of sins."

16

When you love you wish to do things for. You wish to sacrifice for. You wish to serve.

~ Ernest Hemingway, *A Farewell to Arms*

Madison Square Garden was on Eighth and Fiftieth in Manhattan in November 1941, not down on Thirty-Fourth where it is now. Papa commissioned a trailer to deliver Sassafras from Greenwich to midtown Manhattan, where Nicky and I paced the curb impatiently until the horse's equine limousine arrived. The stress was through the roof as scores of highly trained and very valuable thoroughbreds accustomed to fields, fences, and serenity clomped off their vans to the sound of blaring traffic and not a blade of grass in sight. One area was reserved for unloading, and riders tried to move their horses inside as fast as possible.

Usually a model of common sense, Sassafras was unnerved by the horns and chaos of New York City, and for the first time, I wondered if he would rear or bolt. The thought of him dashing wild-eyed down Eighth Avenue had my stomach in knots all that morning.

Nicky hopped up on the platform and came out with Sassafras in tow. I saw Sassafras's eyes dart from right to left and back again. When his hooves hit the pavement, he skidded and tried to gain purchase on smooth asphalt as sparks flew from his shod feet. When he heard my voice, he stopped.

"Sassy boy, it's all just fine. Let's find you a nice stall to rest in."

I spoke soothingly, and finally, he dropped his head and let me stroke his muzzle and feed him a peppermint. Nicky grasped the lead rope close to the horse's mouth. In a few minutes, he'd calmed, and Nicky led him into the building.

"I just whisper in his ear," I told Nicky as we strolled down the aisle, Sassafras between us, walking easily now. "It always settles him. You should try it."

"Hmm. That works with me too, you know. Just whisper in my ear," he said with a smile as he led the horse to his stall. "And what do you whisper to him, by the way?"

"Wouldn't you like to know," I teased, then relented. "I tell him stories about when I got him, what's ahead, and how much I love him."

"Just what I thought. And again, it works with me too." I leaned over and kissed Nicky.

The next day, I woke up refreshed and full of energy after an evening of exhibitions and cavalry maneuvers that had left me speechless with admiration. I put on my freshly laundered riding jacket and breeches. Nicky pinned my number—133— to my back, held me at arm's length, and nodded as if to say, "You look just right."

When I peered out into the arena, I sucked in my breath. The stands were packed with spectators who had come to see the best of the best. Families climbed the stairs, carrying programs and popcorn. I looked hard for a familiar face but the Garden was too big, and the faces blended from this distance. Jedd, who had returned to Ellsworth in September, had promised to be there, but my father was unclear about his schedule—as was so often the case. One hundred percent reliable sixty percent of the time.

The noise was deafening as the preceding class exited the ring to applause and whistles. I pulled down my jacket and did a few stretches as I waited for my turn. Higher jumps were set up for our class, and the arena had just been dragged to smooth the dirt footing.

I watched from the sidelines as my class progressed. Jackie Bouvier had just completed a perfect ride in the fastest time so far on her beautiful mare, Danseuse. I watched with awe as she jetéed around the course as elegant as any ballet at the Met. I sighed at the grace with which she took the water jump and immediately spun to attack a four-foot wall.

I heard the grainy loudspeaker. "Next up is number 133, Finley Hemingway, of Chicago, Illinois, on California Sassafras."

We were on! I ran to the stall area, but Nicky had it covered. In his own riding boots and breeches, he gave me a leg up. I settled into the saddle like it was a comfortable chair by the fire.

"Show 'em how it's done, Tessa."

He stepped away. I swallowed hard and leaned forward to whisper into Sassafras's ear. "You are the most beautiful thoroughbred here, and we can fly like the wind over the high seas."

Sassafras lifted his head. He was polished to a mahogany finish, his black tail swishing, white star on his forehead bright, ears pricked forward. He pawed the ground with one hoof and stomped his right foot twice.

I pulled my helmet on tighter and pressed my leg behind his girth. I stopped at the entrance gate to let Jackie and Danseuse exit.

"You were both just beautiful," I said.

Jackie smiled shyly. "Thank you so much. And good luck to you, Finley."

She knew my name! Sassafras and I trotted into the ring. When he heard the roar of the crowd, he faltered and took a sidestep. I whispered, "We belong here."

We straightened and headed for our course.

I tried to block out the noise and not think about whether Papa was out there somewhere or not. He was closing down the Idaho summer rental house, but wasn't sure what Marty's schedule was or where he might be needed. He'd never seen me ride in a show or on Sassafras at all. I wanted to scream that Madison Square Garden was "where he was needed." Instead, I said, "I understand, Papa."

After the opening circle at the canter, Sassafras and I headed for the first jump, an easy distance and height, soaring over it smoothly and landing well. As we continued, the jumps, distances, and turns became trickier, calling for more talent and balance. Stride, stride, jump, stride, jump, jump, jump. I rode as well and as fast as I dared over walls, twisted turns, water jumps. I wasn't as good as Jackie, but I jumped clean, and enjoyed the heck out of it.

When I finished, the applause was thunderous. I was grinning and high as the edge of the sky. I stroked Sassafras's neck so he'd know he'd done well and then scanned the crowd. Like a laser beam, I spotted him, fifth row, behind the water jump with Max Perkins, Papa's editor, on his right in his signature felt hat, and Jeddrah on his left.

I stood in my stirrups and waved wildly. Papa stood and waved back with both arms straight in the air crisscrossing, whistling his catcall. I came in second, behind Jackie, and as I trotted up for my ribbon, the only thing I heard, the only voice that mattered, even above Nicky's, was Papa's. "Fantastic, Flea!"

I smiled blindly into the glaring lights, seeing only my father in the sparkle and shine, even though I couldn't really see him.

***

It was a cold Sunday in early December. I was in the barn grooming Sassafras, teasing tangles from his tail with a fine-tooth comb and daydreaming about Nicky, as well as about my upcoming Christmas vacation when I'd be baking in the Cuban sun. The serene mood was shattered when Gertie tore into the barn. "Pearl Harbor—you know, our base in Hawaii—was bombed!"

Ten girls popped out of stalls, brushes or hoof picks in hand, the same look of alarm on each face. Rushing to the tack room with a trail of girls behind me, I grabbed the radio and jacked up the volume. We all strained to hear the news through the static. As I sat on the floor, a horse blanket beneath me, Gertie next to me, we learned we'd lost almost the whole Pacific fleet, with thousands of deaths. I shivered and fled to call Mother. Jedd was already on the phone with her father. She waved and looked near tears as I waited my turn.

"Finn, just stay where you are. We'll know more tomorrow," Mother said when I finally reached her.

"But will Papa, Jack, and Nicky have to fight?"

Mother hesitated. "I don't know, Finn."

Papa was in Arizona with Marty. I tried to call him, with no luck. He called me that night.

"Thought something was coming, but never dreamed it would be this bad or that it would be the Japs. I may actually have to get back in the war business. Sorry thing, war."

The next day, in a rare moment of silence, we girls huddled in the living room to hear President Roosevelt declare war. Faces ranged from grim to flat-out terrified. I didn't know what it meant to be "at war" but I didn't want Papa to go. He was forty-two years old and exempt from being drafted. He'd been wounded in World War I while driving an ambulance, and we'd all heard about his love affair with his nurse, Agnes Von Kurowsky, more times than any of us kids cared to remember.

Jack would yell as soon as Papa started, "Not again, Papa. We feel like *we* were dumped by Agnes if we have to hear that story again."

Papa would laugh. One thing no one knew about Papa unless they spent a lot of time with him was that he was really funny. His books and stories are serious yet at home he was very funny, and his letters could be hysterical.

"And you can hear it one more time, Bumb," he'd say. "There's a life lesson here, Mousie and Gig, and you too, Flea. Broken places get stronger." Gig was Gregory.

We'd all moan because we'd heard *that* old saw a million times too, but he'd continue. Usually we all said it in unison before he did. *We know, the broken places get stronger.*

Agnes became a version of Catherine Barkley in *A Farewell to Arms*. We all knew that. Papa was opportunistic in that way. He used people and events that he knew, twisted them a little and added some make-believe. Sometimes he didn't add enough make-believe and clearly recognizable people in his social set showed up pretty much undisguised. That would start the tongues wagging and the phone fights with Max Perkins.

Papa: "Jaysus, Max, it's not that transparent, and I made it a different town."

Max: "Blah blah."

Papa: "Why don't you ask me to write a different story altogether while I'm at it? OK, fine. I'll change the 'Poor Scott' reference to 'Poor Julien.'"

Nicky turned eighteen in March 1942, and he registered for the draft as required by law.

"Maybe your eyesight is too bad, Nicky," I said too eagerly.

Nicky disabused me of that notion. "Tessa, it's war," he said grimly. "Every able-bodied man I know is prepared to ship out. I'd feel ashamed not to go."

Still, he perked up when I visited him in Newport the summer of '42. His family was always pleasant, but reserved, with his mother shaking my hand when I arrived even though it was the third time we'd met.

I ached to lean against the Packard, head tipped back, Nicky pressing into me, closer and closer, my hands in the back pockets of his jeans, pulling him in, kissing him lightly at first, then harder and harder until the world was spinning. I yearned to run crazily along the beach with the ocean roaring, me grabbing the back of his t-shirt, pulling it over his head, and pulling him on top of me. I was obsessed with his nearness and with him. As soon as was decent, we'd scramble to be alone with the horses, the sun, the sea—and each other.

That summer, there was no gas for the Packard. We walked everywhere, and knew every private curve and corner of Bellevue Avenue, Newport. I reveled in the fact that Nicky was so unlike my father. He was always there when he said he would be. One hundred percent reliable one hundred percent of the time. Maybe, just maybe, love didn't always end badly for all Hemingways.

Papa liked him too. "Nick is different," Papa said as we sat around the pool at the Finca on a scorching summer afternoon. He'd met Nicky twice. "You wouldn't know he's rich. Scott always thought the rich were better than the rest of us. He said 'different,' but he meant 'better.' I just figured they had more money than the rest of us."

I repeated all of this to Nicky, and he glowed.

That summer was so different from all previous summers. It usually was us, the Hemingways of Havana, against the world: Papa, me, Jack, Mouse (Patrick's nickname), Gig—and Martha. Now, Jack, although still enrolled at Dartmouth, was constantly talking about enlisting. Marty was away more, and when home, she was often on the phone angling for a position as a war correspondent. She and Papa argued all the time, most recently about her goading Papa to do something more meaningful for the war effort. I didn't like her mockery, but I admired her courage. Papa took it badly.

When Marty did earn a war assignment in Europe, I felt a sadness come over Papa. He was drinking heavily, and seemed angry and depressed often. He took most of it out on Marty.

While Martha tried to keep up a good front when we were there—Gregory/Gig and I absolutely adored her—we all heard the tail end of one heated argument with Papa roaring, "I'll show you, you conceited bitch. They'll be reading my stuff long after the worms have finished with you."

I thought, so this is how a great love ends for us Hemingways—again. But maybe not for me. Maybe I escaped the Hemingway love curse. Just maybe, Nicky and I wouldn't end.

17

There isn't always an explanation for everything.

~ Ernest Hemingway, *A Farewell to Arms*

Nicky started Yale on schedule in September 1942, and I started my last year at Ellsworth. I took advanced elocution classes, hoping it would help me in trial classes in law school. Three months later, Nicky's lottery number was called. I cursed that he was one of the first called up under the reduced draft age of eighteen and had just about accepted that Nicky would be gone soon when he called to say they rejected him.

"Flat feet!" he said with incredulity. "I never even knew they were flat. Maybe the cavalry will take me. Do we still have a cavalry?"

I was ashamed that I felt so happy about his news. It was too much like celebrating someone else's tragedy because at least it wasn't yours. We talked on the phone as often as we could, but it was only when one of us could hop a ride with someone having a war purpose that we saw each other. Nick's family owned a half-intcrest in Armstrong Munitions in Bridgeport, Connecticut, and, on occasion, one of us could hitch a lift on the run between New York and Boston. When it was my turn, I'd crawl in back, straddling the gun and machine parts, and sit on the floor of the truck with legs stretched, vibrating in anticipation of the New Haven arrival an hour and a half away.

Back at school, the mean girls were still mean, but after Prillie knew I went to the spring dance at Exeter so long ago and that I would defend myself if need be, it was as if she went into a coma. She still taunted me, but most jibes landed lifeless at my feet, with no one picking up the cause.

One Saturday morning just after I'd finished cooling out Sassafras, I noticed that my barn cat, Baby, was not lurking as she always did. I snapped Sassafras's saddle pad, our shared signal, but no Baby. I walked outside the barn and scanned the area, but my cat was not there.

"Hey!" I called to several other girls milling around. "Has anyone seen Baby?"

A few heads shook, but one said, "I saw her earlier, Finn. Prillie was carrying her out of the barn in one of those crate things."

"Thanks." I jammed my hands into my barn coat, quickly put Sassafras's blanket on, and slid the stall door shut.

I started walking to the main campus, my speed increasing the closer I got to the dorm. Soon, I was jogging. I strode into the dorm. As luck would have it, Prill was standing in the living room sorting mail. The memory of her insults and taunts swamped me as I snatched her arm and spun her around to face me. This wasn't just about Baby's disappearance.

"Where's my cat?" I demanded.

Prillie gaped at me, a stunned look in her eyes at first, then a smug one. She shook my hand off like it was a scorpion, took a step back, and practically spat at me.

"Get your disgusting hands off of me. I don't know what you're talking about, you lunatic."

Girls began to gather. I was dressed in my riding clothes while she was in cashmere, and I suspect I had a crazed look about me, making this a clear-cut face-off between beauty and the savage.

"You have Baby, and I want her back."

Prillie raised an eyebrow. "You're insane. Go back to the cave you crawled out of," she said, and turned away.

I was sick of being mocked. I seized her arm again. "No! This time I'm not shrinking away. You're going to be accountable for once."

"Shrinking? You, Finley? Hardly the word that comes to mind."

Without thinking and too angry to care, I snapped out the thing I thought would hurt her most. "Really? Well, Nicholas, of the Newport Armstrongs, doesn't seem to mind."

Prillie jerked back as if she'd touched a hot radiator, then said, "There is no cat—anymore. That stupid little mongrel was just perfect for you. Such a pity she met with such a very sad accident."

"No!" I shouted, then grabbed her sweater and pushed her hard against a wall. I jacked her up a little and my thumbs pressed into her neck. I began to squeeze. Prillie's eyes widened and watered. She began to cough dryly and to flail.

For the first time, I knew what it meant to "see red." All I wanted to do was to shut Prill up, stop her. As Prillie made louder gasping noises, I felt two sets of arms pulling me back. Jeddrah murmured, "Come on, Finn. Don't get yourself in trouble over her. She's not worth it." She pried one arm loose.

Another voice spoke from the second set of arms, "Let her go, honey. It will be all right. Let's just move that hand away from her throat." Those arms relaxed the grip of my other hand.

I recognized that second voice, but it sounded different. This one was soothing and gentle. I'd previously heard taunts from that voice. I turned and my eyes widened. It was Joannie Janssen, one of Prillie's quartet of evil, her right-hand girl. *Was this a trick?*

I sprung my hands open and Prillie hit the floor with a thud, sputtering and shaken up, but seemingly unhurt. Prillie staggered up and exploded. "I'm reporting you, you freak! You're going to be expelled! Everyone saw."

I sucked in my breath, realizing I'd behaved abhorrently—criminally, in fact. I would be expelled. I looked down, wondering how I would tell my father. Then I heard a voice from the gathered circle of girls. "I'm not so sure, Prillie. It was all kind of a jumble. A bit of a tussle, actually. Very confusing what happened." It was Gertie.

Prillie's lip curled. "That's how it's going to be, is it?" she said, eyes now slits. She gestured toward me with her chin. "Who's with *that*? Other than the other loser, Jeddrah."

Jeddrah, Gertie, and I stood together. I saw Helen Farwell, who'd been my partner on a history project last year, nod her head. "Me," she said simply.

Prillie's mouth twisted. "You're all pathetic."

She stared at Rachel Warner and Cheryl McAdams, her two girls. They both looked startled, as if so fascinated by the drama playing out in front of them, they'd not realized their leader required them. They perked up, shoved two girls aside, and placed themselves squarely next to Prillie. Another girl joined Prill, who grinned at her. The four of them held hands. Four against four. Joannie stood silent.

Rachel held out a hand to her, a fierce look in her green eyes as if to say, "I don't know what got into you, but come back, and all is forgiven."

Joannie eyed it and shook her head. "You could have crippled Sassafras, and you didn't care. You laughed. If that had happened to Birthday Boy, I don't know what I . . . And you were going to kill Baby, or have one of them do it for you." She jerked her chin toward Rachel and Cheryl. She stepped next to Helen and Gertie. There were tears in her eyes.

Prillie stared, disbelieving, then exploded. "You always were low class. I took pity on you, and this is the thanks I get. Go! Be with the other nothings."

I blinked and turned to Prillie. "Why? I just wanted everyone to be friends and get along. Why are you like this?"

Prillie, recovered, bolted up the staircase away from my reach as if afraid I'd seize her again, but turned back once safely on the landing. "Because I *loathe* you."

The room hushed. I was bewildered that I could cause such strong feelings, and for a moment, was deflected from my purpose of recovering Baby.

"What did I ever do to you?" I asked.

Prillie bent over the railing. "You did *plenty*." She said each word distinctly. "From the moment I set eyes on you, I hated how simple you were, thinking everyone can play on the same field. And your father's a communist and sex pervert who thinks everyone is equal and is rewarded for writing disgusting things. If you'd followed the rules for one year, you could have fit in somewhere. You're not equal to me. No lineage, no beauty, no class. Kind of monstrous, actually. You didn't even know enough to trade on your father's name, although his filthy books are not much to crow about, are they?"

Helen spoke up, her light-brown hair pulled back in a blue, plaid headband. "You're just jealous. Finn's smart, and she is every bit as attractive as you. Her father is the most famous writer in America. And she got your boyfriend. You just couldn't stand it, could you? Well, too bad. Sometimes the nice girl actually does win."

I found my voice after nodding a thanks to Helen. I said, "You're not better than anyone else here. And my cat better be back at the barn by morning or my next stop is the dean's office to report that a grad student from Yale writes your class papers. People tell me things, too."

Prillie blanched. For the first time, she looked alarmed. I headed to the door to return to the barn with Jedd. Prill blurted, yelling at my back, "You don't think Nicholas actually likes you, do you? He'll drop you as soon as he can, and then he'll come for me. He wants to be a journalist, and he's just using you, hoping you'll fall for him so he can get ahead using your father."

I spun back and smiled my brightest smile. "Well, hell, he's a *really* bright one then, because it's working."

Prillie's face drained of color. The next morning, Baby was back and I celebrated with Jedd, Helen, and Gertie over sodas and magazines.

18

Keep right on lying to me. That's what I want you to do.

~ Ernest Hemingway, *A Farewell to Arms*

I set aside two weeks at the end of the summer to visit Nicky in Newport. I would graduate in May from Ellsworth and was relieved to leave it behind. I was particularly eager to share in Nicky's end-of-the-season polo match, to be followed that evening by the Black and White Costume Ball held at Copperbeech Cottage, the home of the top Newport socialite of the day, Victoria Chapple. It would be our first grown-up event together. As an added attraction, I promised to groom for him—prepare his horses for the game.

"All you'll have to do is hop on your horses, play like a banshee, and never worry about a thing," I'd promised him during one of my rare visits to Yale that spring.

Nicky backed me against a wall in the dining hall, one arm high on each side of me. "Really? And what do you want for all of that perfection, Tess?"

He leaned in as he spoke and I curved one arm around his waist, pulling him to me. I whispered in his ear, "All I want is a private dance with you under the stars to 'I'll Be Seeing You' with just the wind between us, Armstrong. Nothing else."

He smiled a slow, seductive smile. "You've got it, Miss Hemingway," he said as he moved in unhurriedly, placing his hands on my hips. He pressed me against the wall and bent close for a kiss. Within a minute, his buddies surrounded us, hooting and whistling. "Smooth move, Armstrong. Maybe you better take it to a motel, lover boy."

Nicky laughed and said over his shoulder, "Could you guys scram? Go have dinner. Go anywhere but here."

Nicky and I turned together, waved at them, and headed out, his arm flung over my shoulder. We were in step and in love, and happy in the way only first love can be.

Jack was at Fort Riley in Kansas, where he'd been accepted into Officers Candidate School. He, like me, spoke French fluently, which was an invaluable asset for the war effort.

"Yeah, who knew, Finn, my French would come in so handy," he said.

I smiled on my end of the phone. "My French is better than yours."

"It is, but don't be so competitive, little sister. And speaking of familial relations, how is our cher père? You hear from him more than I do."

I thought about whether to tell him just the facts or to add my editorial comments. "He's odd."

"Odder than usual?" Jack laughed.

I laughed too. "He scraps with Marty a lot. And he's drinking more again. And you know what happens then. Any little thing that would only slightly bother him when sober leads to some nasty blow-up. They were fighting last time I was there about Marty taking a job in Europe."

Jack sighed. "I hope he doesn't mess this thing up with Marty. I really like her."

"Yeah, tell me about it." I felt my face cloud.

Sensing the downturn in the conversation, Jack changed the subject. "So how's Nick doing?"

"He's OK, but not happy not to be heading to France himself. Or the Philippines or wherever." I hesitated. "He hates that he's home."

"That could change soon." He stopped abruptly, as if afraid he'd said too much.

I was on the phone in the hallway of my dorm. I leaned back as girls shuffled to the bathroom with their totes loaded with shampoo and hair rollers. I held the receiver tighter. "What do you mean?"

He hesitated. "Don't get all Finned-up on me, but I heard that the requirements are being lowered. They're pulling in the almost blind and crippled. Some guys are enlisting before they get called up so they at least have some choice about which branch they go into."

I tensed. "I hadn't heard that." But I had.

It was in that frantic time of uncertainty, and at times, despair, that the Newport polo game stood as a desperate effort to pretend parts of life might continue despite the reality that there were few men left to play, or groom, or drive the rigs.

This was the most privileged layer of society, but still their sons, husbands, and fathers were enlisting and dying like everyone else.

Nicky and I got to the Newport barn early in the afternoon. Partying was in full swing, with picnics set out on blankets; a few more ambitious types sported polished mahogany drop-leaf tables complete with silver candelabras and plates of cucumber sandwiches, deviled eggs, and grape bunches. People milled about sampling each other's spreads and catching up on summer gossip.

"We're part of the gossip, you know," Nicky said to me as we backed the horses out of the trailer and tied them to its side.

"We are? Why?"

"Hmm. Let's see. The beautiful daughter of the most famous writer in America is dating a mere mortal from Newport and is stooping to groom for him, a job usually consigned to the hired help. And just maybe her father will show up. You never know!"

I smiled. "Right. More like son of Newport royalty dating his groom, who happens to be the daughter of crazy man and occasionally banned-in-Boston novelist Ernest Hemingway. And, while I do wish he would show up, I think he's too busy figuring out how to move on to wife number four to make time for daughter number one. No self-pity intended!"

This possibility of wife number four worried me more than I let on to Nicky. The last time I called my father and asked to speak to Marty, he said nastily, "She's gone to Finland to make some money. Barely said goodbye."

However, for the moment, I shook off the concerns about Papa and Marty. I pulled on riding gloves and for close to two hours, I worked to be sure each pony glistened. Soon I had the satisfaction of staring at seven rumps, all with tails tied up perfectly and ready to go.

I glanced at my watch—ten minutes until the throw in. Westport's Rough Riders were led by Nicky's best pal from Yale, Jonah MacGill. While they were teammates at Yale, that day, they were opponents. Jonah rode up to our trailer on a stunning black mare who could barely contain herself. She pranced and sidestepped but looked good-natured, just keen to get the game started. Jonah himself looked dashing in his white riding breeches and English racing-green shirt.

"Hi, Tess! Is Nick around?" he asked.

I looked up, shading my eyes from the sun. "Hi, Jonah. He's already on the field." I pointed.

"Ah, I must have missed him." Jonah twisted and paused. I stood, still squinting, and spotted Nicky hitting a long drive up the field, two of his teammates backing him up in case of a miss and one ahead to get the pass near the goal. I looked at him for a long time and felt a pang of foreboding that next summer, Nicky wouldn't be playing any polo.

Jonah turned back and hesitated. "Look, I may be way off base here, but, uh, may I suggest, Tess, that you watch out for Prill Lamont. I don't know what it is about you, but she never misses a chance to comment on you and Nick, and it's not to wish you well. She's not nice and you are. That's never an even fight."

"Oh, she's here?"

"Yeah, unfortunately."

Jonah's pony was now pawing the ground and bobbing her head while mouthing her bit nervously. I gently grasped the reins and whispered in her ear as I did with Sassafras. She stopped pawing and calmed.

"There's a good girl," I said softly to the hyperventilating horse. "Nothing to be nervous about. Jonah will give you a grand ride." I looked up at Jonah. "She hates me."

He looked confused. I clarified. "Not the horse. She's a love, and we understand each other completely." I continued to stroke her muzzle and gave it a kiss. "No. Prillie. We both graduated from Ellsworth in May, and she hated me then. Prill thinks I'm not good enough for Nicky, and that I took him from her."

Jonah looked serious. "Just ignore her. You're as good as they come." He joked. "Heck, you're too good for Nick, and I love him like a brother."

Jonah turned his horse. She pivoted, all business now, knowing she was about to play. I watched him gallop up to Nicky. They shook hands, chatted a minute, and took their positions next to each other in the lineup. The National Anthem played and a pin drop could be heard. Hats were doffed and hands crossed hearts.

The game started with Westport taking the lead. Newport had to hustle just to stay in the game. By the end of the second chukker (a chukker is like a seven-and-one-half-minute inning), the score was 3–1 in the Rough Riders' favor. Nicky was glum as he handed Sara to me and took Dancing Girl, his best horse, for the third chukker. I untacked Sara, cooled her out, and tied her to the trailer while keeping one eye on the field as the next chukker started. To my delight, Nicky scored, and his buddy Graham King nabbed a goal as well, tying the score at 3–3.

As I watched the last two minutes of the third chukker, I caught someone approaching from the corner of my eye. I hefted a saddle back into the trailer and turned around to be confronted by Prillie Lamont. She was a petite fashion plate in a yellow silk dress and matching straw hat. I froze. I thought I was done with her when we graduated from Ellsworth.

She stared at me. "Ah, Finn. Still slogging it in the manure trenches, I see." I wiped my hands on my breeches, saying nothing. I looked away at the playing field.

"And still Nick's little slave, I see." I was silent. She stood there staring at me. I watched the game as if she were not there.

She sighed. "Ever the poised conversationalist." She paused, one hand on hip, and then continued, voice sarcastic. "Well, I'll leave you to your menial chores. I'm here with Victoria Chapple's nephew, Alistair. He's at Harvard. So glad I dodged that pathetic Nick alliance."

I still said nothing. She took one dainty step away in her heeled shoe, then turned partly back. "Just some friendly advice. For old time's sake. You really should be a bit less of a doormat. But then, for him to notice you at all must be the highlight of your life. Since it will end soon, enjoy it while you can!" She paused. "Must go. Alistair will be looking for me."

Feeling a wave of mischief wash over me, I said, "Honestly, Prill, 'the simplicity of your character makes you exquisitely incomprehensible to me,' so please leave." I was quoting from *The Importance of Being Earnest*, because Oscar Wilde was much wittier than I could ever be.

Prillie, clearly unfamiliar with Oscar Wilde, pivoted fully back, face alive now that she had gotten what she wanted—for me to engage with her.

"What? What did you say?"

I faced her head on. She came up to my shoulder. "I said that 'I misjudged you. You are not the moron I thought you were. You're only a case of arrested development.'" This was Ernest Hemingway, *The Sun Also Rises*.

Her face had blossomed into a blotchy rose color and her hands were balled into little fists. She took a step toward me. "Are you insulting me? Did you just call me a moron?"

I was on a roll. "No. Listen closely. I said you are *not* a moron."

"What? What?" She moved closer and raised an open hand. Just then, Nicky rode up and jumped off Dancing Girl. The spell was broken, and I turned from Prillie to Nicky. He was glowing with good sweat and from the tie score.

"Everything OK here, Tess?" He looked from me to Prillie, his smile waning. "Oh, hi Prill."

I strode to the other side of the trailer and came back hauling Perfect Arc. "Everything's great," I said. "Prill was just going to join her group. We did a little reminiscing, but I need to stomp some divots now that it's halftime. Prill, clearly you won't be participating."

Nick looked down at Prill's heels, sinking deeper into the lawn. "Ha, I guess you're just not cut out for the polo life, Prill. The shoes." He shook his head mournfully, then said, "But you can still cheer us on."

Prillie scowled, then recovered and said brightly to Nicky, "Yes, well I will do that. And I hope to see you tonight at Victoria's ball. Cole Porter is coming. He's a close friend of my mother's, and promised to play something especially for me."

I'd once met him and his wife, Linda, while in New York City with Papa, and he'd been lovely and gracious. Since then, Mr. Porter had been in a horrific riding accident—his legs were crushed—and he often used a wheelchair to maneuver, yet he never held it against the horse.

Nicky threw an arm over my shoulder, gave it a squeeze, then hopped onto Perfect Arc. "We wouldn't miss it for the world, would we, Tess?"

I smiled, flipped Dancing Girl's reins over her head, and led her back to the trailer. With a light kick to Arc's side, Nicky waved and galloped back onto the field.

Prillie gazed after him with palpable longing. She abruptly turned to tiptoe back in the direction she came from but not before flinging a parting salvo at me. "Mark my words. You will rue the day Nick Armstrong walked into your life."

"I will regret nothing except any time I spent hoping you would like me. Goodbye, Prillie."

I turned back to Dancing Girl, unwinding her leg wraps before joining the crowd dotting the field to press down upended grass chunks.

19

A coward dies a thousand times, but a brave man only once.

~ Ernest Hemingway, *A Farewell to Arms*

The evening was clear, and the air was balmy with a breeze off the water. The theme of the Black and White Ball was famous couples. Nick and I were going as Rick and Ilsa from *Casablanca*. I'd been able to pin my hair into a roll back style to resemble Ingrid Bergman's hairdo, and I'd found a white dress that closely mimicked the dress she wore when she asked Sam to "play it again." It was sleek, but not tight, and it hit my leg at mid-calf. I thought I looked sophisticated, elegant, and maybe a little sexy.

Apparently, Nicky agreed, because he wolf-whistled when I walked down the main staircase of his house. He was waiting for me in the front hall. While Newport Horsepower had lost the game in overtime, he was still in a great mood and looked devastating in his Rick/Humphrey Bogart white dinner jacket with black bow tie. His dark hair was still damp from his shower, and it curled around his collar.

"You look beautiful, Tessa," Nicky said as I spun around, skirt flaring a little. He caught my hand and pulled me to him as his mother came around the corner. I quickly stepped back and smoothed my skirt.

She smiled. "Hello, dears. You look lovely, Tess. As beautiful as Ingrid Bergman herself. And you, Nicholas." She took a step back to take in the full view. She held out her arms as if to say, "No words do this justice," then dropped them, and shook her head with a wistful expression. "You look all grown up, Nicholas, and very handsome." She started up the stairs, and turned to me over her shoulder. "I am happy Nicholas found you, Tess."

My heart thumped. "Thank you, Mrs. Armstrong." She turned and continued up.

I whispered in Nicky's ear, "Do you think they'll kick me out because I'm not one of *the* four hundred?" I was referring to the code established by Caroline Astor, who limited her invitations to the four hundred socially prominent people in New York society. Having money alone didn't get you in. The Armstrongs were in; the Hemingways definitely were not.

Nicky winked at me. "It is all so ridiculous."

Copperbeech Cottage was five acres of green lawn surrounding a cream-colored, two-story stucco home. It was slow going for me walking in heels, but we made it. The back of the house faced the Cliff Walk, with panoramic views of the ocean. A fountain surrounded by pink and purple impatiens gurgled on the front lawn.

It was dusk, and I faintly heard music that got louder as the door opened. Drinks were thrust into our hands and I saw a sea of black and white everywhere. Nicky took my hand and led me to the ballroom. We snaked through the throngs as he waved to a few people.

Everything about the room was golden: the sconces, the gilded scrolls on the ceiling, the chandeliers, the mirrors above the fireplaces on each end of the ballroom. Candles flickered on tables and *the* Tommy Dorsey band occupied one end of the room. French doors were flung open to the sea. I could see terraced gardens, more lawn, a fancy iron fence, and then just the sea. Salty breezes poured in along with mist. I stood in the open doorway facing the ocean and breathed in deeply. Nicky had one hand on my shoulder. He leaned in and whispered, "Someday, we'll have our own little place by the sea, Tessa. Not like this, but beautiful anyway."

Still looking out, I said, "I know we will. I can see it."

He held out his arms as the band took up the tune "As Time Goes By." Nicky said, "Hey, our song for tonight anyway, Ilsa." I melted into Nicky. His arm tightened until there was no space between us.

"Later, we'll dance to this with only the wind between us, nothing else," he whispered.

"No, it has to be 'I'll Be Seeing You,'" I said.

"Then 'I'll Be Seeing You' it is," he said quietly.

I closed my eyes and said a prayer thanking God for giving me this. I thought, *Everyone should be given a moment like this once in their lives. Even if it only lasts one night, at least I had it this one time. At least I had it once.*

Nicky pulled back and turned my head toward him. It felt like the room stopped moving, and we were the only ones in it. "Tess, I am hopelessly and completely in love with you, and I would rather die than hurt you or lose you. You need to know that."

I looked at him, a bit misty myself. "I believe you, Nicky. And I love you. Always." I put my head back on his shoulder.

Just then, Tommy Dorsey stepped up to the microphone. He cleared his throat. "Is everyone having fun?"

The crowd roared its approval. Tommy Dorsey took a little bow and gestured to Victoria Chapple, who was off to the side dressed as Josephine in white to her short husband's Napoleon in black and white. "Thank you," Tommy continued, "but it's all due to Victoria. Let's give her a round of appreciation."

Everyone applauded. She curtseyed, clearly pleased. Tommy cleared his throat again. "OK, well if you thought this was fun so far, you ain't seen nothin' yet. It's with pleasure and enormous humility that I yield the floor to my colleague and dear friend, Mr. Cole Porter, who is a beloved friend of Victoria's, and who is going to play a few tunes for you before we take a break. For a man who needs no introduction, I give you, Cole Porter."

A thrill ran through me and I grasped Nicky's hand. He squeezed mine back. With that, a man dressed to the nines in a white tuxedo and black bow tie was wheeled to the grand piano. The crowd exploded into cheering, clapping, whistles, and basic pandemonium. One woman stomped, and a man in back held up a sign that said ANYTHING GOES.

Cole Porter bowed from his chair and grinned. Tommy Dorsey's band played a verse of Porter's "Don't Fence Me In" as Cole waved and smiled. His valet helped him out of the chair and onto the piano bench, where he sat remarkably straight considering the pain he must have been in. A drink was placed on the piano within his arm's reach.

"Ah, good evening, all! Thank you, thank you. It is so brilliant to be here with all of you on this dazzling summer night." He took a sip of his drink. He barely looked at the keys as he began playing "Night and Day," accompanied by a girl with a voice like Ella Fitzgerald's singing the smoothest version I'd ever heard. No one danced. We were all too awed by the charisma of his musical genius. When "Night and Day" ended, he swung into "You're the Top," followed by "Anything Goes." He paused and took another sip of his drink.

Nicky and I were in the front of the semicircle that had formed. People swayed and joined in the songs, and not a foot was still. I could see Prill opposite us with Alistair Chapple. Dressed as a slim Queen Victoria with Alistair as her consort, she'd wrapped her arm through his and was clinging to his side.

Tommy Dorsey handed the microphone to Cole Porter. He began to speak. "I see so many of my good friends here tonight. And there are no friends like old friends." He began to fiddle with a few chords on the piano. "And in that vein, I have to play a little something for a gorgeous young lady out there, and I'm getting some accompaniment. Come on up, guys."

Nicky let go of my hand and was followed up to the front by Jonah and Graham, his polo and choral club pals. Cole Porter played a few chords of "My Heart Belongs to Daddy."

"To Finley Hemingway, daughter of my dear old friend, Ernest Hemingway, who, if I know him, will probably head to France soon to cover the efforts to free Paris, all while he's also writing about it. And then there are we philistines who continue to party here in Newport, doing our part to keep the liquor industry going."

More hoots and cheers. He continued when they quieted. "But we thank Papa and all of our boys over there. So good evening, Finn." He turned and looked at me.

I nodded, a jolt of pride running through me at Cole Porter's acknowledgement of my father in front of this crowd, in front of Prillie. My eyes filled in appreciation for this moment, for this evening.

I said, "Thank you, Mr. Porter. I'll tell Papa."

He nodded. "So here we go. This one is for you and your beau here, Nicholas Armstrong, whose parents have also been champions of mine for decades, even before I was who I am, back in the time when—yes, hard to believe—there were many naysayers. The next one is not, ahem, one of mine, but I love it too, and I've heard it's a favorite of yours. So let's go, boys. This one is for you, honey, from Nicholas." He turned to the crowd and winked. "Folks, we've only practiced this once, so forgive any gaffes, please! OK, boys, let's see how it goes."

He struck a few notes and launched into a slow version of "I'll Be Seeing You." The boys worked the harmony, with Cole's piano riffs torching the spaces between.

My hand flew to my throat. The ballroom was hushed. I could see Prillie glaring at me, but Alistair was smiling pleasantly, oblivious to his date's dagger face. This was a beginning and an end. I knew the war was closing in on me, coming close, just like it had on every family in that room. We all had a shared destiny.

When the song ended, the crowd cheered. Nicky looked at me, head tilted. I smiled, unable to even mouth what I felt: *Thank you. I love you with all my heart.*

Before Cole Porter left the stage, he said, "Now, just one more for our boys who may not be home with us right now, but who are in our hearts always. Let's give them all our love and support and prayers for their speedy return. Because we have to be so grateful for what they are sacrificing for all of us. So if not this year, then home next year, and for now, in our dreams."

He and the band played "Moonlight Serenade." Everyone sang along. *I stand and I wait for the touch of your hand in the June light.*

I thought of Papa, who was supposed to be heading to Europe soon as a journalist. And I thought of Jack and silently prayed for everyone's safe return home. I began to cry softly, as did many others.

We all stood. Many held hands with the person next to them. Some stood with one hand on their heart. One woman ran out, head down, dress floating out behind her. I learned later her son had died a year before in the battle of Midway. All were quiet out of respect for those who had sons or husbands or fathers or friends in the war, or who had already lost loved ones—and that was just about everyone—with no end yet in sight. *So don't let me wait, come to me tenderly in the June night.* Indeed.

20

You won't do our things with another girl, or say the same things, will you?

~ Ernest Hemingway, *A Farewell to Arms*

It was my last night in Newport before going to Cuba for the tail end of the summer. Armed with the nuances of birth control and awash with desire, I hungered for Nicky to make love to me. From my father's liberal attitude about sex, I'd always viewed it as a normal part of a relationship, not complicated by guilt. It was 1943, and the war was escalating. No one knew how the world would change, but we all knew it would. I was eighteen, and Nicky was halfway to twenty. His parents were out at a dinner party; it was the maid's evening off; and we had the house to ourselves.

We were sitting together on the sofa in the library reading when I got up and walked to the window. I stared out at the sea, which was rolling gently in the dusk light. My hands dug into the pockets of my madras Bermuda shorts. I looked up and spied a military plane cutting through the sky, reminding me of the war and all that could happen to us over the next several years.

I turned from the window and gazed at Nicky. His legs were crossed, feet bare, and he was reading the newspaper. I took in his dark hair, blue eyes, fair skin that was tanned a little, straight nose, broad shoulders. I sometimes wondered what he saw when he looked at me. I'd guess long, red hair, high forehead, dark eyes with strong brows, high cheekbones, unfashionably full lips, long legs.

I walked over and sat next to him, picking up my own book, *West with the Night* by Beryl Markham. I was restless, and my mind wandered. I flipped the book over onto my lap and stared at Nicky, wondering about the war and our future.

"So, if you ever have children, would you want a boy or a girl?" I asked Nicky.

He looked over in surprise. "Do you mean if *we* ever have children?" He smiled. I motioned for him to answer the question.

"Well, I don't really care. I guess if I had to choose, I'd like a girl who's just like you."

"Oh, a brilliant child, you mean," I said, amused.

"Brilliant and beautiful."

I thrilled at this what-if game. "What would you name her?"

Nicky set his newspaper aside as I handed him my Coca-Cola bottle. He opened it and handed it back. I took a sip.

"Hmm. I'm thinking." He turned to look at me sidelong. "Anna Hemingway Armstrong."

My heart leapt at the thought. "I love that. Anna Armstrong. It's lovely, Nicky."

Nicky looked serious. He pulled me to my feet and onto his lap. He took off his glasses, and his face softened as he looked at me, hand behind my neck. "Oh, Tess."

I trembled, and reckless energy shot through me.

"I'm eighteen, Nicky, and I know what's good for me."

"Do you?"

I slid off his lap and knelt in front of him, taking his hands. "And I know you, Nicky. I *know* you. You . . . you love peaches but hate pears. You love your shirts soft and forgiving. You smell like oranges and nutmeg. Your favorite color is red. You believe in God. You've read *The Good Earth* seven times. You have the kindest heart. Horses are the loves of your life. You live for dogs, sunrises, the sea, and music. You believe in fairness, and in laughing . . . and in me. I know you, Nicky. You sometimes whistle a tune only I can hear and understand a song only I can sing. Please, please, please, make love to me."

He looked torn. "Your parents . . . I don't want to let them down. And you are wrong." I raised an eyebrow in question. "*You* are the love of my life and what I live for, Tessa. Horses, dogs, all of it comes second." He tucked a loose strand of hair behind my ear.

I rested my head on his knee for a second, then lifted it. "Nicky, I've loved you my whole life, even before I met you. Don't make me beg."

We heard another plane pass over us, and I knew we were both thinking how fleeting the war made everything. I pulled him up with me and ran to the staircase. He sprinted to catch up and caught me from behind. He nuzzled my neck and turned me around. I wrapped my arms around him and buried my face in his neck, inhaling deeply his warm citrus scent. He crushed me against the wall where he kissed me hard.

He towed me up the stairs behind him. I let go and took them two at a time, passing him. We ran to his room, laughing. He closed the door to the cherry-paneled room with its view of the sea and locked it. I was jittery with anticipation and eager to feel Nicky against me.

"You'd better make this worth my wait, Armstrong. I have high expectations," I joked to cover my nervousness as the door latched.

"Oh, it will be worth the wait, Tessa. I do my best work under pressure, niña," he said, tearing back the covers and exposing white cotton sheets.

We fell to the bed's edge, and Nicky played at my throat until my breathing was fast. His hands slipped through my hair and I shivered when they lightly touched the back of my neck. I kicked off my shoes. Nicky was already barefoot.

"Come closer," he whispered, and I slid toward him. He slowly unbuttoned my sleeveless white blouse and I slipped it off. I undid his shirt and helped him out of it. My madras shorts fell off and Nicky's khaki pants lowered and dropped. Nicky unfastened my bra and took a breath as it dropped away.

"You are beautiful, so beautiful," he said in a low voice.

"I'm not, but you are." My face flushed with pleasure, but the room was dim, and I was glad he couldn't see.

"No, Tessa. Really. Look at me." He took my face in his hands and turned it toward him. "Tessa, you are just beautiful. I'll never forget you like this, in this moment, this light. Your hair is almost like fire in this light. I'll always remember."

He pulled both of us up to the head of the bed where pillows were mounded, fresh and cool. I felt smooth and boneless as I slid next to him on the sheets, both of us on our sides, facing each other. I threaded one leg through his, and he responded by moving closer. Suddenly, he stopped kissing me and said, "Are you sure, Tess? I don't ever want this . . . us, to be this crazy thing you did one night that you wish you hadn't. That would kill me."

I put my hand over his mouth. "Shhh. No, never."

Nicky relaxed and touched my face, tracing a line along my nose and resting his finger on my lips. I opened my mouth and drew his finger in. He gazed into my eyes and smiled the gentlest smile. I sucked his finger and let it go. Looking into Nicky's blue eyes, I craved his breath on my neck, tongue grazing my lips, and traveling lower and lower.

While I still had some wits about me, I said, "I'm so sure, Nicky, that of all the crazy things I'll do in life, this is not one of them. I don't think I could bear stopping now. *That* would kill me."

I rolled onto my back, pulling him with me, feeling his weight. His body covered mine, making me feel warm and safe, both thrilled and as at peace as is possible. And my life began—or so I thought.

21

"Maybe . . . you'll fall in love with me all over again."

"Hell," I said, "I love you enough now. What do you want to do? Ruin me?"

"Yes. I want to ruin you."

"Good," I said. "That's what I want too."

~ Ernest Hemingway, *A Farewell to Arms*

Nicky and I ended the summer with a week in Cuba. We knew it might be the last space of time we'd have as the war came closer and draft boards became less selective. Nick was returning to Yale, although he spoke often of trying to enlist, while Jeddrah and I were matriculating at Smith College.

"I need to talk to your father," Nicky said on his last day at the Finca.

I was in white shorts and a loose, blue plaid shirt knotted at the waist. I couldn't wait to get Nicky all to myself. He too was in shorts and a blue oxford shirt with the sleeves rolled up. I held his arm and licked it all the way up, silly, but not caring. He laughed, grabbed me, and kissed me long and slow. My knees weakened and I leaned against a wall in the living room.

"Hey, niña! I have to talk to your father. Don't confuse me. *Ahora*! Now."

I sighed. "Why can't I come?"

"Man stuff, Tess."

"Oh brother. OK. I'll make a pie while you're gone." Nicky laughed again. He knew the only thing I could cook was scrambled eggs.

When Nicky emerged a half-hour later, he practically skipped down the cement stairs in front of the Finca, where I was sunning. He seized my hand. As we strolled through the Finca's gardens, my arm looped through his, butterflies landing on the nearby wildflowers, he filled me in. "I asked your father if I could have the honor of his daughter's hand when the time is right."

I was stunned. I stopped walking and grabbed his sleeve. "Wait! What did you say?"

Nicky stopped too. He laughed. "You look like you saw a ghost. You look positively shocked." He pulled me along. "Keep walking. Good for your circulation. So I said, 'Mr. Hemingway, I know we are way too young, but I want you to know that my intentions toward Finn are all honorable'—I remembered to call you Finn, not Tess—'and I want to marry her if she'll have me, as soon as the time is right.'" Nicky looked nervous, expectant, no smile now.

I exploded. "Oh my God! You asked my father before you asked me! Nicky!" I was breathless, not upset, but shocked, like I had to have heard wrong. While I'd thought maybe someday Nicky and I might marry, it was a far distant dream. He was all I could see, and I believed that if not him, there would be no one for me. He'd just yanked that distant dream into the present. "What did Papa say?"

Nicky put on a serious face and made his voice deep, imitating Papa's inflection. "He said, 'Well, Nicholas, I married Flea's mother when I was only twenty-two, and while I'm not advocating that, age is just a number. And while I appreciate the inquiry, it's Flea you have to ask. She can speak for herself, and if she wants it, I'm all for it. Girl has a good head on her shoulders, and she'll make the right decision. Thanks for the respect though, son.'"

I was aglow. "Oh wow! Wow, wow, wow!" I stopped walking again and spun around, collapsing on the ground laughing, exquisitely dizzy. Nicky was leaning against a tree, bending over with laughter at me. I stood. "But, Armstrong, you have to do better than that. I want a real proposal someday, with some roses and . . . oh, you know, you riding in on a white horse or a black horse or something." I was giddy, over the moon, and punch-drunk crazy. "I always thought you'd want to date some Vassar girls before you made up your mind and all that—you know, to see if you could do better."

Nicky turned me to him and held both of my shoulders. We were almost eye to eye. He said softly, "Tessa, there is no one better. Not anywhere in the world. You're the one." He tightened his grip. "You're the *one*."

He dropped to one knee and scanned the ground as though sure that if he looked hard enough, a ring would materialize from under a spreading begonia bush. He shook his head and rifled through his pockets desperately. He finally pulled from his back pocket a six-inch hoof pick we'd used that morning before our ride.

He gently placed the red wooden-handled pick with its pointy, bent blade, crusted with dirt, into the palm of my hand.

"Finley Richardson Hemingway, with this lowly hoof pick," he began, and grimaced, and we both burst into laughter. He composed himself and began again.

"Tessa Hemingway, with this dirty, yet very functional hoof pick, I pledge my troth to you. I promise to always return and care for you, and the horses, and whoever else comes along, and to always be true to you and only you, through thick and thin, for so long as we both shall live, so help me God. Will you marry me, Tessa . . . someday?"

My fingers closed around the pick. I held it tightly as my other hand rested on Nicky's shoulder. I said solemnly, "Yes, Nicky. I will marry you, and I will be your wife for as long as we both shall live, so help me God, through good times and bad, and this hoof pick will always be with me as a pledge of faith and a symbol of our first promise to each other."

Nicky stood slowly and took me in his arms. He whispered in my ear, "I will get a ring someday, Tess, and I already have a horse in mind for your engagement gift."

I don't think it's possible to be more deliriously elated than I was that day, feeling that the future was bright and limitless and that we could overcome anything. Love could overcome anything.

22

Passini said respectfully, "There is nothing worse than war."

"Defeat is worse."

"I do not believe it," Passini said still respectfully. "What is defeat? You go home."

~ Ernest Hemingway, *A Farewell to Arms*

Marty was conspicuously absent when I arrived for my Christmas visit of 1943. Papa told me he doubted they'd be together much longer. She'd chosen to leave on assignment for *Collier's* in Europe, and Papa was thinking of doing the same. Although I'd heard some of the fights during my visits, I always thought they would work it out.

While I'd respected Pauline, Martha and I were kindred spirits. Marty had my heart, and I loved her. So did my brothers. And I thoroughly blamed Papa for Martha staying away and for the angry outbursts I'd heard when I visited.

We'd just moved out to the pool when Papa hit me with this news. I shook my head in frustration. "God, Papa! What the heck? What did you do to make her leave?" I couldn't help it. I thought, *Here we go again.*

I also realized too late that Papa was pretty drunk already. It was three in the afternoon, and he'd picked me up at the airport. Had I given the fact of Papa's drunkenness more consideration, I might have said little until the next morning.

There was this line for Papa. A few drinks, and he was full of projects and joie de vivre. A few more and he went dark and nasty if you disagreed with him. That line had clearly been crossed before I'd arrived. The boys were nowhere around, and for all I knew, Gig and Mouse weren't coming at all.

Papa and I were sitting at a patio table when Papa slammed his hand down on it. "Goddamn it, Flea! Where's your loyalty? She left me. She's goddamned gallivanting around Europe when she should be here with us. Calls me, sends me letters, but who cares about letters? Where the hell is she?"

I'd heard stories recently of Papa making scenes in town and behaving very badly with old friends. I'd seen his verbal floggings of Marty and knew how she hated it when he got that way. It sickened me, and I knew much of it was the alcohol. Still, I couldn't keep silent.

"But you made her, Papa. You were mean to her, and you made her pay from her own money for every little thing she got. She felt she had to work to support herself."

"That's bullshit, and you know it! Who told you that? Her? Trying to turn my own child against me. You don't know, Flea! She was sleeping with anyone who'd have her, while I'm here trying to work. She abandoned me just when I thought I could get going again."

"No, Papa. You did this! Your drinking and your abuse were too much for her. Pauline took it, but Marty wouldn't! You aren't writing because you drink too much!"

At that, his face went purple. He stood and flung his arm toward the door. "Get out! Sons you expect to turn on you when they want to show they can beat you. But a daughter? I never expected my daughter to turn on me. I thought you and I were *simpatico*, through the best and worst. I was wrong. From today on, I don't have a daughter! Hear me? I . . . don't . . . have . . . a . . . daughter!" He said each word slowly and distinctly.

I took three steps back, stricken, and ran into the house. I quickly called a cab and seized my still-packed valise. I hurried back into the living room where Papa was still hollering, bottle of whiskey in hand. He was waving it, gesticulating.

As I kept an eye out for my cab, I said from a safe distance, "You didn't used to be like this. But now, the world has to revolve around you, the great Ernest Hemingway. What about the rest of us who aren't all that special? What about *us*?"

In a fit of defiance, I seized from the table a sheath of papers he'd been editing and tore them into shreds, tossing the pieces into the air like confetti.

"There! It's the only thing that matters to you." My heart pounded at what I'd done, and I was immediately horrified. I opened my mouth, but a sentence was out of reach. I might have just destroyed some phrasing that had taken him weeks to get right. "I . . . I'm sorry, Papa. I shouldn't have done that," I stammered and recovered. "But I meant the rest."

He stared at the fragments of his work floating across the floor in waves, then glared at me, furious, cold, looking mean, but also a little confused. He started to move toward me. "You! Like your mother, like Pauline, like Marty. All trying to destroy my work, aren't you?"

"No. I . . . she, they didn't, wouldn't . . ." My head felt light, and the room felt too hot, too heavy.

He was weaving, eyes bugging out. Then he bellowed his ugliest words. "You? A lawyer? You'll never be anything because you're weak. You'll never amount to anything but someone's wife and plaything. No courage! You disgust me. What a joke! You in court? Ha! You make me sick."

I was stunned at his cruelty, even though I knew he was drunk. I could tell he wanted to hit me and my blood chilled. Instead, he threw the brown liquor bottle at a wall. I skittered back toward the front door as his anger escalated.

The bottle shattered. Papa raised a fist and shook it, then stepped toward me and pulled his fist back, but checked it. Then he picked up a vase with flowers and threw that too, with force, in my direction. I jumped sideways and it hit the doorframe behind me, where it exploded. Flowers splattered on the wall and pottery bits smashed to the yellow tile floor. The cats flew in ten directions, but good old Negrita, Papa's loving stray dog from Havana, stood stoically near Papa, tail tucked, holding her ground with him in good times and bad.

I tried to salvage something. I pleaded, "Papa, you're killing yourself. I can see it."

He spat, "You know nothing, little girl. Death is like an old whore in a bar. I might buy her a drink, but I won't go upstairs with her. I'm in my prime. Just you wait."

"You're not." I was crying now. "You're not yourself. She loves you, and you just trample it."

"Love!" he scoffed. "If two people love each other, there can be no happy ending."

"Don't say that," I pleaded. "It's not true. Love can last. You try to destroy everyone who loves you, but you're not going to destroy me or make me into something I'm not. Gig cringes when he comes here. Mouse tries to be you. And Jack is . . . Jack just wants you to be proud of him."

Papa rushed at me and bellowed, "I don't need you, Flea! I don't need her. I don't need anyone. I have no daughter from now on."

"Well, that's a really good thing, Papa, because that's exactly how it will end for you. Alone. And you seem to have lots of daughters, actually. Every woman you like who comes through the door is called 'daughter' so I'm nothing special, now am I?" This actually had always been a grievance. He was Papa to the world, and I wanted desperately to be his only 'daughter' but he'd converted it into a general endearment used toward all of his favored women friends. It haunted me. "Don't worry. You'll never hear from me again. And my name is Finley Richardson. From this day on, I'm dropping the Hemingway."

His face became even redder. "Goddamned you, Flea! Ashamed of the old man, now, are you?" he hollered.

I shook my head, then turned and headed for the road to wait for the cab. As I fled, I looked back over my shoulder. The front door was still flung wide and I could see Papa teetering. Then he was on the front stoop, a lumbering bear unsteady on its feet. I stumbled, my knees hitting the gravel, but I recovered and kept going.

I wanted to go back to help him to his chair, tell him to sleep it off, but I didn't dare. I looked back once more to be sure he was OK, but he'd tripped and was on the top step on his knees. Tears were streaming down his face. I crumbled inside but continued toward the road, sobbing into my sleeve. *And love continues to end badly for the Hemingways.* It was like an ice pick in the eye to see him like that, but I turned away and kept going, afraid of losing myself if I tried to save him.

23

"Wine is a grand thing," I said. "It makes you forget all the bad."

~ Ernest Hemingway, *A Farewell to Arms*

A chill went through me when Nicky told me. It was the spring of 1944, and I hadn't seen Papa since the big fight at Christmas. It was like I'd lost my right foot. For more than ten years, I'd talked to him regularly about everything: horses, school, friends, his writing, his next project, my dreams of law school, my worries about the war and Nicky and Jack. Whatever he said was on point and incisive. I craved all of that, and it ended cataclysmically and then, silence.

I tried to stay busy with debate club and government classes, but I found my mind drifting regularly to that last picture of Papa, keeled over and crawling up the Finca steps, a giant felled. Whenever I saw a girl carrying a copy of *The Sun Also Rises* or the local paper trumpeting in bold print that the movie version of *For Whom the Bell Tolls* was playing at the cinema three blocks away, I'd sink into a dull place where all color was bleached out. When I wanted to crow about what I'd learned while working as a file clerk in a law firm part of each Saturday, talking to Papa was no longer an option.

At least once a week, I picked up the phone to call him, but then heard him in my head roaring in that ugly voice, face twisted, "I have no daughter!" I lowered the phone receiver. I knew he was drunk, but *in vino veritas*? Did it take so little to sever a connection I thought was inviolate, through thick and thin, best of times and worst?

I scoured the newspapers for word of Papa's location and health, turning each page with trembling fingers. I finally learned that Papa had gone to France for *Collier's*. I feared for him. I already was in a state of perpetual panic about my brother. He'd dropped out of Dartmouth in the fall of '42 and was stationed in Algeria.

Then the cold splash of Nicky's news felt like the shiver of a frozen blade being sliced across my neck.

"No," I said flatly.

"Tess, I have to. I can't just sit at Yale while the war is going on. My eyes passed the test with the new lenses, and they didn't even ask about my feet. The war will end someday. I'm young and healthy. You and I have been talking about it for months. Now . . . well, it's here."

He looked so handsome in his light bomber-style jacket, hair flopping just a little into his eyes, light freckles on one cheek. I stared at him as we sat on the porch of my college dorm. Nicky had called that morning to say he needed to speak to me and was driving up from New Haven.

"But they exempted you, Nicky," I said, looking away. I didn't want to cry, but seeing him made me start to fall apart. I was terrified, and felt like the last secure thing I had in life was suddenly tottering and falling away too, out of my reach.

"Tess, come on." He lifted my chin so I had to look at him. "Everyone is gone now. Yale is a morgue, and only 4-Fs are there. We both know I'm not 4-F. I can't not go, Tess. Your brother is there. Every pal I had from Exeter and Yale is there. Jonah left last week. Your father was in the war at seventeen. He's over there now."

"Yeah, and what a man he is." I turned away. I couldn't think about my father, too. It seemed no matter where I turned, his dark eyes were boring into me, even when I shut my own to sleep. During my last visit to Cuba, I'd seen for myself the embarrassing boasting and crude talk around restaurant tables late into the wee hours. More than once, I'd simply pushed my chair back and left.

The real reason I needed space from my father was not because of his insults. I actually *could* forgive him almost anything. The real reason was I didn't want to bear witness to his breakdown. It was like watching a once fabulous monument crumble.

I looked up at Nicky and swallowed hard. "I'll never want you to go, but I know everyone feels that way. I'm so scared, Nicky."

Nicky suddenly seemed much older than me. "I know, Tess. I'm scared too, but I have to go. I enlisted in the Marines. I go to Parris Island, South Carolina, for seven weeks of basic training. Then I ship out for the Pacific."

My stomach dove. "What do your parents say?"

"Well, my father knows it's the right thing, but my mother is dead set against it. She said I can work at Armstrong Munitions teaching weapons identification to troops about to ship out. I can contribute to the war effort that way, she thinks. I don't want that."

I looked away. It was done. "What about your horses?"

"I donated all but Arc, Dancing Girl, and Silence to Meadowbrook Polo. They'll take care of them so when I get back . . ." He trailed off. "Tess, I'll make it. I promised you I'd always take care of you. Come on, smile, or I'll remember you frowning until I get back."

I couldn't have our last conversation before he left be gloomy. I didn't know if I'd ever see my father or brother again, and I couldn't lose Nicky too.

I groaned and turned to hug him. As girls walked in and out of the dorm, I clung to him. I felt his arms wrap around me and I tucked my face into his neck, breathing in citrus and nutmeg.

I pulled back and looked at him, wanting to see more, but I saw nothing. I shook my head. "You'd better come back to me, Nicky Armstrong. You pledged on a hoof pick that you'd marry me, and that means something. I only breathe right when you're with me."

A horn beeped. Nicky looked torn. He glanced at the car and back at me. "I promise you, Tess. I'll be back to get you, and then it's forever. Us into the sunset. I gotta go, sweetheart. Write me!"

"I will, every day." My eyes were wet.

Nick started to jog to the car, then turned. "US Marine Corps, First Division. We're heading to someplace in China or the Philippines or somewhere in the Pacific. I'll let you know when I have an address." He threw up his hands and laughed. "Like they'd tell a lowly jarhead like me! I'll be getting a

Marine haircut, but it will grow back, Tessa!" He waved goodbye. So did I.

24

If we win here we will win everywhere. The world is a fine place and worth the fighting for and I hate very much to leave it.

~ Ernest Hemingway, *For Whom the Bell Tolls*

The summer of '44 was the first summer I'd ever spent without my father. The *Times* wrote that he was present at the liberation of Paris in June. I breathed a sigh of relief when I read that he was fine. "Probably drinking champagne at the Ritz by now," I grumped, permitting my resentment to swamp back in once I knew he was safe.

I filled my time that summer working in a law firm in Chicago as a typist. I had lunch most days with the other girls in the typing pool, most of whom also had husbands or boyfriends away at war. I'd hurry home each evening hoping to find a letter from Nicky, but most days I was disappointed. Although I didn't do "real" law work, with the men at war, the partners let me work on drafting pleadings. I was thrilled when one of the vets we represented, just home from France, gained a recovery in a car accident. This was what I wanted to do: help people get what was fair.

The war was far from over in the Pacific, however. I received sporadic letters from Nicky. When one appeared in my mailbox, I'd clutch it like I used to clutch blue ribbons, and run to my room to read and re-read.

July 4, 1944

Hey College Girl:

Not exactly Independence Day here in the land of heat and ... more heat. Sorry I can't write more often, but we are almost always on the move. I miss you more than my limited literary talents can express. Hope all is well at school and that you are keeping Sassafras well ridden! I miss my ponies, but somehow, I don't think they'd appreciate 110 degree temps and 100 percent humidity. What I'd really love right now is dry feet! Yes, dry flat feet.

We're island hopping. "Local Boy Sees the World!" We work our way through jungles and then fight our way back out the other way. The guys keep their sense of humor for the most part. The other day our captain warned us about everything on this island: barracudas, dengue fever, hordes of diseased flies, and told us on pain of death not to eat or drink anything here. My buddy, Bill Mastroni (he's from Casper, Wyoming) turned to me and said, "So why'n hell don't we just let the Japs keep this island?"

I miss you so much it hurts, Tess. Food is OK. Hey, we did have some fun last week. Bob Hope and his troupe came here and entertained. We are all so ready to laugh at anything and well ... he reminds us of home and why we're here. Hope you and Jedd and your family are coping. I'm thinner, but pretty darned strong at this point. I could definitely carry Tessa Hemingway across a threshold! Take care of yourself, amor de mi vida, until I'm home to do it. I love you, Tessa. Don't forget me.

Love, Nicky (Your former polo playing Yalie, but always yours with every piece of my being. ☺)

I teared up at the *amor de mi vida*—love of my life—and at the smiling face he drew at the end. Nicky wasn't the smiley-face sort so seeing that, so out of character, made me laugh through teary eyes, just to have this note, to know he was OK, that he was alive.

The last half of the year passed slowly. As Christmas approached, I felt restless and sad that it was also the first Christmas I'd spend without my father. My mood was dampened further when *Time* magazine blared that "international author Ernest Hemingway and his wife, journalist Martha Gellhorn, have separated for good." *Time* knew before I did. And I felt a stab of pain when Patrick called to warn me that Papa already had some other woman named Mary Welsh to replace Marty.

"Well, Mouse, since I don't see him, I guess it doesn't matter." But it did.

That winter, even Smith College, 250 acres of leafy lanes and sparkling ponds, joined the war effort and had a training center for the WAVES—Women Accepted for Voluntary Emergency Services.

"Jedd, we can join!" I said, excited to think we could help. "We could be mechanics or go to Dayton and work on code breaking." The WAVES had a center for decoding in Ohio. "Maybe I could be a legal assistant. With all of the men gone, maybe some law firms can use help?"

"I'd love to!" she said, but her face clouded. "But you have to be twenty to sign up for the auxiliary. We're only nineteen. They won't take us yet."

I groaned, disappointed. "Well, as soon as we can, we have to. We have to do our part."

25

There will always be people who say it does not exist because they cannot have it. But I tell you it is true and that you have it and that you are lucky even if you die tomorrow.

~ Ernest Hemingway, *For Whom the Bell Tolls*

The telegram arrived at five on a Saturday evening. We were all heading out to eat at the dining hall. I'd forgotten my rain hat, and it was pouring. Jeddrah ran back with me as I clambered upstairs to retrieve it. I sprinted back down the stairs, my pleated skirt fanning out around me. When I tripped on the bottom step, I thought Jeddrah would laugh. Instead, her expression was frozen.

"What's wrong?" I asked, glancing around for a cause of concern.

She pointed to the front door. The buzzer was ringing, and a man in a Western Union uniform stood at the door.

It's not for me, it's not for me, it's not for me. I breathed in short spasms, and my legs felt like they might not hold me up. "It's not for me, Jedd. I'm sure of it."

Jeddrah nodded. "I know."

She walked slowly to the door, opened it, and took a thin envelope. Her hands shook, and when she turned back to me, her eyes were shining. She stopped as if it were impossible to take one more step and nodded almost imperceptibly.

I stepped forward and took the envelope. My name was in bold block lettering, and when I saw it, I leaned against the wall for support. *To Tess Hemingway.* Only Nicky, his family, and his friends called me Tess. With hands shaking so badly it took three tries to slide open the flap, I slipped out the thin sheet of paper. It read:

> *Dear Tess: We regret to inform you that Nicholas ... a loss to all of us ... With sadness, I remain ... Jackson Armstrong.*

I slid to the floor, my back to the wall. Jeddrah caught me and sank to the ground with me. My hands wrapped around my head as if to keep the news out. The telegram fluttered to the floor.

I whispered, "No, no, no, no. Not Nicky. Oh, God, no, no."

Jeddrah wrapped her arms around me as tight as a vice. She was shaking, too. "Oh, my God. I'm here, Finn," she said, voice weak. "I'll take care of you. I'm here. You'll get through this. Oh, my God."

My head was now in my hands and the sobs would not stop. I was broken. "No, I won't get through this. Oh, my God. Nicky, you promised me. You said you'd come back for me." I began to rock. "I'm dead, Jedd. I can't ..."

"Don't say that," Jeddrah said, panic in her voice. She moved closer and draped herself around me, more loosely now, like a shroud. I was cowering against the wall, and Jedd was literally over my back, encircling me and trying to stop my quaking; we were almost one in our huddle.

"Leave me, Jedd. Please, please, please. Leave me." I was crying so hard that breath was hard to catch.

"No, I won't leave you." Jeddrah stayed where she was, stroking, soothing, a bit like loyal little Negrita, Papa's faithful stray, who, even when unsure how to comfort, stood firm in solidarity, never leaving her charge.

"I need to go home." *But where was home?* Jeddrah's grip loosened and she sat back on her haunches. I glanced about frantically, jumped up and grabbed my coat. I didn't want to be here when the girls returned from dinner. "I have to get out of here."

Jeddrah stood too, nine inches shorter than I, and uncertain. She seized my arm and pleaded, "Finn, stay here. We'll decide tomorrow. You can't be alone. I'll make you some tea."

Tears streaming, I said, "I have to go. I want my father. I want Papa." I flung my thin trench coat over my shoulders and tore out into the pouring rain. The coat ballooned out behind me like a cassock billowing behind a fleeing monk. At the porch stoop, I stopped and stared into the dim fogginess of the early evening, cold sheets of rain making the view foreign and hostile.

I scanned the landscape, not knowing where to go. My eyes passed over a shape, slid back, and stopped on a dark figure standing next to a solid maple tree. It was a man in profile, Irish cap pulled low, biggest shoulders I'd ever seen, rain hitting the cap and absorbed by it. The head was tilted. It rotated slightly toward me as if testing the waters, then the figure faced me fully.

It was Papa. Papa, whom I hadn't talked to in seventeen months, who told me I wasn't his daughter anymore, who said he needed no one.

None of it mattered. He was here.

"Papa, Papa, Papa!" I screamed, and ran out as if to my deliverance, my hair streaming out behind me. It was soaked in seconds, and my feet splashed through dark puddles. Papa's face lit as he opened his arms. I was enveloped in wet wool and warmth. He closed his arms around me and I dug my head into his neck. It smelled like smoke and soap—familiar, safe, home.

"Papa, Papa, he promised me. He promised he'd come back," I sobbed. "Oh, my God. What will I do?" I burrowed deeper into Papa's neck.

"I know, Flea, but sometimes even good people can't keep promises. The Armstrongs called me yesterday. I had to come even though we . . . well, you know."

Papa's voice dropped, and I knew we were both crying for Nick and for Jack, who was now a prisoner of war in Germany. I looked up at that face I loved so much—dark eyes, beard, lined brow—and sobbed, knowing my life was over. "Papa, I'm done."

Papa took in a ragged breath, then said, "No, Flea. You're not. I know it feels it right now, and for today, you are done. Tomorrow's not here yet."

"It will be, and he'll still be gone. I'm done, Papa. Nothing matters anymore. He'll still be gone tomorrow."

"But you won't be. The first and final thing you have to do in this world is to last and not be smashed by it. We are all broken, Flea. That's how the light gets in. Through the broken bits."

I covered my mouth with my hand as the horror flooded back. "Oh God. Oh, my God." I couldn't catch my breath but struggled to talk. "Papa, I don't think I'll make it."

Papa drew in a second strangled breath and finally said, "You're home, my only daughter. And you need to go on and make Nick and yourself proud." He took me by the shoulders, forcing me to look at him. "No one you love is truly lost, Flea. Not ever. I can't explain it, but they stay with us. I know it's impossible to feel that now." Papa pulled me into him. His voice broke when he added, "My darling daughter. I couldn't love you more. The well doesn't get any deeper."

I thought about Prillie's words. *You will rue the day you met Nick Armstrong.* I did rue that day, because I wasn't sure I would survive his loss. I remembered my first lesson about love from my childhood: *Love always ends, and usually badly.* Indeed.

26

There is only now, and if now is only two days, then two days is your life and everything in it will be in proportion. This is how you live a life in two days. And if you stop complaining and asking for what you never will get, you will have a good life.

~ Ernest Hemingway, *For Whom the Bell Tolls*

I returned the next day to Cuba with Papa to find his new woman, Mary Welsh, in the kitchen washing some dishes and setting the table, perfectly at home. She had an ease with Papa that made clear this was not a brand-spanking-new relationship.

There had been only two more weeks of my junior year of college when I left. Jack had been released from the prisoner of war camp a few weeks ago, and my elation was now replaced by devastation over Nicky. Jeddrah was working again that summer at Greenwich Hospital. We spoke on the phone weekly. More and more responsibility had been promised her. I envied her certainty about the future. My dreams of Nicky and law school were over. I had no dreams anymore.

For the first month after the telegram, I lay dry-eyed in my room, broken, drapes drawn. Cats wandered in and out and at times, little Negrita would sleep with me, but I barely noticed. I couldn't move that first month. Getting out of bed meant I had to accept that Nicky was gone. My red hair stuck out in every direction, and a shampoo required more energy than I had. Fifteen pounds fell away, and I was already thin.

"Flea," Papa called each morning. "Join me on the boat. Get out of that cave. Come on."

My room was a medium-sized square with a window facing east. The old tile floor glowed, and I'd thrown down a rug of red and gold that Papa had brought back from Africa. I loved the wallpaper of yellow rosebuds and curving green leaves that covered the walls and ceiling too. With the humidity, it curled at the edges, but I loved it anyway. I'd made a million plans staring at those rosebuds when I'd seen nothing but possibilities ahead. Now I saw only ends. I saw now that the buds weren't opening as I'd always assumed. They were dying, closing up, their day in the sun past. Like me.

I rolled over in bed, stared at the ceiling, and fingered the hoof pick. The hoof pick. Our promise. Then I looked around and saw the rose buds closing up.

"Not today, Papa, but thank you," I called back.

"Sweetheart, you need to eat. Let Miss Mary make you some eggs. Or I'll make my soon-to-be famous toasted breadies."

I smiled a little at Papa's strange words. "Thanks, Papa, but I'm not hungry."

I could hear him still standing at the door. Long pause. "OK, Flea. But you have to come out for dinner."

I didn't. In fact, I did nothing. After another week, my father came into my room and sat on the bed's edge. As he stroked my hair, he seemed without words, which was unsettling. Finally, he said, "You have the courage to go on, Flea. I know you do, and so do you. This is about dragging yourself up when you see absolutely no reason to. It's about faith and hope in the face of tragedy, and nothing is more tragic than love gone away. But that's all there is to live for when you boil it down; the faith and hope you will survive to love again."

I said nothing, finding it ironic that Papa believed love was hope. It seemed so transient in his life.

Two weeks later, a telegram came for me. I cringed when Mary spoke through the door, "Finn, a telegram. Do you want me or Papa to open it for you?"

I winced. She called him Papa. Marty never did—she called him Ernest, or The Pig when things were degenerating—and my mother never did. Pauline sometimes did. I thought it was a little affected for Mary to call him Papa and for him to call her Miss Mary. She was maybe in her late thirties, sturdy, and dressed casually most of the time. Miss Mary? Quite contrary? It sounded like she should be eighteen with blonde braids, wearing a flowery sundress and sandals. But then again, I was becoming quite the young curmudgeon.

"No, thank you. I'll get to it later," I said. I did not want another telegram.

Instead, Mary slid it under my door. Contrary, indeed. I sighed and reached under my bed for my helper, a large bottle of rum. I took a big swig, grimaced as it went down, and wiped my mouth on my arm. I felt ashamed. I hated it when Papa drank and left behind his modest, self-effacing self to become a bombastic jerk, but I was overwhelmed by my own problems.

I was disgusted with myself for turning to the habit I hated in him. I'd been proud of Jeddrah for fighting her addiction and beating it into submission. Yet even knowing the damage drinking could do, it was an accessible salve—very accessible in my father's house. For a few hours, it took away the memory. For a few hours, life was fuzzy, edges blurry, and sometimes, with enough swigs, I even forgot Nicky was gone. Sometimes I dreamed of flying down a beach road in a maroon Packard with the cream top down, him driving, me with a bronze-colored kerchief on my head, leaning way out, arms open to catch as much sea breeze as I could. Then my mind would flit to a picture of Nicky pulling on a pair of argyle socks while giving me a slow smile or dipping a finger into a jar of peanut butter and popping it into my mouth. I could almost hear Frank Sinatra singing Cole Porter's "Night and Day" with Nicky and me joining in. With a few more swigs of the rum, I could even sleep an hour or two. Sometimes I could hear "I'll Be Seeing You" without disintegrating, because I forgot he was gone. This was about the barest of survivals, only until the next day.

I was pretty sure Papa knew about my drinking. On the rare occasions when I came out of my room, he would look at me over the tops of his reading glasses with worry lines on his brow and ask if I was OK. Mary would flutter around, not knowing what to do with me. The boys stayed out of my way.

By the end of the month, my room was a decomposing mess; clothes in piles, air stale, blinds drawn. The telegram of last month stared reproachfully at me from the corner of my dresser. I'd look at it occasionally, assuming some condolence, and declined to face it.

Other than hoping his death was fast and painless, I had no interest in the details of Nicky's end. I knew that his unit had been cut off from the rest of their battalion by the Japanese after landing in Okinawa. Return shelling had killed Nicky's entire unit. Every last one. I didn't need to know anything else.

Papa rapped once on my bedroom door early one morning, opened the door and poked his head in. "Flea, are you decent? If not, you have about thirty seconds to make yourself so."

I groaned. "I'm decent, Papa. Come on in."

Papa was still wearing a head bandage from a minor car crash a week ago, and he looked like a wounded, jaunty pirate. He headed for my window and cracked open my blinds. A sliver of sun crept across the floor, making a lightning bolt. He sat on my bed. It creaked.

I rolled to face him. He touched my brow and brushed back my tangled hair. His face looked worn to me. He was only forty-six years old but had always been accident-prone. Still, he was a handsome man with bright eyes that caught every nuance.

I stared at him, aching to be normal, wanting to say, "Good morning, Papa. What's up? Fishing, or just swimming and eating?" Gloom hung around me like a haze in a cigar parlor.

His face softened when he looked at me. "You look so much like your mother now, Flea, in this light. The way she was when I first met her." I smiled just a little. Papa could be sentimental. Never about his childhood or his own parents, but about my mother and his children.

"Anyway, I had Sassafras brought in. He's in the stable where he usually is. Arrived last night. Plain ornery he was, too. Didn't want to go into his stall, but this morning he seems fine."

Under any circumstances other than those, I would have leapt up, hopped on a bike, and raced down the road to the farm where Sassafras was boarded. I stirred, but couldn't get up.

"Thanks for doing that, Papa. I know it's expensive for just two months. How are you feeling, by the way? Still trussed up, I see."

Papa shook his head. "I'm fine, Flea. And the money is fine, too. Much as I hate every movie ever made of my books—they changed the damned ending to *A Farewell*, for Christ's sake—it pays better than anything else. But hell, it's humbling. They buy the rights and can make a whore of a saint, and you have no say. Jaysus, the best way for a writer to deal with Hollywood is to meet the producers at the California state line, throw them your book, they throw you the money, and you drive like hell back the way you came."

I smiled for the first time in weeks by this comical image. It was so Papa and so funny, but I couldn't laugh. I wondered if I ever would be able to.

"Anyway, still getting good money for *Bell Tolls,* so the Hemingsteins are solvent for now."

"Thanks, Papa, but I just don't feel like going to the barn today." I didn't want to tell Papa what really was keeping me in bed. I couldn't shake the selfish idea that Nicky hadn't had to be in the war. He'd been exempted. He could still be here with me, planning the summer, riding, and heading back to school. I should have fought harder to keep him here, maybe even cried. I couldn't put all of that into words.

"I know, Flea, but sometimes you have to get up even when you don't want to." Papa stared at me for a long time. "I know it's incomprehensible to lose someone you love, and the pain is like a hot poker dug into your heart and then shoved down your spine and back up, just in case you didn't feel it on the way down. But Nicky died for something that mattered."

I rejected his thinking. "No, Papa. He didn't have to go. The war was almost over, and he didn't have to go. We would have won whether he was there or not."

Papa was quiet for a minute. "And if he'd stayed home when everyone went, that would change him too. He'd live with that self-anger and self-disappointment for the rest of his life. And maybe he'd resent you. That can kill a man faster than almost anything, in spirit anyway."

I said nothing, picking on my blanket. Papa sat still for a moment. "Do you ever read my books, Flea?"

I raised an eyebrow and lay back deeper. "Of course, Papa. I've read all of your books."

"Have you seen me writing them here and in Key West?"

"Well, yeah, sure."

"Does it look easy?"

I sat up and fluffed my pillows so I would not be at such a disadvantage lying on my back. I shifted my weight. My pajamas of pink and pale green bunched up everywhere, but I smoothed them.

"Um, well, it looks like you're focused, Papa, but it's not . . . it's not like ditchdigging, it doesn't seem." My thought petered out.

Papa chuckled low in his belly. "Well, Daughter, I'll tell you. Writing sure is easy. All you have to do is sit down at the typewriter and bleed. And of course, the first draft of anything is shit. But you try the best you can to distill what you know into something that is truer than if it really happened. And to do that, for each sentence I write, there are eighty more in my head that I'm not writing, but they make that one sentence possible. Does that make any sense to you?"

I nodded.

"When I write stuff like 'Man can be defeated but not destroyed,' or 'The coward dies a thousand deaths, the brave but one,' do you think I flipped it down on paper one morning out of thin air because it sounded tough and manly?" He ended on a self-mocking tone.

I shrugged. "No. I know you work hard at it," I said lamely to someone who looked at words like they were new each time he saw them.

Papa leaned forward as if it were important that I understand. "Everyone has an opinion, so I can only speak for myself. I believe what I put down on that paper, or I couldn't expect someone reading it to believe it. And *that,* my daughter, is what makes writing real." He paused. "Flea, you're entitled to your opinion about Nick, but I don't think he had a choice. All men were drafted, and he knew he was capable. He wasn't going to hide or fake it for fear of being killed. And I don't believe he's destroyed. He was part of something, and it takes each man in an operation like that invasion, each man pulling his weight, to succeed. He mattered. For you to think he didn't, diminishes him, and I think that's wrong."

I sat a little taller and propped myself up on one elbow. "Do you really think that, Papa?"

"I do, Flea. Nick was a good man who fought bravely for his country. He loved you with every breath he had. I hate war, but don't take down a good man who did the right thing."

I pulled my knees up and wrapped my arms around them. I was silent for a minute. "I guess I didn't look at it that way. I just wish he didn't go. I know it's selfish."

"And how would it work if everyone felt that way? War is a sorry scene, but some things are worth fighting for. And it takes each man doing his job to prevail. Don't turn something honorable into shit, Flea."

I fluffed all my pillows. I stared at Papa with fascination. "OK. Maybe you have a point." I thought for a second. "So how *did* you become such a good writer, Papa?"

Now Papa shrugged. "For a long time now I have tried simply to write the best I can. Sometimes I have good luck and write better than I can."

I slid one foot tentatively out and touched the floor.

27

There is nothing else than now. There is neither yesterday, certainly, nor is there any tomorrow. How old must you be before you know that?

~ Ernest Hemingway, *For Whom the Bell Tolls*

I started going to the barn most mornings before the blistering Cuban afternoon temps kicked in. However, I found the habit of rum sipping to be a tough one to break, especially on the days when I heard Tommy Dorsey blaring from the radio, or when I spied a Packard zipping down the road. On those days, a Bloody Mary in the morning, a hefty cocktail before dinner, some wine with dinner, and then a nightcap seemed to settle me enough to sleep the sleep of the drugged. Papa scowled a few times when he spotted me with a glass in my hand, but said nothing.

The thought of returning to college for my senior year was daunting. I felt years older than my classmates. While they'd be excited to go to parties at Dartmouth or Amherst, hoping to find their future husbands, I was done with that. I'd found and lost my future husband forever. The prospect of law school was not even a possibility anymore in my mind. Everything had reached an end for me.

Jedd, on the other hand, was excited about going back to school and was focused on her medical school résumé. Few women applied and even fewer got in. She had connections though, and her father was supporting her 100 percent. Her mother was baffled as to why she would want to work when she didn't have to, but had no other comment.

"Finn, it will be a good year. Then graduation and we are launched into the world! We have to decide which law school you'll go to," Jeddrah said during one of our Sunday night phone talks.

"Yeah, let me know when you have it figured out," I said, talking on the extension in my room. My dream of law school and being a female avenger had moved behind some shrubs, covered in a veil of fog on some distant continent. I had no energy to resume that challenge. Jeddrah laughed, and I added, "In fact, I'll drink to that."

The laughter stopped and the line went silent. I'd told her about my three new boyfriends: Captain Morgan, Jack Daniels, and Johnnie Walker.

"It's not funny, Finn. Does your father know?" The irony of our role reversal was not lost on me.

"Sorry. Um, I suspect my father suspects. He *is* the king of the bullshit detectors, after all, as he is all too keen to tell you."

All Jedd said was, "Hmm."

We talked about our classes, what we needed for our room, and hung up. The phone rang again, but I made no move to pick it up. I had one friend who'd just hung up, and the other one was dead. There was no reason for me to answer the phone. It stopped ringing, and I assumed the housekeeper had picked it up.

"Finn, phone for you," Mary called.

I grimaced and called back, "Who is it please?"

"They didn't say."

I sighed. Mary was all about my father. She was nice to us kids, but I think she was a man's woman, not a woman's woman. She and I never had common ground except Papa.

I wearily lifted the receiver next to my bed. "Hello?"

"Tess?"

Nicky! My heart skipped and I gripped the bed sheet so hard my fingers cramped. The name only Nicky and his crew called me! Could it all have been some horrible mix-up? Just as quickly, I knew there would be no miracle for me. It wasn't Nicky's cadence. He would have said, "Tess! What a crazy mistake! I said I'd be back and a promise is a promise, niña! Grab your horse and let's go. Ye of little faith!" And then he'd laugh, and everything would be right. No, this wasn't that.

"Yes?" I said tentatively. Something about this male voice still registered as familiar, and he'd called me Tess. "I mean, yes. Yes, this is Tess." I sat up straighter, paying attention.

"Uh, this is Jackson Armstrong. We sent you a telegram a few weeks ago and never heard from you. We weren't sure you got it. My wife and I were concerned."

My mind swished about. Telegram? Ah, right, that day when Mary slid it under the door and I put it, unopened, on my table. I stretched as far as the telephone cord would allow, but I couldn't reach it on my bureau.

I was embarrassed. "Oh, Mr. Armstrong, I'm so sorry. I . . . I never opened it. I didn't know it was from you."

There was silence, and I suppose it did not make sense to him.

"Well, OK. Look, Tess, Nick's will was read a few weeks ago. He wrote it just before he shipped out. He left you his three horses and the money remaining in his trust to help you support them for a while. I know it's not a very practical idea, and we can make arrangements for them if you can't accommodate them. I played too—polo, I mean—and our club would be willing to . . ."

I bolted upright, boozy haze suppressed. Those horses were a part of Nicky. "No, sir. I . . . I want them. Please, I would like very much to have them. Thank you, Mr. Armstrong." I paused. "How are you and your family doing, sir?"

There was a long silence on his end. He sighed. "We're enduring, Tess. It has been hard on Nicholas's mother and of course, me too, but mothers and sons, you know how it is. It seems the tightest bonds are mothers and sons, and fathers and daughters. Somehow, it cuts to the very essence."

Indeed.

"And you, Tess? How are you doing?"

"Enduring, sir."

***

The Armstrongs' Newport "cottage" was on the ocean at the far end of Bellevue Avenue and was fronted by a circular stone drive lined with trees. Mr. Armstrong answered the door. Nicky's mother stood behind him in shadow. Her dark hair was loose, but I noticed white streaks I'd never seen before. I hadn't gone to Nicky's funeral. I'd been too distraught when Papa removed me to Cuba.

When she looked at me, I saw blue eyes sunken and a scattering of freckles that disappeared into her hairline—Nicky's looks. My spirit rose and plummeted as it all came back. She stepped forward and handed me a sealed envelope addressed to me but without postage.

"It was among Nicholas's things, Tess. I guess he hadn't had a chance to mail it, and I wanted to be sure you got it. I couldn't bear you . . . couldn't bear you not getting his last letter. I hope it says all happy things." Mrs. Armstrong grasped my hand, leaned in and clung to me in a desperate hug, so different from her usual composure. I hugged her back and almost fell apart completely. My legs weakened. She continued. "My God. Please know he truly loved you, Tess. How will we . . ."

She moved back and left the sentence unfinished. She turned away, shoulders shaking. I watched her walk away and seized the doorjamb to steady myself. Mr. Armstrong's shoulders dropped, then he straightened. "Good luck to you, Tess. If I can ever do anything for you—anything—please tell me. It would be an honor."

***

We—Jack was helping me—put my four horses in a row in the Smith College barn. I now had Sassafras plus Nicky's three. Jack had been released from a POW camp in April 1945 just around the time of Nicky's death, and he was a pretty good hand with a horse. I couldn't bear to have new nameplates printed, so Nicky's mahogany plaques were screwed into the stall doors of his three. Perfect Arc, Owner Nicholas Armstrong. Sara's Silence, Owner Nicholas Armstrong. Dancing Girl, Owner Nicholas Armstrong. When the last one was up I wept in the stall, my head on Dancing Girl's neck.

Once the horses were settled, I bee-lined for my favorite tree on campus near the pond. I sat, back against the tree trunk, legs crisscrossed, and pulled Nicky's letter from my back pocket. I wanted to read it alone at our spot, the spot where we leaned close, and shared secrets, and plotted our future. I unfolded the thin, blue paper. It was dated two days before his death. I stared at the familiar writing, and could almost hear Nicky's voice.

Dear Tessa:

I don't have much time, but I just wanted to drop you a line. It's three in the morning, and I'm not sure when I can write next. I want you to know that the thought of you keeps me going here. I see us someday in a cottage by the sea with our horses out back and a couple kids running around, feeding the ponies carrots and hay, and us laughing, with a couple of big dogs thrown in for good measure. I really see that, Tess.

I want you to know that I feel good we didn't wait. Some nights, the thought of being together again is the only thing that soothes my mind enough so I can sleep. It is the dreamiest of dreams, and I keep it tucked inside as just mine, to be pulled out when I need it to sustain me. When things get rough here, I think of you, your touch, your smile, your legs wrapped around mine. A lifetime of that would not be too much. I just wanted you to know.

Anyway, I have to run. Some days are wicked here, but the men are good men. I will make it back . . . but if I don't, and I know I will, but if I don't, please know I feel I've been loved enough to last a lifetime. I just hope you feel like you have been, too. I missed nothing in life that mattered. I love you, Tessa. Always move forward, but please don't forget me. I love you always and forever. So, Tess, not to be too cute, but I'll be seeing you in all the old familiar places, because you really are in my dreams every night.

Love, Nicky

I slumped against the tree, closed my eyes for a few moments, and wondered how many times your soul could die. Then I smiled ruefully at the foolishness of thinking I could outfox the Hemingway love jinx. It would not be thwarted, ever.

Nicky. Nicky. I will never forget you, your smile, and your gentle touch, and those nights when I shivered just to feel your *leg crossing over mine, or your voice when you breathed my name like a prayer: Tessa, Tessa, Tessa.*

28

I loved you when I saw you today and I loved you always but I never saw you before.

~ Ernest Hemingway, *For Whom the Bell Tolls*

I began riding all four horses on a regular basis. With my focus on my classwork, as well as on the horses' care, I barely noticed the months passing until one afternoon I headed to the barn and couldn't escape the fact that that day—the third Saturday in March, 1946—was a grim day for me. It was Nicky's birthday. My grades were far from stellar after midterms. To top it off, I had learned the night before—from a newspaper article, no less—that Papa and Mary had married in Cuba on March 14. *Great, just great. Thanks for letting me know, Papa. Yet again no notice or inclusion.* Although I'd known the marriage to Mary was coming as soon as the divorce from Martha was final, a heads up would have been a nice, familial touch. I growled. What the heck? Sometimes I agreed with Faulkner that Papa's problem was he thought he had to marry every woman with whom he fell in love.

I wanted to call Papa and confront him about the marriage, but I didn't have the verve. I shoved all of those dark thoughts aside and set my mind to riding my four horses. I'd had a drink before breakfast, another at noon, another at three. I had a full flask in my pocket to supplement after that.

By the time I got to exercising Dancing Girl, my last horse, I wasn't sure of anything. I stayed on her back just barely, and only because she slowed when I was close to falling. I didn't remember putting her away at all. I did recall vaguely promising myself I'd be back first thing in the morning to groom her properly. *I put a blanket on her for sure—or did I? I didn't feed her when she was still hot, right? I'd remember that, wouldn't I?* I do recall shuffling back to the dorm resolved never to let this happen again, this neglect and failure to . . . well, failure to do right by Dancing Girl and the others.

I staggered up the stairs to find Jedd studying. She looked up when I entered. Her lips flattened and her eyes narrowed.

"Finn, you're drunk. Good God. This is not good at all. This stops now."

Fortunately, I was not a belligerent drunk like Papa could be. I smiled at Jeddrah. "Jedd, come on. No big deal. I'll be fine in the morning."

As she shook with anger, I burst into laughter. "You should see yourself, all puffed up like a self-righteous pigeon!"

Jeddrah was unimpressed and unintimidated. "Finn, sleep it off. You're in no condition to listen to reason. We'll talk in the morning."

I woke up at six with a head-cracking hangover, but stumbled down to the barn. Although I always saved Dancing Girl's workout for last, I liked to greet her and Sassafras first, because I loved them best. My mind was still whipping through my less than perfect life when I tripped on a stone, looked around, and noticed, even in my semi-stupor, that something was wrong. The barn door stood wide open.

I rushed in. The aisle was dark and I flipped the switch, flooding the space with light. The cement center aisle was still messy from last night. I stopped and listened. I heard the customary morning munching of last night's leftover hay and murmurs of contentment. I inhaled the scent of leather and oil. A few heads poked out and I saw that Dancing Girl's stall door was gaping open. I ran to it and knew what I would find: horse gone.

My heart raced. I stared, stunned, rubbing my brow. When did I leave here last night? God, I couldn't think! *I closed the stall door tight, right? I latched it, didn't I?* A slimy, cold sensation started to slither up my spine. Had I even brushed her down and put on her blanket? I couldn't remember. I ran outside to see if someone had turned her out or if she'd escaped and was grazing nearby, but no horses were visible.

In a panic, and sober as a teetotaler from terror, I stuffed my pockets with grain, grabbed a halter and lead rope, and tore toward the woods behind the stables, calling her name. I hurried down a trail we'd ridden many times, alternately running and walking. Periodically, I would stand still to listen for any horse sounds. After an hour, I was deep into the swampy part of the woods and my riding boots were soggy and mud-covered.

"Dancy!" I screamed intermittently, in a half-hysterical, half-despondent voice. I'd been drunk last night, and Nicky's best mare was gone because of that. I'd let him down in the most shameful way. Dancing Girl could be out on the road, or if she'd been wet when I put her away—and who knew? I sure didn't—or if I'd fed her too soon after her exercise, she could have colicked—a deadly abdominal condition—or developed one of a multitude of other deadly conditions. I'd learned long ago that "healthy as a horse" was a misnomer.

Shattered and scared, I pulled the back of my riding jacket down and sat on a damp log to catch my breath. Tears of self-loathing rolled down my cheeks. I dropped my head to my hands, not knowing what to do. The sun was pouring down through the naked branches of early spring, but I barely noticed.

Finally, I headed back to campus, hoping the horse had returned, as horses often do. I heard a noise. I listened and heard it again. It was a low moaning. I spun around and raced up a hill, thinking the sound was over its crest. I was right. Not thirty feet ahead of me, I saw the beautiful bay horse down on her side with no blanket on and saddle marks visible from a negligible grooming. She was visibly shivering, and in that moment, I truly yearned to trade my life for hers. I groaned and skidded down the hill, stumbling into a tree, rappelling off of it, and veering from the path to where she lay. I knelt beside her and stroked her velvety neck. Her eyes rolled back to see me. She puffed out little, quick breaths, and her ears twitched.

"It's OK, girl," I said. "Simple as pie. Come on, Dancy. Let's get you some help."

She raised her head, but it was now back down on the ground. She seemed exhausted and unable to get up. "OK, girl. I'll just give you some help." I looped the halter over her ears, fastened it, and clipped on the lead rope. I stood and pulled. I held out some grain, but she had no interest. Finally, I grabbed a fallen branch and poked at her. Her eyes went frantic. I hated scaring her, but a fearful horse will do all it can to get on its feet.

As I prodded, she rocked herself into a lying down position, head up though. With extreme effort, she stuck out one front leg and leveraged the bent front leg under her to gain purchase. She pushed hard. I pulled on the lead rope to give her an assist. With a grunt, she rose clumsily. She was shaky, but stepped forward and followed me up the hill to the trail. When she tried to stop, I kept her moving, knowing that if this was colic, she had to keep going.

It took us two hours to get back to the barn. The forced march was paced for a snail, but a steady snail. "Come on. Wow, that was weird, huh? Wait until we get back. Nice fresh hay, a warm blanket, and a mash. Won't that be great?" My babbling seemed to soothe her.

When we got back to the stable, I rushed to the barn manager's office to call the vet. In the meantime, I sponged Dancing Girl with warm water to clean off the caked-on mud and tossed a wool cooler on her. I walked with her, letting her drink small sips of water. When the vet arrived, I almost cheered with relief.

"Is she going to be OK?" I asked repeatedly. The vet and his assistant didn't answer, just kept shaking their heads. Finally, I shut up. The vet gave Dancing Girl a shot and stood up. I stared anxiously at him.

"She's not in good shape, Finley. Seems like she just missed having a full colic by a hair. Keep walking her for the next two hours. If she tries to lie down, don't let her. Keep her moving. If she starts to get very lethargic, call me again. If she shows some interest in food, she'll be OK. You found her in the nick of time."

The horse doc turned to leave, then pivoted back. "Finley, I don't know how this happened, but you'd better change your barn protocol. Someone has some explaining to do."

I was too ashamed to speak. I nodded. "Thank you, Doc. I understand."

He nodded grimly and left. For the next couple of hours, I walked Dancing Girl around the indoor arena. We shuffled through the dust and kept the lights dim. Sometimes, she'd dawdle a full length behind me. Sometimes though, she'd be right next to me, docile and confused. I stroked her muzzle or threw an arm lightly over her neck, pulling her closer, planting a kiss on her nose. I told her my stories and my secrets and my plans . . . how she'd play polo again this summer with Graham and Jonah . . . how I might go to NYU Law School next year . . . how I'd loved Nicky as you can only love a first love and a last love. He'd been both.

And I vowed never to have a drink again. Nicky's death wasn't an excuse for selfish, irresponsible behavior. Except for one instance, I never drank a drop again. I still had to figure out how to endure this darkness and these grief-haunted nights, but I knew that I couldn't let everything that came before poison everything that came after. If it did, my life was over and, as my father always said, the business of living was to survive.

This is where before and after divides. Before Nicky died, I believed I could outsmart the Hemingway love curse; that I in my arrogance was better than my father was, than my mother was, or than Pauline or Martha were. After Nicky died, I knew I couldn't avoid my family destiny. After his death, I accepted it. While after Dancing Girl's episode I chose to live cleanly and responsibly in Nicky's honor, I also knew that love was over for me, just like it was for all of us Hemingways. My father could keep trying to get it right, but I was done.

29

Thou wilt go now, rabbit. But I go with thee. As long as there is one of us there is both of us.

~ Ernest Hemingway, *For Whom the Bell Tolls*

The summer of 1946 started out with élan, a time of new beginnings and with the hope that I maybe could forge a fresh path in law school, even if I was dragging sadness in my wake. Jack had met a war widow and seemed ready to shut down his playboy ways. Papa was looking forward to spending time with all of us kids in Idaho in August. I'd stopped drinking altogether and was thrilled to be accepted to NYU Law School. I'd brought my college grades up by the end of the year and my entrance scores had been high. I looked forward to being able to support myself someday and was determined to be the best trial lawyer in the state of New York, righting all wrongs that crossed my path, but not before enjoying some family time out west. As for Mary, Papa's fourth wife, it seemed her hope for a little Welsh/Hemingway baby was about to come true.

"Flea, buenas noticias! Good news! Miss Mary has a bebé on the way. Due in spring. We'll have her speaking Spanish and English before she can walk. I thought we could have little baby Bridget and Negrita share a crib, but Mary took umbrage at that."

Papa sounded happy and excited on the phone call. *Maybe Papa would break the Hemingway love curse with Mary.*

I bucked up. "That's fantastic, Papa. Give Mary my best. I'll see you soon."

"Can't wait. You're my barometer, Flea. Always have been."

What the heck did that mean? I wondered, while I finished packing for a few weeks in Idaho. The good vibrations fled quickly. Papa and Mary had paused for an overnight in Casper, Wyoming, en route to Idaho when Mary woke up in excruciating pain, apparently the result of an ectopic pregnancy. Within hours, her fallopian tube had ruptured.

Papa rushed her to the Memorial Hospital of Natrona County, but no surgeon was available when they arrived. Mary fell unconscious, and the intern on duty—poor kid—told Papa to prepare his last goodbyes to her.

Here are two things about Papa. One: not only was he 100 percent capable of grossly exaggerating the importance of his actions, but you could almost expect that he would. It was his storytelling nature to make the story more dramatic. Throughout my childhood, I'd heard stories grow exponentially with each telling, so Papa's original supporting role suddenly exploded into a starring one by the fifth retelling. He exaggerated less with me, and the boys would always look to me for the version closest to reality. Two: Papa was magnificent in a crisis. He transformed into what I think of as his true Midwestern self: calm, cheerful, kind, take-control, and humble.

Papa cabled me at my motel in North Platte, Nebraska, where I was staying on the way to Idaho. His telegram sounded upset, but direct: *Flea, hang a left above Casper and get to Memorial Hospital. Mary dire. Need you here. P.*

I was out the door in ten minutes and arrived mid-crisis six hours later. I raced off the elevator of the modest hospital and headed toward a voice that sounded for all the world like a general rallying the troops for battle. Nurses were scurrying in and out of a room in response to pleasant but specific commands. As I rushed in, I spied Papa in a surgeon's gown and face mask. His father was a doctor, and he was familiar with many of the procedures of a general practitioner, in addition to having rudimentary medical training as an ambulance driver. Under other circumstances, I would have found this scene hilarious.

"Flea, just in time. Here, hold this pan until I need it. Nurse Holmes, we'll need more plasma sooner than we thought, so I'd appreciate it if you could run for some right now."

"Right away, Mr. Hemingway." A pretty blonde nurse in a crisp, white nurse's dress and winged hat spun and hustled out of the room.

When I saw the blood, I got woozy. I grabbed the end of the bed and steadied.

"Flea, stay afloat. I need you solid," Papa said.

I straightened and followed all commands to get water and towels. Papa asked the intern, who had pronounced Mary just about dead a mere forty-five minutes before, to please probe for a vein. Papa cleared a line for plasma, inserted a needle, and kept vigil until Mary began to regain color and breathe. When the actual surgeon arrived in a flurry of self-importance an hour later and learned that Ernest Hemingway had taken control of his OR, he seemed miffed, mortified, and relieved that Mrs. Ernest Hemingway had not died on his watch.

There was no doubt that he and the hospital staff knew Papa had saved Mary. No exaggeration on this one. And Mary knew he had saved her. I think at some of her worst moments with Papa, Mary summoned up this testament of love, swallowed hard, and kept her head high, assuring herself that deep down—really deep down—Papa loved her.

Everyone close to my father knew that when he was his good self, he was as good as it gets. When he wasn't, however, the sun stopped shining.

***

When we finally got to Idaho after Mary's recovery, I met Logan Grant. Logan was in his mid-thirties. I'd just turned twenty-one. He was often around, checking on our wood, or on our heat, or on the water system. I wasn't sure what else he did, but his "howdy, ma'am," hat-tipping habits amused me— very un-New York. I was surprised when I heard he was a doctor.

"What kind of doctor?" I asked him as I chopped wood, pausing to push back hair curling on my brow.

"Bones," he said as he grabbed the ax from my hand and started chopping. I grabbed it back.

"I like to chop wood," I said. "What do you mean 'bones'?"

"I fix bones, and I also do a little writing on the side."

"Huh." I raised the blade and dropped it with force. Logan looked like he wanted to retake the ax but saw that I meant to keep it, so he leaned against a tree and watched, hands in pockets, his Stetson tipped down.

"What does that mean?" he asked.

"What?" I asked, as if I didn't know.

"That 'huh.'"

I leaned on the ax handle, appraising him. Idaho's late August days were starting to cool. Logan had gray-green eyes, dark-brown, wavy hair that could use a cut, a square jaw, and the longest black lashes I'd ever seen on a man. He didn't smile a lot, but when he did, it was a lovely reward—a sun-breaking-through-clouds sort of thing.

I finally said, "In my experience—and I've broken my collar bone twice and my arm twice—bone doctors tend to be a little lacking in empathy. You know, just set that bone and out the door. Writers are the opposite. They want to know everything, every why, how, and when, then they use it in their next piece. I tell Papa nothing that I don't want to show up in his next novel. That's all. They seem like very different careers."

"Ah, therein lies the paradox and the mystery, Finley. Doesn't it make you want to know more about me?" He smiled, and there was the sun breaking through—well, what I said before.

I shrugged. "Seems to me you're talking in riddles and trying to make it sound deep, Logan."

"You're on to me, Finley." He took off his Stetson, hit it against his leg to clear the dust, and put it back on. He reached over and took the ax back.

"My turn," he said quietly. I gave it to him and flopped into an Adirondack chair.

"So how did you meet Papa?" I asked.

As he raised the ax overhead, he said, "I met your father two years ago when he started renting. He wanted to fish, so Bill McNeill, over at the lumberyard, asked me to show him the best spots, and we struck up a friendship. I keep a sheep ranch going too, just a couple hundred head, and he enjoyed watching me work the dogs." He finished chopping, stacked the wood neatly near the door, tipped his hat, and hopped into his truck. "See ya, Finley. Don't break a bone when I'm not looking."

***

The next afternoon, I pulled up to the First Methodist Church of Hailey, Idaho, slammed on the brakes, and ran to make my AA meeting before the doors locked. I flung open the side door that led directly to the church hall, a room with fluorescent lighting, tan linoleum floor, and walls of creamy yellow. The hall was full of sunlight, with each window framing a mountain.

"We're a small group today, so let's go crazy and form a circle up front," the leader called. As I turned to sit down, I saw Logan Grant across the circle from me. He gave a little side-to-side wave. I raised an eyebrow and waved back, a side-to-side gesture mimicking his.

I'd asked Papa to join me at the meeting, but he'd laughed. "You go along, Flea. I really respect your decision. It's a good one. But I like my whiskey without a side of religion."

He knew he should stop drinking, but he still liked it too much to try to curb it. He said it took the edge off. Yes, it took more than the edge off. When I told Jack I was going to AA, he said I wasn't really an alcoholic.

"You just drink too much sometimes," he said as he chugged a beer.

"Uh, that's called an alcoholic, Jack."

"You were depressed and had a right to be."

"The end result is the same. I can't drink."

"Geez, Finn, you're really striking out into uncharted waters for this family. Watch out, or we may start to shun you like baboons shun their young who've been touched by humans. We may not be able to relate to someone who doesn't drink," he said, finishing off his beer and squashing the can on his forehead as he bugged his eyes out. He leapt around the room making monkey noises and scratching.

"You're disgusting, Bumb," I said, laughing and tossing a crumpled piece of paper at him. But I was clear; I didn't intend to do a toxic death waltz with a bottle of whiskey.

After the meeting, Logan ambled up to me. It was the first time I'd seen him in anything other than jeans. He was wearing a blue button-down shirt and blue blazer. No Stetson. His hair was combed, and he had a light tan. He looked good.

"Drink?" he smiled.

"Ha-ha."

"I meant coffee, Finley."

I ignored his question. "So," I asked, "what are you doing in AA?"

"I could ask you the same," he said, leaning against the wall. "But the short answer is that Kentucky's finest bourbon was my drug of choice for easing stress until I went into an operating room under the influence five years ago. Fortunately, with assistance, no harm done, but it scared the daylights out of me. Came to AA the next day and never stopped coming. You?"

"Pretty much the same."

"So, coffee?"

I was glad I had not run out the door ragged. I was wearing a mid-calf navy dress that flowed nicely.

"Sure." I nodded. "Your car?"

He nodded, and we headed out, waving to a few people as we left. As he opened the passenger door for me, he asked, "How do you like spending time out here with your dad and mom?"

"Mary's not my mother," I said too quickly. "She's my father's fourth wife. I'm from wife number one."

"Ah, I wondered about that."

I shrugged. "Mary's fine, and I love it out here. Whenever I see some of your trails, I dream of getting on one of my horses and riding until we want to stop. Out east, there is always an end to the trail. Out here, the land seems endless."

"It is pretty country, isn't it?"

"Sure is. Did you grow up around here?"

"Yep, just across the border in Wyoming, in a little place called Jackson Hole. My father raised some sheep, but he didn't really have a head for the business end."

He started the car, and the radio blasted to life with Jo Stafford singing. Logan switched it off and drove the three blocks to the Big Rock Café in downtown Hailey. As we pulled over to park, I admired again the wide main street of the town with the mountain range jutting behind it like a Hollywood backdrop.

Our coffees arrived, and Logan asked, "Hey, how are those horses of yours? Your father told me a little bit about them and your fiancé, Nick. Sorry about that. I was in France, and half my buddies didn't make it out." Logan looked like he might cry. "Anyway, your father said you still ride a lot. How do you do that in NYC?"

"I have my best horse in the city, Dancing Girl. She finds it odd to be riding through a park. The other three are at a barn in Greenwich. I only get out there on weekends. Sassafras is older and not well. I'm afraid I won't have him much longer. The other two were Nicky's and are just wonderful." I took a sip of coffee. "Nicky left me some money, so that's made the horses possible. That money will be gone soon though, and I can't keep more than one." The thought depressed me and made me feel heavy. I tucked my hair behind my ears and hesitated. "They pretty much kept me sane after Nicky died. Without them, I don't think I would have survived, and I mean that literally. They were a reason to get up."

The waitress took our order and quickly returned with my steak and eggs and Logan's bacon and eggs.

"Sounds like those horses are more than just pets," Logan said as he peppered his eggs.

I picked up my fork. "I couldn't sell Nicky's horses. I could donate them to the polo club, but the thought of them not being someone's personal ponies is . . ." I started to feel sick at the thought, and my face must have clouded. I took a breath. "Sorry."

Logan's face softened. "You don't have to talk about it if you don't want to."

"It's just that it will kill me to lose them." Logan was quiet and listening. "Anyway, I have almost a year to figure it out. Maybe I have a secret aunt who'll leave me a stash."

Logan smiled and sat back. "So tell me about him."

"Him?"

"Nick. Tell me about Nick."

That stopped me. I put down my fork, wiped my mouth, and gathered my thoughts. Sometimes I didn't want to share anything about Nicky, and sometimes I wanted to crow from the rooftops about how lucky I was to have had what I had, even for too short a time.

I took a sip of coffee. "Ah, Logan, there is so much and so little to tell." I looked down at my hands, my fingers wrapped around my mug. "He was all I ever dreamed of in the world. He loved horses, and laughing, and the sun, and reading, and driving his Packard with the top down, and the wind blowing through our hair, and . . . me. With some people, you're not sure about tomorrow, but with Nicky, I knew."

Logan eyed me intently. He leaned forward on the table. "You *were* lucky. It's got to be hard to lose that."

"It was," I said quietly, then brightened. "But those horses carry his spirit, and I couldn't stand not knowing that they're well cared for and loved."

Logan motioned for more coffee. "Horses are special. You can only ride 'em because they let you. Kind of like women." My eyebrows shot up. He colored and added, "Oh, no, not that way; I meant you can only love them because they let you. It can't be forced." He paused. "Nicky sounds like he would be a hard act to follow."

"No one has to. There will never be anyone else for me."

"You can't know that, Finn. You're what, twenty?"

"Just turned twenty-one." I fiddled with my coffee cup, placed it on the table, and put my hands in my lap. "There will never be anyone else for me."

Logan looked away, and I felt the "élan" of new beginnings sinking under the weight of old endings.

30

And who understands? Not me, because if I did I would forgive it all.

~ Ernest Hemingway, *For Whom the Bell Tolls*

My first and second years of law school passed smoothly, but I was happy to be back in Idaho for a few weeks at the end of the summer before starting my final year. Stretching out on the sofa, I savored my last week of vacation sobbing as I read the last page of *Green Dolphin Street,* a *New York Times* bestseller. The door burst open as Papa and Logan Grant tromped in, trailed by two shaggy dogs, and a third smaller one with a limp.

"So, what's up?" I asked. It was midday, and the sun was streaming through the two front windows. The modest cabin had only five small rooms, a kitchen with eating space, a living room with a dining room table, and three small bedrooms. The views of the mountains made up for any deficits in the accommodations.

After checking to be sure it was unloaded, Papa put his rifle in the corner and looked at me. "Hey, what's wrong, Flea? Looks like you were crying."

I looked up with a sniff. "I was crying a little, but just about this book, *Green Dolphin Street*. God, what a love story. So sad."

"Aren't they all?" Papa said.

"No, not all love stories are sad, Papa. Yours are, but not everybody's are."

"Yeah, tell that to Tolstoy, Stendhal, Shakespeare, and Flaubert."

I laughed. "No, really. In this one, there are these two sisters, one shy, the other one outgoing, and the hero loves the shy one. Then the hero, while drunk, asks the wrong one to marry him, easy mistake, Marguerite and Marianne, and . . . oh, it's just so sad."

Papa trudged over to his chair and started to pull off his boots. He was grinning at me. "You must think I never read anything, Flea. I read that book last year. Like to scope out my competition." He got one boot off, then leveraged the other one. It went flying and crashed into a wall.

"Shush! Mary is napping," I said, finger to lips.

"Sorry. But really, Flea, I know what's out there." He had lowered his voice to a stage whisper. Logan greeted me with a nod of the head and sank down on the other end of the old sofa. I shifted my legs to make space. The small hobbled dog got up too and promptly fell asleep between us. Papa turned to Logan.

"You know, Logan, week after week, my publisher gets these letters from Hemhaters about how disgusting my books are. They don't like my subject matter, bullfighting, war, hunting, fishing. They ask, 'Can't Hemingway write about something pleasant?'"

Papa pulled a bottle of whiskey from the side of his chair. It was noon. A glass mysteriously materialized, and he poured. He took a gulp and set it down on his side table with a thwack.

I shot him a look and another shushing warning. "Mary's resting!"

"Oh, sorry." He continued in a diminished voice. "But, Jaysus, do they think I can't write about roses? All my books are about love, for Christ's sake, how to get it, how to lose it. If all a reader sees in *Sun, Farewell,* and *Bell* is people at war, or dying, or going to the corridas, then the hell with 'em. Let them read Gertrude Stein's sludge. By the way, did she actually write anything in the last two decades other than that Alice B. Toklas autobiography that isn't?"

I rolled my eyes. "Don't start on Gertrude, Papa, especially since she's dead now. Next thing, you'll be talking about Scott, Zelda, and the Murphys, and then back down memory lane."

"Them's good memories for the most part, Flea. Just ask your mother. Very good memories. Someday, I'll write about them."

"I'd like that." I'd love to read his version of those years. I like to think of him when he was young and in love with my mother, the way they look in their wedding photos.

Papa held the bottle out to me. I held up my hand in a "stop" gesture. "Uh, no, Papa. Remember? I'm in AA."

Papa jerked back like he'd touched a sizzling coil. "Sorry. I'm an idiot, Flea." He quickly stowed it under his chair. Papa put both feet up on an ottoman, took another swallow from his glass and picked up a folded sheet of paper. "Hey, Flea, did I tell you I got this letter from Max last spring? I'd heard he was not too well, but he sounded good. Wanted to know when my next opus would be ready."

Papa held out the letter to me. Max Perkins had been one of his closest friends. For years, he was the sole conduit for Scott Fitzgerald and Papa. They both wanted to know what the other was up to, but wouldn't contact each other directly. I unfolded the letter.

> *Dear Hemingway:*
>
> *I'm trying to get away, but stuck here working with some fascinating new authors. That doesn't mean I forget the old. Yes, I too thought Edmund Wilson's criticism of Bell was dead wrong and below the belt unfair. Fortunately, most of America agrees with you and me, as its sales continue to be red hot.*
>
> *Wolfe is still a pain in my side, but new author James Jones is proving promising. Hoping he follows my suggestion to scrap his old novel and focus on his new war manuscript with the working title of "From Here to Eternity."*

The letter went on to say he'd love to visit that summer. The letter was dated April 13, 1947. Max died in June. I handed the letter back. "I miss him. He was always so humble. And that hat; I loved that hat."

Papa's eyes got shiny. He nodded. "Yeah, that hat." Papa swiped at an eye before changing the subject. "Logan, what will you do without Miss Mary, me, and the kids to divert you? We'll be gone in a few weeks, too."

Papa turned to me. "Logan writes about conservation." He took a swig. "You'd love Africa, Logan. Most beautiful countryside you'd ever want to see."

"I'd love to see the nature there, but no offense, Papa. No hunting for me."

"Understood, son," Papa said. I too hated those dead animal heads on the walls in Key West and Cuba. Papa knew it, and it was an agree-to-disagree situation.

"So, Logan," I asked. "Are you still married?" He'd never worn a ring, but I'd asked him early on. Today, he hesitated. Papa and I both turned to look at him.

"Simple question, Logan," Papa said with a chuckle. "Or not. Just ask *Life* magazine about my marital status."

Logan fiddled with his shirt buttons. "Yes, sort of."

"Sort of?" I asked.

"Janet and I started to live separately last year, but we're not divorced."

"Yeah, I've tried that a few times. Never works," said Papa, as he picked up a magazine and started reading. "Either divorce 'em or stay married. No in between."

Logan fidgeted. I took pity on him and changed the subject. "Whose dogs are these?" I was used to animals following Papa home and then staying.

Logan spoke up. "They're mine: Bouviers. Herding dogs who'll give their life for you."

I ruffled the curly fur on the head of the dog flopped against me. "First thing I'm doing when I get back to New York is get a dog." As if on cue, the dog licked my hand.

Papa looked up from his magazine. "Yup. I love my critters. Couldn't pry my Negrita or my Boise from me upon pain of having to listen to Faulkner recite some of his never-ending sentences."

Logan pointed at the dogs surrounding us. "Take one, Finn. I have too many, and only took the limping one because they were going to put her down. As a pup, she jumped too close to a tractor and her leg got caught. She's really sweet, and I couldn't let them kill her. Or take one of the others. They are all great, and I don't need three."

I looked down at the gray brindle dog with a white spot on her chest and crooked leg. Her short tail wagged like a short metronome, and round, dark eyes looked up at me.

I said, "Her. I want the hurt one. What's her name?"

"Tess."

31

For what are we born if not to aid one another?

~ Ernest Hemingway, *For Whom the Bell Tolls*

Jeddrah and I had lived in the midtown apartment since our move to New York after college. It was a cozy but plain space that was mid-way between NYU and Columbia, its glory being a wood-burning fireplace. Jeddrah took the subway up to Columbia, while I grabbed one down to NYU. Dancing Girl was happy at Claremont Stables in Central Park. And Tess, also known as Mess, because she was, had taken to the city, choosing to defend Jedd and me instead of sheep.

Papa was footing the bill for law school, as well as my share of the apartment and all living costs. My money from Nicky was ending soon, and I couldn't ask Papa to subsidize four horses. He was also covering my car rental for trips to Idaho, food, spending money, Mary's parents, alimony to Pauline, tuition for the boys and me, subsidies to all us kids, and trips to Cuba for all of us multiple times a year. I'd also heard that getting a job as a woman lawyer might not be as easy as it was during the war, when jobs needed filling desperately, so that made me anxious. Practicing law was all I ever dreamed of doing, and I detested being a financial burden. I wanted a job as a lawyer when I finished school.

That Christmas, the Finca, Papa's home in Cuba, was quiet, but festive. His new dog, a scraggly Springer Spaniel stray he named Black Dog, was always in his wake. Papa had brought him back from Idaho, hand fed him, and built trust.

On Christmas Eve, Mary made a delicious fish dinner, and we swam in the pool at midnight. I got Papa a gift certificate to Abercrombie & Fitch, which he pinned to his shirt; he got me a buttery Italian leather briefcase for "when you're a real lawyer, Flea. Gotta look the part."

I also had received a Christmas card from Martha just before I headed to Cuba. She was still traipsing the world, covering crises, and ended noting that there was no need to tell my father that we were in touch, as he still blamed her completely for that divorce.

She was right about that. It was only regarding his marriage to my mother that he took blame for the demise. And no matter what anyone says, my mother never got over him. The only complaint she ever voiced was his exclusion of her from *The Sun Also Rises*. She said more times than I could count, "I just wish he'd included me in *The Sun*. Everyone else was in it, except me. I cried a lot about that after he left. But it all turned out OK, right? It came to an end. That's all."

It came to an end all right, a bad end, with my mother crying in the dark.

***

The first letter from Logan Grant arrived that spring. It was chatty, going on about the wicked weather in Idaho, his insane surgical schedule, and repairs on his cabin. I smiled and responded in kind. I wrote about the famous law school contract case known among law students everywhere as the case of the hairy hand, and of the perils of a western mountain dog in New York City, including photos of Tess at tourist attractions: Tess on the steps of the Fifth Avenue Library, Tess at the Statue of Liberty, Tess at Radio City Music Hall, Tess taking a carriage ride through Central Park, Tess in a Yankees cap. Tess gimped her way happily down 5th Avenue, and every kid who saw her gave her hugs.

I started to look forward to Logan's letters. Then one day in the spring, he wrote that he would be in New York City.

Finn, I have to be in your town for a meeting with the editors of a new magazine on conservation issues. If you're around, I'd love to have dinner or whatever you can fit in.

I looked over at Jeddrah, who was sitting at our kitchen table studying a colored page of a human skeleton. Her blonde hair hung over her shoulders and she wore thin, horn-rimmed oval glasses. I said, "Hey, Jedd, listen to this. What do you think?"

I read her the letter. Jeddrah looked at me over the tops of her glasses. "It sounds like he wants a date with you."

"It does? Really? No, I don't think so," I said. I ran a hand through my long, red hair and studied the letter. Jeddrah herself was dating a fellow medical student, Robert Drake. She was the happiest I'd ever seen her, and we spent hours discussing how melodious Jeddrah Drake sounded. Then we tested Dr. Jeddrah Drake and ended up laughing at our obsession with her name change, but we were twenty-four, and it didn't take much to make us giddy.

"What should I say to him about dinner?" I asked.

"Isn't he still married?"

"He was last year."

"Well, dinner is just dinner; just don't get into some ugly, sordid affair." Jeddrah's eyes widened. "You don't want to be the backstreet girl thing, like in that Charles Boyer movie."

I laughed. "I'm not going to be the backstreet girl, for heaven's sake. You watch too many movies. And I don't think he likes me that much."

"What will your father say?" Jeddrah closed her book.

"Nothing, since he is not in charge of my life." I was sitting on the floor brushing shaggy Tess, who was not cooperating. I eyed her crusty beard as she shook her head stubbornly and gnawed on the rawhide chew. "I don't need his approval."

"Hmm, if you say so," said Jeddrah softly.

***

Logan stayed in New York for four days. We had dinner together every night and rode in Central Park twice. He teased me for not providing him with a big western saddle.

"Sorry, we don't have those big old horns you can hold onto for dear life. Just adjust, cowboy," I said. He laughed, gave a kick, and took off at a gallop, with me giving chase.

We went to the Bronx Zoo, where Logan spent hours looking at the environments for the animals and making notes. The last night Logan was in town, we went to Toots Shor's for dinner. I was always treated royally there, as it was a favorite haunt of Papa's when he was in town. The comedian Jackie Gleason, as funny off stage as on and also a Papa pal, was often there too. That night, he was there with an entourage of twelve.

When Toots pointed me out, Jackie sauntered over, cigarette dangling from one side of his mouth.

"Finn! How's the old man? He afraid to come and face me himself?" Jackie did a little jig and gave me a huge hug. As I introduced Logan, Jackie waved his cigarette at us and turned to Toots. "Toots, on my tab."

I tried to protest, but Jackie turned back to me. "No discussion, Finn. Tell Papa I still owe him from the last time. Just remind him, Belmont, Little Jello, third race. He'll know. Good night, sweetheart. Enjoy the night." Jackie and his group moved into a private back room.

While we were eating, Toots came around to our table. "Finn, how's Ernie?" Toots called Papa "Ernie." Most of his friends called him Papa, or Ernesto, or Hem. He hated the name Ernest, and only Ingrid Bergman, and sometimes Mother, got away with calling him that. "Get him up here! We'll take him to Abercrombie's, serve his favorite scotch." Toots winked and hurried off to greet some other luminary.

Logan shook his head. "So, student girl, you seem to still get around. And Jackie Gleason is picking up our bill?"

I shrugged. "Don't be too impressed. Rumor has it Toots never lets Jackie pay."

When our dessert arrived, I spoke up. "Why didn't you bring your wife, Logan?"

He looked surprised. "Actually, I filed divorce papers last week. Janet has someone else."

"So you'll be free soon?"

"Seems like I will."

"I was thinking that when I'm out in Idaho, might you and I . . . see each other?"

Logan sat straighter, took a sip of water, and rearranged his napkin. "Finn, I have really thought about that possibility and with all due respect, I'm not sure that's a good idea."

He must have seen my confusion because he rushed on. "I like you a lot. I'm sure that's obvious. I did think at first that maybe someday . . . But now that I know you, I have to say that you're more complicated than I'm up for. You're clearly still in love with Nick, and I think we're better as friends. Honestly, Finn, I don't want an angst-filled love affair that I can never feel good in, if you don't mind."

I swallowed, and in my heart, I totally understood. I *was* too messed up. I said, "Of course, Logan. That makes total sense."

I patted his hand. I was disappointed, but I was mostly relieved.

32

Luck is a thing that comes in many forms and who can recognize her?

~ Ernest Hemingway, *The Old Man and the Sea*

"Your résumé is impressive, Miss Hemingway, but we've found that women don't stay long. Do you intend to marry? Have children?" asked a senior partner at Jones McKinley, a law firm in midtown Manhattan.

It was my first real interview with a law firm, and I'd worn a navy-blue suit bought for the occasion. The night before, I'd gone over and over my answers to standard questions and practiced being strong yet demure. I tried not to let my nerves take over as I was ushered into a paneled office with an oriental rug and leather chairs, leather loveseat—well, leather everything. I gave a firm handshake and looked the senior partner in the eye.

"No, sir. I don't intend to marry, and I need to practice law as a career. Forever."

The senior partner smiled indulgently. "I'm sure you'll change your mind when the right fellow comes along, dear. You are such an attractive girl."

I wanted to scream, but instead swallowed hard and conjured up a smile. "No, sir. I won't. I want to do litigation. I won't change my mind, sir. I just want a chance."

A bark pierced the air. "Litigation! Dear, that's for the men. It's too rough-and-tumble for you girls. Long hours and late nights. The women can't work long hours with our men."

I rushed to answer. "Sir, I love long hours and late nights. I need little sleep. Almost none. I was tops in my moot court class, sir. I prefer litigation," I added limply, for fear that I was losing him altogether. "Even if it's just the litigation preparation and research. Yes, that would be swell . . . perhaps."

His lips retracted into a thin line. "I'm sorry, but you aren't what we had in mind for a new associate. Good luck, Finley."

I hung my head, then nodded. "Thank you anyway, sir."

After a few similar interviews, I was discouraged, but true disillusionment hit like a wrecking ball after I had lunch with a woman lawyer, another Smith grad, named Brenda Vaughn. Brenda had worked for a New York firm during the war, but left to be a housewife and have a child when her legal career hit a dead end.

I'd never suspected things were this bad for women. Unknowingly, I'd been sheltered. Pauline, Martha, and Mary all were journalists of note, and Papa and his pals respected their talents. Papa's actress friends traveled, were independent, and negotiated contracts. While a professor at law school once looked at me quizzically when I bubbled about doing litigation, no one confronted me with the stark fact that not only might I never be hired, but litigators were a closed club. Drafting wills and doing research in a back room was the best I could hope for. During the war, women had a place, but not anymore.

Brenda and I met for lunch at Luchow's on a rainy day. Luchow's was a well-known German restaurant in the East Village. She was standing out front, and when I gave a single tentative wave to be sure it was she, she grinned and waved back. I liked her at once. She was about thirty-four years old with short, sandy hair, a pointed chin, and a pert nose. Her camel swing coat swirled as she spun to open the restaurant door. As soon as we were seated, she dove right in. I listened, and my spirits plummeted at the harsh realities.

"Honey, if you get a job at all, it will be a miracle. During the war, they let us do all sorts of work, because the men were away. There was no one else to do the work. A friend of mine was even allowed to go to court once. We all did our own typing—we had no secretaries—and we filled in typing when they were busy," said Brenda, lighting a cigarette. "But when the men came back, we all lost our jobs. The few who were allowed to stay on typed for the men, and the lucky ones did research." Brenda shook her head. "I graduated top of my class at Columbia, and I was typing for a guy who was bottom of his class from a no-name law school in Oregon."

I gulped. I'd known a career in law would be uphill, but I was dumbfounded as Brenda went on. "You'll have no one to have lunch with, Finn, so get used to being lonely. The men go to their all-boys clubs for meals. All golf outings are men only. And forget another woman being hired. If you get hired, you just met their quota for the decade, a quota of one."

Brenda took a puff of her cigarette. "Oh, and the secretaries will hate you for putting on airs of being a lawyer—better than them—even when you don't do anything to suggest that."

I took a sip of water. "But I want to do litigation. I took three times the classes in trial practice. I feel I could do a first-rate cross-examination with a little experience."

My voice started strong and trailed off as I saw Brenda's eyes open wide, then soften. She placed a hand on mine and quietly said, "You'll never see the inside of a courtroom, Finn. Maybe you'll prepare a brief, if they let you, but go to court? Argue motions? Never in your lifetime."

At that, I felt my face drain of color and my shoulders dropped. I sat back, defeated. "Really?"

Brenda shook her head. "I'm sorry, Finn. Didn't they tell you it's just not possible? Clients don't accept it, and while judges can't forbid it, they'll give no weight to what you say, so the firm can't allow it."

When we parted on the street, Brenda gave me a hug and held me at arm's length by the shoulders. "Finn, if I can help in any way, or if you just want someone to talk to, call me. I'm sorry to give you bad news, but you may find something. Maybe times will change faster than it seems. Stranger things have happened, darling."

That night, sitting on the floor around the coffee table, I told Jeddrah about my lunch. She shook her head. "There have to be exceptions. You'll get hired; then just show them you can do it."

"Jedd, you don't get it. Look at this." I shoved a copy of the most recent *Harvard Law Record* at her. Its headline read, "Women Unwanted."

Jedd read the first few paragraphs, but I rushed on. "It says in a survey describing characteristics most desirable in applicants for law firm jobs, on a scale from minus ten to plus ten, being a woman was a minus 4.9, lower than being in the bottom of your class or being a Negro or Jewish." I stabbed at the paper. "Look, it says that ninety percent of firms won't even interview women because, and I quote, 'They don't stay in the law, they can't work as hard as men or make the same kind of trips, and the clients prefer not to have them.'"

I lifted my head, triumphant in relaying this bad news and being vindicated in my bleak outlook. "You're a doctor. Your skills are obvious. In law, someone else has to believe in you."

Jeddrah looked doubtful and turned back to the article as if looking for the silver lining. She finally looked up at me. "Well, you *are* a lawyer, and you just have to show them."

When I told Papa about the situation, he was still for a minute, then said, "It's not fair, Flea. But life is easy when you have nothing to lose. Sounds like you've got nothing to lose, kid, because they don't want you at the table. Make them need you there. You have to pull on gumption almost too deep to dredge up. It's there, Flea. You're worthy. Show 'em."

"But, Papa, it's not that. I think I could do a really good job, but it doesn't matter if I'm great. One look at me in court, and I'm nothing. The judge won't listen." I paused, the crush of disappointment swamping me afresh. I felt I'd climbed Kilimanjaro only to find a whole other mountain I didn't know about jutting far above and behind it. "I wanted to practice law to make the world fairer. And now they won't even let me in the door."

"Oh, you're in the door, kid. You're in the door. Now kick it wide and drag a few in with you."

33

Have faith in the Yankees my son. Think of the great DiMaggio.

~ Ernest Hemingway, *The Old Man and the Sea*

In June of 1949, I flew to Paris to attend Jack's wedding. I hadn't seen Mother in a while, so I was happy to get over there and catch up.

It was a mixed time for me. I had just completed my final year of law school, and the bar exam awaited me. However, I had no means of support, and to my consternation, getting hired as a woman lawyer seemed nearly impossible. I'd had an inflated expectation, as there were many women working as lawyers when I started law school. The war had made that possible. But now, the pickings were slim indeed. I dreaded the possibility that I'd wasted three years of study and my father's money, not to mention my passion for the law and enthusiasm for practicing it.

To add to my distress, Sassafras had passed away the previous year, and I deflated whenever I gazed at photos of him and me in our salad days. I still had Nicky's three horses and couldn't afford them. My stomach knotted whenever I thought of placing them elsewhere. Mother had paid for my flight to Paris, as well as for my dress, and I couldn't tap her for money. Papa was already more than supporting me. On the flight to Paris, I tried to clear my head and just enjoy Jack's wedding, his new bride, Byra, known as Puck, and Paris, the old hometown.

I also was stewing about my father. He wasn't attending this shindig. Jack was the first of us kids to get hitched, and it seemed to me Papa owed him an appearance. Jack's wedding to Puck took place at the American Church in Paris with a reception at Mother and Paul's apartment on La Rue de L'Université, a pleasant, sunny, two-bedroom place on the left bank. Papa sent regrets. He was working on *Across the River and into the Trees* at Finca. It didn't go unnoticed by me that he'd visited Venice just that past April—where a new young woman, Adriana Ivancich, had caught his eye—yet couldn't make it to Paris a few months later for his son's wedding.

The reception's unexpected highlight was the appearance of Alice B. Toklas, Gertrude Stein's companion. Gertrude had been Jack's godmother. In a surprisingly melodious voice, Alice greeted the guests as if it were *her* wedding, and she flitted around the room in a large, pink hat with feathers, a beige shirtwaist dress that fell to mid-calf, and her usual sandals, leaving everyone whispering, "Who *is* that delightful little woman?"

Mother glowed in a teal-blue suit, but she also looked older. I was thrilled to hear she and Paul planned to move back to the States soon, probably to New Hampshire.

The wedding was touching enough to bring tears to my eyes, and I was ecstatic that wild Jack seemed to have found happiness and stability in his life.

"And how is your father, Finn?" Mother asked after the reception when we finally were alone. Mother had kicked her shoes off, put her feet up on a coffee table, and sipped a glass of leftover champagne. I nursed a ginger ale.

"He's . . . OK. But he never seems really happy. He and Mary travel a lot, but he's generally sniping at her. And then there is this girl, Adriana. I guess it's some flirtation or something, but everything is Adriana this and Adriana that. I could scream every time he says her name. Gig thinks she's attractive, but Jack and I think she looks like a spider. Mouse hasn't weighed in." Gig was Papa's nickname for my half-brother, Gregory.

Adriana Ivancich was of old Italian nobility that had lost most of its wealth, and Papa seemed completely infatuated with her. She was eighteen years old. Papa was forty-nine. Adriana had thick, black hair, hazel eyes, a thin face and a narrow, curving nose. She was tall, trim, and intelligent. Picture a carved Venetian woman's face, all angles and shadows, and you're close to a version of Adriana. That spring, she was all I heard about in Papa's calls and letters.

Mother laughed and rolled her eyes. "Oh dear. Yes, your father and his women. Always a challenge. Poor Mary. But Finn, your father is under a lot of strain. *For Whom the Bell Tolls* is a hard book to follow. It's been oh what? Nine years since he's come out with a novel? That has to grate on him."

"That doesn't excuse it all, Mother. This . . . this girl is leading him around like an old fool, and if I have to hear about her 'elegance and style' one more time, I think I'll . . . oh, I don't know. I'll turn purple or something." I gritted my teeth for emphasis.

"You sound a wee bit jealous, darling." Mother took a sip of her drink.

"Jealous of that . . . that manipulative, creepy girl? No, Mother. Hardly." I protested too much.

"You've always had his most focused attention, and now he's diverting it." She raised an eyebrow.

"Most focused attention? Are you kidding? The world and every socialite, his work, and the next Mrs. Hemingway, whoever she may be, have his focus, not me."

Mother looked away, then said quietly, "I think you haven't been paying attention, Finn. And have some empathy, sweetheart. It's not easy being almost fifty, with each book a new start." She smiled kindly, and I could tell she was thinking about him and her.

Later, when I blasted him to Jack, he just shrugged. As we sat in his pretty hotel suite while his new bride, Puck, was out shopping, Jack said, "Geez, Finn. Have you ever thought what it's like being him? He has to always top the last book; someone is always waiting to take him down; he has to be the most-manly guy on the field; he has to please Mary, who can be a handful; he has to not eat or drink too much if he wants to write well, and you know how he loves to eat and drink; he has to support all of us to some extent, plus his various family members, Mary's parents, two homes, a staff."

He paused to put his feet up on a cocktail table and sip a beer. "Let the guy keep working if he wants to. I'm OK with it. And then there's you, always whispering in the background, 'Love me best, Papa. Please.'" He said it in this high, frantic voice. My face tightened. "And he does, as you know; or should know." He paused to answer a knock at the door and carried in yet another bottle of champagne sent by Scribner's.

He resumed his seat. "I know you mean well, Finn, but cut the guy a break. Papa has enough to do without worrying about your fragile ego, too."

I felt like I'd been slapped, especially after Mother making an almost identical comment. I crossed my arms over my chest. "This is not about my ego. I'm just asking that he remember he has a family, for gosh sakes. Geez, I thought you'd agree with me, Bumb."

Jack sat back, ever relaxed, and took another sip. "Well, yeah, he can be remote sometimes, but it's who he is. He loves us. Let it go at that."

"That's OK with you? He gets a pass at being an insensitive lout because *it's who he is?* I think it's his way of telling us that he's more important than we are."

Jack wiped his mouth with a napkin and shrugged. "Well, he kind of is. By a lot. And you need to be OK with that, because to change the bad, you'd change the good. He's a package, all of it. He'll always come through for any of us. Even for Mother."

I snorted, but thought about it all the way home on the plane, whipping myself into a frothy frenzy by the time we were over New York. While I understood Jack's points, some were just wrong. Did all of us matter so little that not only could Papa skip his oldest child's wedding, but also the chance to see all of us together: Mother, Jack, and me?

The next morning, I dialed his number in a fury, tapping my foot as I jabbed the dial. It was early, so he likely would be clear-headed. Papa answered on the first ring.

I wasted no time on preliminaries. "Papa, I can't believe you didn't go to Jack's wedding. What the heck! Jack's your firstborn. Are you going to skip my wedding, too, if I ever get married? Let Chink walk me down the aisle instead of you?" Chink Dorman-Smith was one of Papa's oldest pals.

"Sorry, Flea, but I have to get it all down while it's churning," Papa said in a matter-of-fact tone. "I spoke to Jack. He and Puck understood."

I warmed to my anger. "No, he didn't. He was being nice because he adores you. I'll bet you'd be on the next plane to Venice if Signorina Adriana were to suggest a break from your writing."

I was met with dead silence. I waited for the explosion. Instead I got a sigh, and that was almost worse. It was unexpected. More silence followed. "Papa? Papa, are you still there?"

"I'm here." He paused, then said slowly in a heavy voice, "Flea, it's getting harder to do. Used to just flow out. Sure, I'd have to edit to death—the first draft of anything is shit—but the rawness was there. The power that I could shape the next day. Now, I have to wait longer, and it doesn't always come. I thought I had something here and was hot on it. Just couldn't leave it, 'cause it might not come back. Now I don't know if it was anything to begin with."

He stopped abruptly, and I heard something I'd never heard in his voice before: a hint of despair. It rattled me, and my rage flattened. Papa took a breath. I thought he was going to say more, but he didn't. I'd never heard him voice doubts about his writing—not once.

"Oh," I stammered. "I didn't know. I'm sorry, Papa. But might this be what you call writer's block?"

"I wish. This is its ugly, grisly, fire-breathing cousin, Flea, not so easily banished by a good night's *sueño*."

Sueño: dream. I didn't know what to say to make him feel better, so I just said what I felt. "I love you, Papa. I'm sorry."

"Thanks, Flea. I'll get through this. You know, it's good to have an end to journey toward, but it's the journey what matters in the end. I'm on the journey."

***

I needed money badly. I was working hard on my job interviews but in reality, I had only my weekend Macy's job, and bills were piling up. I did have the Hemingway name, however. It's hard to convey what it was like to be a Hemingway in 1949. To me, my father was just the busy, exasperating, smart, sometimes drunk, sometimes charming, astute, hilarious, loving man whom I saw two or three times a year. To other people, he was a brilliant writer or despicable, overrated reprobate who was always doing something good or bad enough to be worthy of *LIFE* magazine or the People section of *TIME* magazine. People who had never cracked the spine of a Hemingway novel or short story all knew Hemingway. He was everywhere for his persona, and his writing was beside the point. Curiosity about him—and therefore about me, to some extent—was unquenchable.

College students carried around *The Sun Also Rises* like an identity card. *A Farewell to Arms* had been a best-seller, and it didn't hurt that the 1932 Helen Hayes/Gary Cooper film had become a classic. *For Whom the Bell Tolls* just kept selling, and the movie had been Oscar-nominated. Newspapers and magazines followed Papa's travels in Africa, Italy, Spain, and the Caribbean, and he seemed right at home staring out from the cover of those magazines.

With alarming regularity, Hemingway updates were printed in the People section of *TIME* magazine on Papa's fishing and shooting exploits, and a whole article was written about his favorite drink, which supposedly was Death in the Gulf Stream, a concoction of gin, lime juice, and a dash of bitters. In fact, his favorite drink was neither Death in the Gulf Stream nor a Mojito, the other alleged favorite. It was actually a very dry martini served very cold.

When he and Marty got divorced, the *New York Sunday Mirror Magazine* ran an article titled "Bell Tolls for Three of Ernest's Wives." *American Weekly* published an article called "Hemingway Sets the Style," claiming Papa had set short hair as the ideal for American women and declared him a trendsetter. Trendsetter! Boy, they should have seen how he dressed at home. Even when he went out, he shunned ties. He wore the same pair of loose khaki shorts endlessly, usually tied with rope or that not especially attractive Gott belt.

Not long after the trendsetter article, the *New York Post Weekend Magazine* announced, "Papa looks virile enough to make bobbysoxers swoon by the droves," and *Holiday* covered him fishing on his boat, *Pilar*, as he talked about his life in Cuba. Sales at Abercrombie & Fitch soared when Papa revealed it was his store of choice for outdoor gear and clothing.

The coverage never stopped, and Papa was a bona fide forerunner of today's celebrity machine. Most days, even he couldn't live up to his touted persona. A media frenzy ensued whenever he appeared in public. He claimed it was all "too damned much" that everyone wanted a piece of him. As collateral damage, people were interested in me.

A few times a month, I'd receive letters asking me to endorse a hunting product or model riding breeches or sit for a paid interview and photo shoot about being Hemingway's daughter. I refused all interviews. Papa stopped talking to his brother when he spoke to the newspapers and told his mother early on not to talk about him for public consumption. I'd always shied from this reflected fame, but now I was considering a few offers to pay for the horses until I could find full-time work.

Before I could react, however, I got a letter from the Greenwich stable stating that Arc and Sara's Silence had been sold to cover their costs. As I read in disbelief, my heart clutched, and I sank onto a kitchen chair, letting the letter flutter to the floor. The board fees were overdue, but I thought I'd get a second notice. *Nicky's horses.*

When I told Papa, he was livid. "Jaysus, Flea! Why didn't you tell me? Christ! I could have sold another of the old stories to the movie people and paid for the board for years. That Lillian Ross article made me out to be semi-illiterate, which just made people more interested. They wonder how this *imbécil* from the backwater of Chicago wrote anything readable. *El tonto* could barely speak English. How do you like it now, gentlemen?" *El tonto is a dim-witted fool.*

Lillian Ross, a journalist befriended by Papa, had published an article in *Cosmopolitan* in May 1950 about Papa, claiming it was an "affectionate" portrait of a great writer. She feigned shock at the negative reaction, but that article helped to build her career, which made it sickening to me. She made Papa sound like a Neanderthal with such conversational gems as, "Book is like engine. We have to slack her off gradually." Or as a total non-sequitur, "How do you like it now, gentlemen?"

I was wounded for Papa, even if it was his own fault in part. He'd trusted Lillian and hadn't taken the interview seriously. As one of Papa's biographers, Jeffrey Meyers, wrote later, "She repaid his generosity with meanness," and established her reputation at his expense.

On my summer visit, I ranted against the article and Lillian for about twenty minutes without pause. As Papa read his magazine on fishing reels, a relaxed look on his face, he never looked up as I stomped around the long living room and gesticulated wildly, calling Lillian a two-faced weasel and a snake. I paced and roared. Finally, I ran out of steam. He looked up pleasantly.

"Are you done?" he asked.

Nonplussed, I said, "I guess so."

"Then have a seat here." I took the seat across from him. He took his glasses off, leaned forward, and looked straight at me. "I appreciate your loyalty, Flea, but I like Lillian as much as I like anybody, and anything she or anyone else writes about me, good or bad, is their own impression. I will not edit it or correct it. Except for dates or place names. Lillian's piece is OK with me, and so is Lillian."

He put his glasses back on and reopened his magazine.

Still, 1950 was not our best year. For him, in addition to the Lillian article, there was a rash of negative publicity about the new book, his first book without the sharp eye of Max Perkins: *Across the River and into the Trees*. Critics savaged it, calling it trivial, tawdry, embarrassing, and distressing. His model for the main character was Adriana Ivancich. Mary was pretending she was just one more of the young women my father collected for his entourage but she was more.

I met Adriana at Christmas and loathed her. I tried to give her a chance and stayed up late one night sitting around the pool to chat one-on-one. However, when she told me that, "Mary should be grateful to me, because I did not walk away with Ernesto. I could have, you know," it was all I could do not to strangle the girl.

All hell broke loose when rumors began to swirl, first in whispers, then in roars, that Papa and Adriana were having a scandalous affair. Adriana and her mother packed their bags and left. He wrote to me shortly after her departure.

Dear Flea:

Been a bit stormy down here, and I don't mean the sea, kid. But writing going well, and when that's the case, I can stand the rest. I'm pissed at Charlie Scribner about a few things, but would never leave. He's pissed at me for criticizing Scott, especially now that he's long dead, and for commenting on their new up-and-comer, James Jones, in a not flattering way. Shit on that. I can have my own opinions and they don't have to agree with his, but I'd rather keep a friend, meaning Charlie, so I've vowed to tone it down.

And yes, Adriana is gone. No one to practice my Italian with. With Marlene, it's always English, but German if we are angry. And with you, Fleasiliscious, it's English or our own combo of Spanglish or midaho (Midwestern Idaho speak, in case you need a translation of THAT).

Have you seen Hotch lately? He's working too hard and I want you and him to come down soon. Leaving an old man to his own devices is dangerous, mi querida. Lousy book review on Across the River from Time. But New York Times and Newsweek were OK, so I guess the Hem House will eat this year. Starting a new book that may be something good. Different from my usual. About a woman. Put my favorite into my heroine, Elena. Ha! That will get you thinking! We'll see.

Black Dog is having rough time with heat. I'll stop this boring letter here or maybe you've stopped reading already. I love you, Flea, and I am so proud of you.

Con mucho amor para mi hija hermosa,
Papa

"Hotch" was Aaron Edward Hotchner, a young writer whom Papa met when he was sent to Cuba to interview my father for *Cosmopolitan* magazine. The interview had been something of a bust, but Aaron had become a great pal, sidekick, and true friend to my father right up to the end. I came to love Hotch too. He lived in New York City, and we had lunch every few months to compare notes on my father and on life. He was Ed to his friends, Hotch to Papa, and Aaron to me because that was how he introduced himself the day we met and for me it stuck.

As for me, the loss of the horses was so devastating that Jeddrah rarely left me alone for fear I might start to drink again. I went to AA regularly and didn't succumb, if for no reason other than it had almost killed Dancing Girl. However, my efforts to find the purchaser of the horses in the hope of getting them back were unsuccessful, as the stable refused to provide any information.

"Flea, any progress in finding them?" Papa asked regularly during our phone calls.

"No, Papa. And even if we find them, I can't afford to buy them back."

"Jeez, Flea, I'll front the money. You can repay me in legal services, just in case I'm ever sued by a jealous husband, or by Mary, or by anyone else I've offended. Since that group is ever expanding, I think I have a great chance of recouping what I lay out in spades. In fact, I may be the only client you'll need to fill your time." I laughed, something I wasn't doing much of these days.

I tossed at night worrying about the horses and could only fall back to sleep by convincing myself that only someone who really loved horses would have bought them together. If I considered that was not the case, I might never sleep well again.

34

This was a big storm and he might as well enjoy it. It was ruining everything, but you might as well enjoy it.

~ Ernest Hemingway, *For Whom the Bell Tolls*

On the day of my arrival in Ketchum, Idaho, that summer, still without job prospects but with ideas, Logan Grant showed up at the cabin. He looked rugged in his jeans, brown cowboy boots, Stetson, and a tan shirt with the sleeves rolled up.

He gave me a hug. "You always said you wanted to ride these never-ending trails. Here's your chance, Finn. Let's take a ride."

I smiled at him. "You look . . . giddy, or something. You look terrific, actually. What's up?"

"I'm in love. It agrees with me. You must be, too, since you look great; but then you always do."

I felt a funny little stab when he said he was in love. "Really? Who's the lucky girl?"

"You'll meet her. Let's go."

I grabbed a denim jacket, pulled on some riding boots, and called out, "Papa, I'm going riding with Logan!"

"Have fun, Flea. See you later!" Papa called back.

I ran outside and hopped into Logan's pickup truck. Ten minutes later, we pulled up to his barn in a cloud of dust.

"Follow me," he said, heading to his six-stall barn with one wide center aisle, three stalls on each side, each with a clean blanket hanging on a bar outside of its sliding door and a fresh bucket of water hanging on a hook inside. All six horses were munching on fresh hay.

I inhaled deeply, savoring the scent. Clean straw bedding, fresh water, oiled leather, sweet hay. "You keep a good barn, Logan," I observed. I hugged myself, happy to be there.

"Thanks. I try."

As I walked a few steps into the barn, I looked into the stalls, peering at each of the horses. At the second stall I stopped, almost paralyzed. I held my breath, disbelieving. I grabbed the stall door and slid it open. A mirage—it was Sara's Silence. I pivoted and looked at Logan.

"You? You bought them?"

He nodded, hands shoved into jeans pockets. "Say hi to Arc, or he'll be inconsolable."

I couldn't move. I turned back to Sara, not believing what I had seen, and reached out to touch her, as if still not sure she was there. She took a step forward and nuzzled my pocket, her old trick. I usually had a peppermint or two in there.

I stroked her neck, tears streaming down my cheeks. "I'm sorry, girl. If I'd known, I would have brought you a treat." I turned to Logan. "How did this happen?"

He shuffled his feet a little and tipped his hat back. "When you told me about them and your money woes, I contacted the barn you mentioned and asked them to keep me posted. When they said the horses would be sold, I couldn't let that happen. And hey, I can always use a good horse. Arc has turned out to be one hell of a range horse. And you already met the new love of my life, Sara's Silence." I now understood his little joke earlier.

I thrust my hands into my pockets to stop them from shaking. "While I should probably kill you first since I've been sick worrying about what happened to them, now that I know, I am bowled over. You can't know what this means to me, to know that they're well and loved. I don't know what to say. Logan, I am in your debt forever."

Logan smiled. "I was going to tell you, Finn, but I was afraid you wouldn't let me bail you out. I knew you'd be coming here in a few weeks, so I thought it would be a good surprise. Heck, you did *me* a favor, really. I knew they'd be great horses, sight unseen, and they are."

He added, "But look, you're starting to sound like some *Madame Butterfly* character with all that in your debt forever talk. You owe me nothing. Just ride them when you're here, and we'll call it even."

I shook my head, tears flowing freely now. "You've made me so happy today, Logan. You don't know."

He handed me a handkerchief. "That's enough for me. Hey, saddle up. You don't think I'm going to tack up for you too, do you?"

He tossed me a brush. I caught it and laughed. In fifteen minutes, we galloped out for the ride of our lives.

***

That night, Papa was blessedly sober. We sat outside in two Adirondack chairs as Mary cleaned up after the dinner I'd made: trout on the grill with a slice of bacon on each one, plus corn on the cob. Papa had a glass of water next to him. He was trying to cut down. His doctor said it was vital, and he was working intensely on a book about a woman named Elena who was in love with a childhood friend named Jonathan. He wanted to be clear and clean to work on it.

"So, niña, ready to hit the job search again when you get back?" His eyes were bright and he seemed relaxed, legs stretched out.

"I am, Papa. So, we'll see."

Papa smiled. I had all of his attention. Papa could be a bit "out of sight, out of mind," but when you captured his focus, you had all of him.

"Good, Daughter, good. I hope practicing law will be all you expect it to be. Hard for a woman to find someone to look up to career-wise. No real heroines for you yet, 'cept maybe Marty's Eleanor Roosevelt. You'll be it for the girls coming up behind you."

I smiled, finding it hard to see myself as a role model for anyone. "For right now, Logan Grant is my hero. Can you believe he bailed out my horses and brought them all the way out here? Never said a word."

I reached over to Papa. He took my hand and held it firmly. I sighed, settling into the chair, taking in the pink western sky with the mountains jutting up, and treasuring the shared time with my father.

I'd been thinking a lot about Logan and said, "Is it moral of me to just accept Logan's gift, Papa? Shouldn't I, like, become his slave for life or something?"

Papa laughed. "I don't know. What's moral is what you feel good after doing, and what's immoral is what you feel bad after doing. My particular failing is that even when I know the difference, I don't always choose the right one."

I laughed too. He re-crossed his legs. "You know, Flea, sometimes you have to let people do something for you, and let them have the good feeling. Don't rob them of that."

I thought about that, then thought about him and all of the bickering I'd heard between him and Mary lately. I said, "You're right. So are you and Mary going to get divorced?"

Papa let go of my hand, tipped his head toward me, scratched his beard. "Haven't we had this conversation before, except it was about one of my other wives?" He sat back and looked at the sunset for a minute. "No, I don't think so, Flea. I'm too old to get divorced again, and the other one is too young, and she doesn't love me. Sometimes, I think that if two people love each other, there can be no happy ending. Someone always leaves first in one way or another, but the alternative is worse, so I choose to wake up every morning and hope for love. Sometimes, it's enough for just one person to feel it."

I shook my head. "I think both have to feel it. But you may be right that the ending is never happy."

"Well, aren't we two rays of sunshine?" He laughed, and I did too. Black Dog sat at Papa's feet and he reached down to pet him. "So, speaking of love, are you and Logan keeping company?"

"No. I kind of wanted to, but he's smart. He sees through me. Said I'm too complicated and still have feelings only for Nicky. He said he'd rather skip all of that turbulence, so to speak." I turned to look at him to see if he understood. He folded his hands across his stomach and stared straight ahead.

"You can only be who you are, Flea, but being alone's not easy. I'm alone a lot, and it's necessary, but solitary. Just me and the old Smith Corona. Same blank piece of paper every day when I face the typewriter. But you don't have to be alone, Flea. Life is richer when you share it. You may have Nick in your heart forever, but that may not be enough for this Earth. A good man or woman to share it with, well, it can almost make you immortal on the good days."

35

Think of what you can do with what there is. Now is no time to think of what you do not have.

~ Ernest Hemingway, *The Old Man and the Sea*

Back in New York, I spent most of my weekends perfecting and mailing out applications for jobs of any sort. I applied to be a secretary in at least twenty law firms, an assistant to copy writers in thirty-three ad agencies, and a beat reporter for a small newspaper in Brooklyn.

I passed the months working tables at a deli a few blocks from my apartment, taking any hours I could get. I already had lined up added holiday hours at Macy's, wrapping gifts. Jeddrah thought that was hilarious, since I was the worst wrapper of presents of anyone we knew. Tons of Scotch tape wrapped like a tourniquet featured prominently in my gifts.

Finally, I got a call back for a second interview with the Madison Avenue advertising firm of Getty, Chatsworth. I'd met with an associate initially, AJ Packer, a man in his early thirties with dark hair and a mustache, and now was meeting with a senior partner, Humphrey Reed. He was on the phone when I was ushered in, but he waved a cigarette in the air and motioned for me to sit.

"No, that won't work. The design has to be fresh and catchy, like the one you did last year. Some humor is OK, but Stan didn't like the guy looking dumb in the new one."

I looked around the office. A degree on the wall from Dartmouth. A photo of a pretty woman in a wedding dress on his credenza. I looked at Mr. Reed, who blew out a smoke ring over his left shoulder.

"Yeah, OK. I need it on my desk first thing tomorrow." He hung up, rammed his chair back, and stretched out his legs. "So, Finley, you want to be a secretary to one of our associates, I see." He picked up my résumé and scanned it, one finger tracing down the page. He frowned and looked up. "You finished law school? And passed the New York bar?"

I spoke slowly, recalling my last interview and how my law degree had hobbled me. I needed this job, and said what I thought he wanted to hear.

"I thought law school would be good training . . . background, you know." He looked doubtful. I raced on. "But I would be thrilled to assist any of your associates. I type ninety words per minute, am organized, speak fluent Spanish and French, if translations were ever necessary, and make a perfect pot of coffee."

He stared at me. "Stand up."

"Excuse me?" Now I was confused. *Was there a height requirement for this job?*

"Stand up," he said again. I stood.

"You're tall. How tall are you?"

I colored. "I . . . I'm five ten, sir. I may look taller with these heels."

"Yeah, you do." He sat silent for a few seconds and looked back at my paperwork. "How are you about working late? Have to get home to the husband and kids, do you?"

I looked down, fidgeting and slouched a little. "I'm not married, sir." I shifted my weight awkwardly. "May I sit down, Mr. Reed?"

He nodded. "I admit that I have hesitations about hiring a woman who went to law school. It suggests . . ." Here he paused and gazed up, as if the word he wanted were in the upper corner of the room. "It suggests a possible arrogant attitude that is not desirable in one of our girls." He swiveled more. "However, your skills look good, and your lack of a home life is fortuitous." He looked as if he were going to explain what "fortuitous" meant but instead shook his head. "In fact, I think I'll keep you myself and move Molly." He slapped his hand on his desk. "Congratulations, Finley. You start on Monday." He stood, and I shook his hand again.

"Thank you, Mr. Reed. You won't regret this."

He flashed me a gummy smile, dark eyes bright. "I'm sure I won't. See you Monday."

I turned to leave, hand on the doorknob.

"Oh, Lee, please be on time; and wear flats here. You don't mind if I call you Lee, do you? Finley is a bit too fancy for a secretary, don't you think?" He turned away with a chuckle.

I stiffened, hand in place. No one had ever told me my name was too fancy, or that I couldn't wear heels. I said, "Lee is fine, sir."

***

I was at my desk by eight on Monday, a pile of documents already sitting on my chair for copying. Lena, the receptionist, had just finished a call and walked over, her glossy, dark hair swinging across her shoulders.

"Hi, Lee! Mr. Reed asked that you go pick up a portfolio from Mr. Packer." Lena leaned in and added in a lower voice, "Hint! Don't ever get stuck alone with Mr. Packer."

I was curious. "Why not?"

Lena moved her arms in every direction. "Octopus."

I smiled, comprehending. "Ah. Thanks."

Lena crooked a finger for me to come closer. "And worse. He knocked up a girl in packaging. Nice kid too. She's back home in Omaha now. He's a married cad." She frowned. "Stay away from him."

I nodded, feeling disgusted, and watched dozens of young women surge out of the elevator, laughing, dressed up, lipstick, perfume, heels. I looked down at my flats, sighed, and stood to get the requested portfolio.

I hustled down two floors to AJ Packer's office, where Molly was smoking and eying me up and down. "Don't get too comfortable. Mr. Reed likes variety. You're the flavor of the month. See you down here soon."

Just then, AJ Packer popped out of his door. "Molly, I need . . ." He saw me. "Finley, I heard Humph Reed kept you for himself, clever girl." He gazed at me as if I may have warranted a second closer look. "Good for you. Come on in for a minute."

I was in a hurry, but he motioned enthusiastically. I stepped in. He closed the door behind me. "Take a seat."

I balanced on the chair and gazed around his office. The easels were where they'd been when I first interviewed, but now, instead of an ad for an Austin-Healey, there was an ad for Lucky Strikes with the tentative tagline "Be Happy, Go Lucky."

His office was smaller than Humph Reed's, with a view of the sides of buildings instead of the New York skyline. However, as my eyes glided past a wedding photo, they slid back and I held my breath a second. Dressed in white, with an ornate veil framing her heart-shaped face, was an icy blonde, a proud princess. It was Prillie Lamont, my old prep school enemy. There was no mistaking it. I clasped one wrist hard and bit my lower lip. She was married to AJ Packer.

AJ turned to me with a grin. "So, how's it going, Lee? Ha, I heard you got a name change courtesy of Humph!"

I lifted my chin. "Yes. Lee is fine though, sir. As for the work, I just started this morning, but everyone seems very nice. Thank you for asking."

"Just don't let old Humph overwork you. And if there's a lull in his work, he'll let you do some errands for me. We work as a team here, you know."

I nodded and rose. "Thank you, Mr. Packer. That's very kind advice. I hate to run, but I have to start a project for Mr. Reed."

He stepped out from behind the desk and snaked an arm around my waist, pulling me in. I swung away quickly with a laugh to soften my haste. "I'm very grateful to be here."

After about a month, I got used to the routine. Coffee for Mr. Reed, mail, typing, dictation, get lunch for Mr. Reed if he wasn't going out, a few personal errands for him or, sometimes, for his wife. If he ate lunch out, he was jovial when he came back, commenting on my outfit, or making suggestions for better ways to dress or wear my hair.

"You should dress like Lena, Lee. Show off that nice figure of yours. And more lipstick would brighten your face. You're pale, as so many redheads are. You're only young once."

For an ad man, he was pretty clichéd in his compliments, but I said, "Thank you, Mr. Reed. I will keep that in mind."

I was still applying for legal jobs, but this position paid my rent and food. I didn't like it, but experience was experience. I just hoped this wouldn't be forever.

One Monday as I was distributing mail to the junior partners and associates, I literally ran into AJ Packer as I rounded a corner.

"Whoa there, Lee. Near collision. Big weekend, I assume! Head still in the clouds?" *More clichés. No wonder we lost the Schlitz account.* He laughed, but it wasn't a nice laugh.

"Oh sorry, sir. I better slow down." I forced a chuckle. I liked him even less knowing he was married to Prill. "Here's your mail, sir."

He flipped through the bundle, then pivoted back. "Hey, Lee. My wife said she knows you. Prep school or something. It threw her off when I said we had a new girl named Lee Hemingway, but then I recalled that your real name is Finley. Small world. She remembered you well." He laughed again. "Said you were pretty wild in your day. Had a boyfriend you went off with on the weekends. Still waters and all that." He stared at me in my loose blouse, black, pleated skirt and flats as if I were in a slinky nightgown. "We should have dinner sometime."

I blinked and was silent. He added quickly, "Of course, I meant all of us. You, me, and Prill. Old times, you know."

I leaned against the wall, feeling weak, breathing fast. Having seven teeth pulled would be delightful compared to having dinner with him and Prill. And I hated what he was so blatantly suggesting: that I was fast and loose and available—to him—for the plucking. I touched my throat and took a deep breath, then finished the mail delivery.

36

My big fish must be somewhere.

~ Ernest Hemingway, *The Old Man and the Sea*

"Hey, new girl! How are you doing?"

I looked up and saw a cute man standing in front of my desk, hands in his pockets, three-piece suit, blond hair sweeping across his brow.

"Um, I think you're newer than me. But I'm fine, thank you, sir." I returned to my typing, but he stood there.

"That's it?"

I tilted my head. "It seems to cover your question, sir."

He jingled some coins in his pocket. "'How are you' was not really a health question. It was an opener."

I wasn't sure what he wanted, but I knew who he was. His name was Michael Jenner, and he was the newest partner at Getty, Chatsworth. Unmarried, handsome, and all of the girls were whispering about him.

"Opener for what, sir?"

"Conversation. See, this is how it works. I say, 'How are you?' You say, 'I'm pretty well but a little tired today. And you?' I say, 'Great so far but it's only noon.' And so on. You have to do your part; Lee, is it?" I nodded. "I'm Michael. Michael Jenner." He held out his hand.

I shook it and said, "I know who you are, sir. Nice to meet you."

He raised an eyebrow. "You're getting the hang of this conversation thing. And you don't have to call me 'sir.' It makes me feel like one of the older guys. 'Mr. Jenner' is fine. But if we were ever to be alone," he leaned in closer and lowered his voice, "if we were ever alone, Michael is better. I'm your neighbor, just down the hall. Stop in any time."

He headed to his office with a jaunty walk, reminding me of Danny Kaye, as if he might just break into a dance step on his way down the hall. I returned to my typing, smiling to myself.

A few minutes later, Lena stopped by, atwitter as she alit on the edge of my desk, slender legs crossed. Leaning forward, she whispered, "Hey, hey, hey. I heard Mr. Jenner stopped by to talk to you. He's a real humdinger, don't you think? Not like some of these crumbs around here! Tell me all about him when you get a break, Lee."

I liked Lena and her feminine ways. She always had chip-free, shiny, red nails, perfect hair and makeup, and luscious high heels. I stopped typing and took a sip of my coffee. "Ha! I wish I had some juicy gossip, but there's nothing to tell, Lena. He just said hello."

"Well, he didn't say hello to anyone else," she said in a singsong voice. "We'll just have to see!" She sashayed away, snatching looks from all the men in the vicinity.

At lunchtime, as I pulled a brown bag from my bottom drawer, a shadow crossed my desk. I looked up to see Michael Jenner grinning at me and shaking a finger.

"You know, you don't look like a Lee to me. What's your middle name?"

I stood. "Richardson."

He frowned. "No, that doesn't work either." He paused. "Spin around, Lee."

I laughed. "I'm not going to spin around."

"Then do a dance step. Come on. Just one step." He cocked his head. "Come on. Work with me on this, if not on that conversation thing."

I sighed and did a waltz step, twirling at the end and flinging my head back, red hair spilling over my shoulders. Michael Jenner said nothing. I raised my eyebrows expectantly. Then he said softly, "You're lovely, Lee."

I stared, then broke the spell. "You're funny." I seized my lunch bag and joined the throng of women heading to the office kitchen. I stole a look at him over my shoulder though as he stood in the same spot, watching me.

Later that afternoon, Mr. Jenner's secretary handed me a note on her boss's stationery inside a sealed envelope. "Here you go, Lee. From Mr. Jenner."

I set it aside until she returned to her station and opened it.

A drink? MJ

I marched into his office and left the door open. Michael Jenner was paging through a report, pen in hand. He looked up as I sat in one of his guest chairs.

"Why the full corps press, Mr. Jenner? You have every girl in here hanging on your every move. Why me?"

He sat up and pushed his chair back. He looked surprised, then said, "I don't go for the low-hanging fruit. I prefer quality to easy."

I was quiet for a moment. I used to flirt, but that version of me was gone. "If what you want is a challenge, go see Sallie in the mail office. She's beautiful, sassy, and by all accounts, a handful, in every sense of the word. I'm not interested in games. I'm not interested in dating. I just need my job."

He crossed his arms across his chest and pulled his chair into the desk so he was closer. We both spoke in low voices to avoid each word carrying to the outer office.

"Well, you definitely are not a Lee. A 'Lee' would have said, thank you for thinking me special, Mr. Jenner. A 'Lee' would have said, where shall we meet for a drink."

"That's a game too. And I don't drink. I'm an alcoholic."

His eyes widened. "How do you know?"

"I drink to avoid sadness, and I don't stop until I wake up disgusted with myself."

"Hey, that's just about everyone I know." He added quickly, "I'm kidding. Good for you for dealing with it. But I still would like dinner. I'm not scared off that easily."

I shook my head. "No. Thank you. I have a dog, and I head home right after work."

He got up and sat in the chair next to me. "I love dogs. This is perfect. Get the dog, and we'll get coffee somewhere. We'll drink it on a park bench with little Fido. Come on. What do you have to lose?"

I looked down. "My dog isn't little. She's particularly large. Oversized, some might say. And I know nothing about you."

"What do you want to know? I'm thirty-five, not married. In fact, never married. I was born in Fargo, North Dakota. Couldn't get out of there fast enough, but the parents are still there. Went to Yale. Joined Hebb Gorman out of college, then was recruited here six months ago. I played tennis in college, love animals—especially particularly large dogs, oversized are my favorite—and am very clean."

"Clean?" I asked, amused. "That's a new one."

A smile played on my lips. He saw. "No, really. I take a shower twice a day. Everyone says, 'There goes that Michael Jenner. Wow, is he clean!'" He leaned closer. "There, I see a smile. I barely recognize you with it. Hey, it's just coffee. Come on, Lee." He was wheedling, but in fun.

I sighed. "OK. But the dog comes."

"Absolutely. I wouldn't have it any other way. Great excuse to get away from me if things turn bad. Gotta walk my dog! OK! Saturday it is, at four o'clock."

I turned to leave, then looked back. "It's Finley."

He took a step closer. "What's Finley?"

"My real name."

He grinned and snapped his fingers.

***

"He sounds like a real charmer. Maybe too charming," said Jeddrah as we walked through Chinatown, heading to Jimmy Wong's Dim Sum Garden for an early Friday dinner.

"Exactly my thought," I said. "And I don't have the energy for dating."

Jedd stopped. "Turn toward me, Finn. You're too tall for me to do this right. Take you by the shoulders, look sternly into your eyes, and say my piece."

I laughed and did a military quarter turn to face her. "Shall I squat too?"

She laughed. "No. As you are! Finn, it's six years since Nicky's been gone. You can go out, you know. I loved him too, but what I really loved was you two together. Finding someone doesn't mean you forget him. Promise me you won't push away love."

I wanted to laugh at her tiny earnestness, but her words came from a place of deep caring. And if truth be told, she'd voiced my inner fear: to even be mildly diverted by another man felt disloyal to Nicky's memory.

I swallowed and smoothed my outer expression. "I promise, Jeddrah."

She un-tensed her stance and turned to resume our walk. "OK. Now that that's clear. But be careful. There are a lot of bounders out there."

"Bounders?"

"Yup. My friend, Hannah—the one from London—says that's the English word for a really terrible cad."

I laughed. "OK, I will be sure to avoid all bounders."

The next day at three thirty, I skipped down the stairs to make it to the coffee shop by four. In my flat white Keds, I half-walked, half-ran to be sure I wouldn't be late to Helène's Café. As I entered, a little breathless, I spotted Michael, who stood and motioned me over to a table in the back. He looked nice in a blue oxford shirt and khaki slacks.

He motioned to the seat opposite him. "What about the dog? I have dog biscuits and was all set to move to a table outside." He dug in a pocket and pulled out two large dog cookies.

"I left my pup home. I felt I could manage you without the added protection—this being a public café and all."

He sat back and laughed. "I took the liberty of ordering you a coffee and some cakes for us." He was leaning on one elbow, chin on hand. "So I've been wondering for the past week, what is a nice girl like you doing in a place like Getty, Chatsworth?"

I tested my coffee to see how hot it was. It was very hot. I took a sip and grimaced, but not because of the coffee. "Geez, do all of you ad guys save your brilliance for your work? The clichés abound in that office, and that one is an old doozy that no woman liked even in its day."

He raised an eyebrow. "Fair enough. OK then, for starters, why the heck are you called Lee if your name is Finley?"

"Mr. Reed said Finley is too fancy, and he renamed me Lee."

Michael shook some sugar into his coffee. "Well, that's just plain weird."

The waitress set our cakes in the middle of the table. I was starved, and grabbed a beautiful chocolate éclair. "Tell me about it."

Michael took a napoleon. He tried to cut it with a fork and layers of filling squeezed out in all directions. We both laughed as it slid entirely off his plate. He put down his fork.

"Well, I've met my match."

I lifted another éclair and put it on his plate as the waitress cleared the distressed napoleon. "Try this. It's great."

"Thanks. Any relation to *the* Hemingway?" Michael asked as he picked up the éclair and took a bite.

"Ha! No. Otherwise, I might take a try at some of those jingles you fellas turn out. Do you like the work?" I changed the topic as soon as I could, burning with my own hypocrisy. *No games, indeed, Miss I'm-no-relation-to- Hemingway.*

He wiped his mouth on his napkin. "Hemingway's work? I love it! Madison Avenue work? Yup, I also am absolutely crazy about it. I see a product, and immediately start running ideas in my head. How to sell it better, present it in a zippier way, target a particular market. Sometimes I start drawing design layouts and jotting down slogans on a napkin, something catchy. I don't come from money, and I'm sick of being at the bottom of the heap because of it. I love this work and intend to dominate this world." By now he was gesturing and jotting down shapes on a paper napkin. "See? I look at this bottle of plain old ketchup, red and white and poised to season some lovely Hélène pommes frites." He held it up. "I think, what can I say that makes you think this is better than any other ketchup in the world. What can I say or show so that every housewife in America rolls down the aisle in A & P and wants *only* this one. Only this one is good enough for her family. And I start playing with words, and doodling with colors, and framing a campaign. I start thinking about whether to focus on Mom, or on the kids, or on a theme of home and apple pie, serious or use humor in the ad."

I leaned forward on an elbow and took the bottle of ketchup from him. "Hmm. And I just see a bottle of ketchup."

Michael shrugged. "It's a gift. I also want a new Caddy every two years, and a house on the Upper East Side with a summer place in Newport, and invites to the biggest parties in the city. I intend to run Getty, Chatsworth in five years, whatever it takes."

He was out of breath when he finished and looked embarrassed by his declaration.

I shook out my napkin and placed it in my lap. "You, Michael Jenner, are very ambitious, and I mean that in a good way."

"Yup, and that's the only way to get where you want to be, Finley. You have to visualize it in full detail, and never let them see you worry about it. They'll use it against you. Nice for these swells born to it to act like they don't care. That's because they are there—top of the mountain—without having to earn it. But I care plenty, and I don't care who knows it. And I'm going to the top, whatever it takes. I *am* going to run Getty, Chatsworth in five years. Whatever it takes."

"The operative phrase is 'whatever it takes,'" I said, taking a bite of my éclair.

He reddened a bit. His blond hair flopped into his eyes, which were sea green and alert. "Sorry. I think big."

I waved my fork in the air. "No need to apologize. You're honest."

"So, what do you want out of life, Finley?" He motioned to our waitress and mouthed, "Check please."

"I want to be a lawyer, go to court, help people, and win cases. I finished law school and passed the New York bar. I want—no, I will die if I don't get to practice law."

Michael sat back, tipping his chair on its back two legs, mouth open a bit. He lowered his chair and licked his lips. "Well, who would have thought it? A 'Lee' would have said that she was waiting to meet Mr. Right and have three children, in that order, and passing time until then. So how come you aren't married? You're twenty-four or so?"

"I'm twenty-six." I looked down, wondering how much of the Nicky story I wanted to tell. "I already met Mr. Right, but the war had other ideas," I said wryly. "He died. No interest after that."

Michael pursed his lips and tapped his cigarette pack. He took one out and offered it to me. I shook my head. He lit it while still looking at me. "Are you still in love with the first guy? I mean, I know he's gone, but feelings don't always follow reason. Is that why no one else has ever been 'the one'?"

"That's part of it. But I have no interest in looking."

Michael took a sip of his coffee. "I think it's trust. You don't trust anyone—at least, this is my hypothesis—with your heart. You gave it away once and look how that turned out. Even though of course it wasn't his fault, it still feels like abandonment and betrayal."

He nodded. "You will trust someone again someday." He snapped his fingers. "Hey, did you ever read your namesake's book, *For Whom the Bell Tolls*?"

I squirmed. "Um, yes, I have."

"Think about Maria. Robert loved her as much as a man could love a woman. But in the end, I'll bet when she ended up in Madrid and he was gone, she felt like he'd deserted her. Of course, he didn't. He died. But I'll bet that's how she felt. Feelings defy logic."

Michael looked at me and shook his head. "And what are you doing about that dream of yours? To be a lawyer."

"I'm still applying for jobs, but since the war ended, there are no jobs for women in law. I haven't given up hope, but I have to pay the bills, so here I am."

The check arrived and he paid quickly with cash. We started to walk uptown when Michael glanced at his watch and made a face. "It's five thirty, and unfortunately, I have plans tonight. What are you doing next Saturday?'

I looked at his boyish face and open smile. "Nothing."

***

I'd been seeing Michael for about six months and, for the first time in years, I felt like I might be able to fall in love again. Jedd and I were at our little corner grocery store where we took turns holding Tess outside while the other went in to buy supplies. Once we'd completed our list, we headed home.

Jedd asked casually, "Is this thing between you and Michael serious?"

She'd met him for the fifth time the previous Friday when we all went to dinner: Jedd and Robert Drake, Michael and me.

I shifted my grocery bag and switched Tess's leash to the other hand. "I think it might be. He's very kind, and seems to understand me. I'm relaxed and happy with him, Jedd. Tonight, he has to be in Greenwich, Connecticut, at the big boss's house. John Chatsworth's house. Some sort of gala, but just for the executives. Tomorrow we are going to the park and we just have fun." I hesitated. "It's not like with Nicky, but Michael really supports me in what I want to do. He said he hopes to have kids someday but that he has no problem with a wife who works." I raised my shoulders in a "who knows what's next?" gesture. I looked at Jedd's face, and it was a strange combination of guilty and fearful, not open and smiling like usual. "Why? What do you think of him? What does Robert think?"

Jeddrah dawdled in answering. "I think he's smart and witty. I just wonder if you really know him, and why couldn't you go to this thing at the boss's house? He seems busy a lot of Saturdays."

I rushed to his defense. "He travels all the time for the company. He needs to, you know, to make it to the top by the time he's forty. He said then he can lighten up."

In reality, I had noticed in the past couple weeks that he'd been stopping by my desk less often, and we'd been seeing each other more out of the office than in the office, and on Sundays more than on Saturdays. I attributed it to professionalism—low key on the office romance stuff—and lots of work and travel.

Jedd nodded. "That makes sense, but . . ." She bit her lip.

"What, Jedd?"

She stopped walking and her face clouded. "Um, Robert said he saw Michael out at Le Café des Artistes last Saturday night when he stopped for a drink with the other doctors. He was at a back table with a blonde woman. Robert said they seemed cozy."

I was stunned. I was sure there was an explanation. I hadn't slept with him, despite his pleas, but I wanted to. I wracked my memory to recall what Michael had said about last

Saturday. "Um, he told me that he and some of the guys were working on the new Pontiac ad."

Jeddrah said quietly, "Robert said it didn't look like work."

I felt my slim grasp on excuses slipping. "I can't explain it, but he wouldn't lie to me. There has to be a reason. I'll ask him tomorrow."

The next day, Michael arrived at the apartment at noon. Jedd had tactfully left to meet Robert for lunch. Michael bounded in like a Labrador puppy, grabbed me, spun me around in a dance dip, and kissed me.

"What a great day, Finn! Gorgeous October in New York. Let's take a walk in Central Park, get a boat, row a bit, and have dinner at Tavern on the Green! What do you say?"

I pointed to a chair. He raised an eyebrow, puzzled, but walked over and sat. I sat across from him. "How would you describe our relationship, Michael?"

He cocked his head. "What a weird question, Finn."

"Tell me."

"OK." He took in a breath, then let it all out. "I would say it's close."

"With a future or without a future?"

He looked nervous, turning the class ring on his finger. "Finn, what is this? Thinking of you not being in my life is not something I want to consider." He looked straight into my dark eyes with his bright-green ones.

"What were you doing last Saturday at Le Café des Artistes with a blonde woman?"

Funny, but *I* could almost feel *his* mouth go dry. He cleared his throat and swallowed. "She's an old friend."

"You told me you were working on a job with the other guys."

He fiddled with his shirt buttons and stuck a hand in his jacket pocket. "I didn't want you to be upset. I did work all day, but met her for dinner."

"Who is she?"

"Does it matter?"

"Yes, it matters."

As if through gritted teeth, he said, "Maribeth Chatsworth."

I repeated, staring ahead without seeing, "Maribeth Chatsworth, only child of John Chatsworth, co-owner of Getty, Chatsworth?" I looked at him. He nodded. "I never considered that you were seeing other women, Michael. How old a friend is she? Don't tell me she grew up in North Dakota?"

He uncrossed and re-crossed his legs. "I met her about three months ago."

"Ah, not so old a friend after all then," I said flatly.

He cleared his throat, diverting his eyes. "Definitions differ."

"Don't," I snapped. "Don't try to be glib. Are you dating her? Does she know about me?"

He stood and walked over to the window. He was silent.

"Michael, are you dating her and forgot to tell me?"

He spun and faced me, his face white. He gulped like fish on a dock, then blurted out, "I . . . I'm engaged to her. We announced it last night at her father's house. Getting married at Thanksgiving. She's pregnant, Finn. And she knows I used to see you. I told her I broke it off."

I sat motionless, stunned. He walked over and knelt, taking my hands in his limp ones. "I don't love her, Finn. I've never loved anyone like I love you. Don't leave me. We can still be together. She'll be busy with the baby, and she bores me to death. You . . . you and I . . ."

"Stop," I said, whispering. I pulled my hands back, my gaze tunneling into his eyes to see what I'd missed. *How had I been so duped?* "Why, Michael?"

He shrugged. "She liked me. I met her at an office party at John's house a few months after you and I started up. All of a sudden, her father was paying more attention to me, giving me better and bigger accounts, calling me son." He took my hands again and shook them. "Finn. Finn, listen! You have to understand. I had a golden pass to go around the hurdles, direct to the end zone, make it to the top fast. I had to take it."

"An easier path to the top of Getty, Chatsworth by the time you're forty, whatever it took. That's what you said. I just didn't know I would be part of the wreckage on your way up."

I pulled my hands back and wrapped my arms around myself, fearing no one else ever would, humiliation maximized.

He walked back to the window and stared out. "Finn, don't be like that. Come on. We had a good time, and it doesn't have to end. You and I—"

I cut him off. "There is no 'you and I.' Get out." I strode to the door. "Out. Now!"

"Finn, it doesn't have to be like that. I really do love you."

"Get out," I whispered. "Don't ever contact me again." *You bounder!*

His eyes were wet. The tears in my eyes remained unshed. Family Reality Rule #4: Love always ends, and usually badly, for the Hemingways. Eternal bliss is not for us.

***

As I straggled in on Monday, there was a buzz in my wake wherever I went: the ladies' room, the lunchroom, the elevator, my desk. I heard bits of conversations.

"I don't think she even knew."

"He's engaged—and not to Lee. To Mr. Chatsworth's daughter!"

"Geez, poor Lee. Played for the fool. Can you imagine the humiliation?"

I wondered if Michael was hearing anything other than, "That a boy! Marrying the boss's daughter! And with a kid on the way to cement the deal. You'll own this place in a few years, Jenner!" A wink and more congratulations. "Better choice than poor old Lee. She can't give you a leg up like Maribeth can."

No embarrassment for him. He tried to call me on Sunday night, but when I heard his voice, I hung up.

I didn't tell my father or my mother. I felt enough like a losing proposition. No law job; a boyfriend who didn't just two-time me but was engaged; and I was barely able to pay my basic expenses. I was so far from my childish goals of making life fairer for others, finding true love despite the Hemingway love blight, and wanting to impact my father where it mattered that I felt almost as low as I could get.

My only consolation was that I wasn't at rock bottom. I'd been there, and I wasn't going back.

37

Everything about him was old except his eyes and they were the same color as the sea and were cheerful and undefeated.

~ Ernest Hemingway, *The Old Man and the Sea*

I phoned Jackson Armstrong, Nicky's father, the day after the Michael Jenner debacle. I pocketed my pride and asked if he might put in a good word for me at Sloane White, the firm that did his legal work. I felt awkward asking, but I remembered Michael's grit and determination to go after what he wanted, with no obstacle being too big. While I had no desire to emulate his ethics, I did grudgingly admire his focus. And I was darned if I was going to let his betrayal derail my plans to become a "real" lawyer.

I had stayed in touch with the Armstrongs through Christmas cards and letters a few times a year. When I told them of my plan to go to law school, Mrs. Armstrong had sent a personal note of congratulations, noting how pleased Nicholas would have been. "He always believed in you, Tess," she wrote.

Jackson Armstrong was as good as his word, and I heard from Sloane White a week later. An interview was set up, and it went smoothly, like most others, but I knew I wasn't wanted. The usual questions were asked.

"Planning to have children, Finley?"

"No sir. I don't plan to marry or have children. I want to practice law." My vigor in presentation had waned, and I hoped I didn't sound like a robot reading from a script.

A sharp look and some notes taken.

I stayed head down in paperwork at Getty, Chatsworth whenever Maribeth Chatsworth Jenner floated in, pretty in her sunny yellow coat and matching hat, carrying her cute newborn baby girl. As the office girls oohed and aahed over baby Marion Jenner, Maribeth flaunted her status as daughter of the big boss and wife of his heir apparent.

Michael had the good grace to have his office moved up three floors so I didn't see him daily. I thought that was that until Humph Reed called me in just eight weeks after Michael's baby was born. I sat, expectant. Maybe a raise? I'd been at the firm over a year, and all of my reviews had been stellar.

Humph Reed leaned forward. "Lee, I'm sorry, truly sorry, but we have to let you go."

I froze. "Did I do something, sir? My work, I thought, was always well done? I—I need this job, Mr. Reed."

He sighed and tapped his pen. "You're a great worker, Lee. It's just that Maribeth Chatsworth, I mean Jenner, isn't comfortable with you working in the firm. Michael spoke up for you, but Maribeth's father had the final word. I'm really sorry. I'll give you a terrific recommendation. You have a week of vacation coming. When you're back, I can give you two more weeks of work." He looked pained. "I'll miss you, Lee. You always were a cut above. Good luck to you."

I was actually wringing my hands at this point. I took three short breaths and stood.

"Thank you, sir. I appreciate that." I held out my hand. He stood and shook it. I returned to my desk in a fog.

As I waited to hear from Sloane White, knowing it would be a polite, "No," I decided to visit Papa at the Finca. Going to Cuba would be a quick escape, but it now took on a bit of a pall too, knowing my job was short-lived. I hoped to avoid telling my parents that I'd lost my job.

When I arrived in Cuba, despite it being hurricane season, the air was clear and I could see the palm trees distinctly on the distant Havana hills. The blue pool sparkled, and I inhaled the fresh scent of flowers just past full bloom. The high grass in the field was silvering. Even the cats who ran out to greet me seemed fuzzier, as if anticipating the cooler weather, which in Cuba meant eighty degrees. I stood on the white cement steps of the Finca and lifted my head to the sun. The farm was so lovely that my spirits rose.

I slogged into the Finca, suitcase dragging, to find solid, tough Mary sitting at the kitchen table, sobbing. I'd often felt sorry for Mary over the years. Papa could be sweet to her, but at times he could also be dismissive, rude, and cutting. Once, to my horror, I saw him toss a glass of wine in her face. When I confronted him the next day, he said, "Butt out, Flea. I'll consider your advice when you've been married a few times."

Once the previous year, late at night, I'd heard Papa yelling, "You were nothing when I found you, and you're still nothing. Scavenger! Camp-follower!"

Mary screamed back. "Stop it! You can't make me leave you. That's what you want so you can have your darling Adriana. But I won't do it. I'm Mrs. Ernest Hemingway and always will be."

"Face like Torquemada! And can't have children. You're a fine bargain!"

"You can say whatever you want. I'm staying!"

It pained me. I'd never heard anything like that with Pauline. Even with Marty, it hadn't been that bad. I was hurt on Mary's behalf, particularly about the no children comment. If this were where love led, I wasn't going. Now, I dropped my bag and stooped in front of her. "Mary? God, what's wrong? Can I help?"

I grabbed a tissue and pressed it on her. Mary jerked her head up when she heard me and frantically dabbed at her tears with a sleeve. Her round face was blotchy, and her blue eyes were swollen.

"Oh, Finn. We didn't expect you until this evening. Your father is at jai alai."

"I caught an earlier flight. Mary, what's wrong?"

Mary smiled weakly. "Oh, nothing, dear. It's just that your father was supposed to meet me and some of my friends at a restaurant downtown yesterday. He arrived late, with a Havana whore on his arm. It's just so humiliating sometimes, but he thinks it's funny. And that horrid Italian girl, Adriana!"

I exhaled. Sometimes it was hard being Hemingway's daughter. I couldn't imagine being Hemingway's wife. I wrapped my arms around her. "You know Papa. Tomorrow, he'll be all sorry, and will go out of his way to entertain your friends. And it will pass with Adriana, like always."

She tried to smile. For the first time, I truly felt her agony and doubts about sticking with a man who was generous, self-centered, loving, cruel, bigger than life, and yet filled with insecurities and booze that led to hideous behaviors. I too, in the relationship with Michael, had been disposable to his bigger dream. I could be his mistress but not his wife because Maribeth offered an immediate short cut up the ladder to success. Mistress or nothing, and I chose nothing. For Mary, she could be the wife but only on my father's terms, which were lousy terms. I felt sad for her and a little bit for me.

That night, as I sat with Papa and Mary around the pool, I saw more of his dark side. This trip was beginning to feel like a very bad idea, not the respite I'd expected. Mary had set a drink on his table and he'd lashed out.

"Christ, Mary, this martini is practically lukewarm. I like 'em cold. Cold! After seven years, you'd think you'd know that."

Instead of saying, "Well then, make it yourself, big shot," she looked embarrassed, seized the glass, and hurried back to the kitchen.

Papa turned to me. He had a glow. "Flea, Adriana may come back with her mother after all. Mary's in some silly huff about it."

I was silent. He spoke as if the incident with Mary was of no import and her pain was irrelevant. I couldn't hold back, despite knowing it was dangerous to start a conversation once he was pretty well soused. I sat forward and slammed down the magazine I'd been paging through. "Jesus, Papa. What is it with you? This ridiculous thing with Adriana, and the way you're treating Mary. It always has to be about you. Sometimes I wonder if you care at all about Mary, or me, or the boys."

Just then it all flashed back to me. So many times. An admirer would approach in a restaurant, gushing compliments. Papa would graciously invite her—and her three friends, usually—to join us. That alone irked me. My parents divorced when I was two, and I saw my father only in the summer and at Christmas. I begrudged sharing my swatch of time with interlopers.

Chairs would be dragged over and the seating reconfigured as they squashed in, greedy for their story to tell back home in Philadelphia, or Cincinnati, about having a drink with Hemingway. I would end up jostled to the opposite side of the table, as far as you could get from Papa, with one of the trespassers elbowing me into obscurity.

I'd eye the girls, noting how sleek and polished they were compared to me with my red hair in a bedraggled ponytail, my splotchy T-shirt, and my wrinkled shorts. With a flip of hair over one shoulder, the gusher would say, chin tucked, "Oh, Mr. Hemingway, I'm such a fan of yours. Where do you get your ideas? I could never think of even one story to write."

Papa would gaze up as if considering an answer to the chief *New York Times* book critic. Then he would say something like, "Well, Janice, I decided when I was about sixteen that I would write one story about each thing I knew about. Hunting, fishing, girls," Papa would say, looking over his shoulder for our waiter, glass held high to signal another round. "And call me Papa."

Janice, or her facsimile, would lean in, then say in a breathy voice, "But how do you know you'll have another idea every day to keep going, Papa?"

I would grimace and roll my eyes from my devalued seat. Noticing my eye roll, Papa would wink at me like we were in this together, like it was our joke. But today, my disgust was deep.

I plunged on. "I thought that whole Adriana thing was done." I was boiling over, my fists clenched tight.

Papa's face drained, then reddened. He turned to me, eyes just slits. "Shut up, Flea. You don't know what you're talking about."

"No, I see it, and I try to ignore it because you're so busy and important—you are. I know we—me, Mary, the boys—are nothing compared to that." I swung to face him. He was clutching the arms of his chair and leaning forward as if ready to spring.

I had to get this out. It had percolated for more than twenty years. I leaned forward too, pressing my hands together, wadded tissue and all.

"But, God, Papa, even Mother. You'd better give Mother the respect she deserves. Write something for *her*, goddamn it! Not for your Adriana. Your dedication in *The Sun* to Mother and Jack meant nothing. You wrote about every person in your life at that time, even the minor ones, except her! She used to cry about it. She'd been written out of your life, she said. You broke her heart." I whispered the last words, accentuating each one.

His eyes went wide, then he closed them for several seconds. When he opened them, he looked stricken. His high color drained. He held the chair arms tighter and sank back into the chair, his breathing heavy. The room fell silent, and I too went still.

Papa said nothing for a full minute. Then he sat up and began turning a matchbook from side to side on the wooden table between us, tapping and rotating it. Tap, rotate, tap, rotate. I felt clammy and nervous, not knowing if this was over or if the other shoe was about to drop.

He stopped flicking the matchbook, picked up his tumbler of whiskey, took a big swig, and smashed it down on the table. It shattered, and I saw he'd cut his hand. Blood dripped onto the table. He ignored it.

Sounding dead sober, he said, "You were the one I loved the most. You were the one I trusted. Now I find it's another mask you put on. Fuck you, Flea." He got up and walked outside, slamming the door.

***

I was awake all night and got up the next morning preparing to go. This trip sure went bad fast. After packing my few things, I gazed around my bedroom with its yellow rosebuds, wondering if this was the last time I'd see it. I remembered our last battle with its accompanying bitter estrangement so complete and breathtaking that my life was cleaved forever into the "before" and the "after." Papa too recognized the impact of that blowup. He forever referred to it as *la mala corrida*—loosely translated as "the bad bullfight." And for Papa, nothing could be worse. *La mala corrida* could mean many things, but all of them were bad: a loss of honor, discredit all around, regret everlasting, shame, chances lost, death. When Jack complained one Christmas that Papa and I never said a cross word to each other, Papa shook his head.

"I wish, Bumb. You remember when Flea and I had that big blowup?"

"Yeah, sure. But it seemed to get patched up just fine." Dear go-with-the-flow Jack.

Papa tipped his chin toward me. "Ask Flea about *la mala corrida*. Enough bad there to cover a lifetime."

It had taken no less than Nicky's death to bridge it and allow healing to happen, both of us being too stubborn for anyone's good. I feared there was nothing big enough out there that could ever bring us back from the brink like the blast of sanity after Nicky's death.

I dragged my bag to the front hall, planning to call a taxi. As I walked into the kitchen for a cup of coffee, I saw Papa coming in from his morning walk carrying a thick sheaf of pages. He was dressed in his usual loose shorts, wire-rimmed glasses, and short, white beard that was neatly trimmed. I stood my ground, bracing for scorn and accusation.

He spied me and waved. "Flea! Top of the morning, lass. Ready for another gorgeous day in paradise before heading to that hellhole called Nueva York? How you stand it is beyond me. Have to shoot me and bury me there to get me to stay."

I was so surprised I almost lost my grip on the coffee cup. There was no question he fully recalled our conversation the night before and had chosen to forget it. He forgot nothing, even when drunk, sometimes repeating whole conversations verbatim from a sloppy, booze-filled dinner discussion. No, this was a choice on Papa's part. I felt like I'd gotten a reprieve.

I thought fast. "Good morning, Papa. What's on for the day?" Two could play this game.

"Working on that project, the one with Elena and Jonathan. Going good. Hit a dry spot but trudged out of it and back on good earth again." He lowered his voice. "Between you and me, I never could write my best in Mary's Tower." Mary had a tower built for the cats and Papa's writing, but he still preferred the house. Papa headed for his big desk in the living room, Black Dog and Boise at his heels.

We spoke no more about Adriana or writing something for Mother. I left three days later, a second *mala corrida* narrowly averted.

38

Why do old men wake so early? Is it to have one longer day?

~ Ernest Hemingway, *The Old Man and the Sea*

I was two months into total unemployment with no income when the letter from Sloane White arrived. I opened it with lackluster interest, knowing it would start out with the usual "Dear Miss Hemingway, we regret to inform you" language.

Instead, it trumpeted, "Dear Miss Hemingway, we are pleased to inform you . . ." A thrill like no other vibrated through me every time I read that line, and I read it a lot. I tingled for days and carried the note with me for almost a year, folding and unfolding it as if fearing the words would change.

On a raw day in mid-November 1953, I was nervous but elated to start my first job as a *lawyer*. Sloane White was one of the best and biggest firms in Manhattan, and it was Jackson Armstrong's law firm. Mr. Armstrong had put in an insistent word for me, or I wouldn't have been hired. I later learned he'd gone so far as to threaten to move his mountain of expensive and continuous legal work from the firm if I weren't offered a position.

After my six months of training at Sloane White, I was advised that they were placing me in the Trusts and Estates division. I resisted. I knew I couldn't ever go to court, but I pleaded with the managing attorney, Warren Lind, to put me in litigation research and preparation.

"Mr. Lind, I will be good at this. Please, you won't be sorry. Let me try." I sat on the edge of my seat in my black suit and white silk blouse, hair in a French twist to look older and serious.

Warren Lind sat behind his desk, leaning back hard in his red leather chair, hands steepled. He gazed at me with pale-gray eyes. I fidgeted with my blouse bow. Then he said, "Finn, we like you here. You're not pushy, and you fit in well with the other women, the secretaries. But litigation is not for women. The clients don't accept working with a woman. But maybe in the office. Maybe the research. I'll talk to the men and let you know."

I tried a closed-mouthed smile. "Thank you, Mr. Lind."

He gave me a tight smile back, and I was dismissed. However, a week later, I was assigned to the litigation department on a trial basis. I spent my first two years at Sloane White preparing depositions I wasn't permitted to take and poring through law books to craft arguments I wasn't permitted to make in court, and fashioning positions to decimate the other side's claims. I sometimes felt like Papa, who was always searching for not just a good word, but *the perfect* word. I similarly dug not just for a case on point, but the best case on point that would crush our adversaries.

I died a little as my colleagues made the arguments that I, a legal Cyrano de Bergerac, wasn't allowed to make. Handing over my research to lead counsel, I'd sit mutely at counsel table, or worse, behind counsel table on the benches reserved for spectators. I'd mouth the argument along with my colleague, him hitting the words and cases I'd gone over with him. Still, I was elated for our side when we won a ruling due to my research.

After court, I'd return to my tiny office with its small window, a place I loved. I closed the door when I needed serenity and opened it when I hoped for more work. My door was almost always open. When my name plaque went up, I felt a jolt of pride: Attorney Finley R. Hemingway. Each morning, I stared at it to be sure it wasn't a mistake. Then I'd step in, hang up my coat, look out my window to see if the old lady across the way with her purple kerchief had put her cockatoo out on her balcony yet, and I'd get to work.

The day I met Carter Kane, I'd started the morning by tripping on the sidewalk, breaking my heel as it snapped off in the subway grate, snagging my stocking, and tearing the cream cuff of my navy-blue suit. I had no scheduled appointments and longed to get through that day under the radar. The men would notice my torn attire, and in this blue-blood law firm, a turned head was cutting. It was close to noon, and I'd just started to cross-reference a deposition for Warren Lind when I heard two voices outside my open door.

"Who's that?" I heard a low voice ask.

John Hannon's voice chimed in. He was my direct boss, sixty-two, and almost totally bald. He said, "That's Finley Hemingway, one of our associates. Been here about two years."

"A woman?"

"Well, yes. It was a tough decision, but there were factors."

Quiet. Then, "Any relation to . . .?"

"Uh, yes. Daughter."

At times like that, I wished I were Finley Richardson.

"Really?" The word was drawn out a bit. "Any good?"

"Actually, she's outstanding. Smart as a whip and quick on her feet. Tops in trial practice at NYU. Shame we can't send her to court. She'd eat them alive, legally speaking."

I heard a sniff. "So then why not use her in court?"

John sighed. "Well, Carter, women aren't accepted in litigation. Hell, they're barely accepted in law. Takes jobs from the men, and it's the rare one suited to the rigors. It took our most valuable client's threat to remove his business if we didn't hire her to get her in the door. No one wanted her. Judges would wonder why, if the case were that important, we didn't send a man, a real lawyer. Shame. She may be the one who could have made it, but that's life."

"Seems pretty unfair to me," said the other man, who then added in a teasing tone, "Hey, I thought *I* was your most valuable client."

"Second-most valuable, Carter. You don't have enough disasters to keep us busy full-time. This other fellow does. And, yes, it is unfair, but she *is* here, so we did our part." John paused, sounding politely defensive. "Actually, she came up with some creative ideas on your case. I'd hoped the three of us could talk. Come on. I want you to meet her."

John Hannon rapped on my open door, and my life changed.

"Finley, I have someone I want you to meet. Can you spare us a moment?"

"Of course. Come in." I stood. As I recalled my stumble that morning and my tattered attire, my confidence sank. Carter Kane looked important. I stayed behind my desk, hoping I could remain there.

Carter Kane was tall, about forty-five, light-brown hair thinning and combed back, blue eyes, fair complexion. He wore a well-tailored navy-blue pinstriped suit over a crisp, white shirt and red paisley tie. He stepped around John and thrust out his hand.

Before John could make the introduction, he said, "Miss Hemingway, I'm Carter Kane. Delighted to meet you."

I smiled. He was aggressive, but I was comfortable with that. "Just call me Finn, please. Nice to meet you, Mr. Kane."

"And call me Carter."

John cleared his throat and got into the conversation. "Finn, Carter's is the divorce case you've been working on." John turned to Carter. "Carter, as you may know, the only basis for a divorce in New York is adultery. While you believe Mrs. Kane is involved with that Italian fellow, it's tough to prove, and she'll never admit it. Without that, no divorce is possible without some, um, creative staging. Finn had another idea though that I'd like to discuss. Let's move to the conference room."

I felt my pulse quicken. The men walked side by side ahead of me as we headed to the conference room overlooking the East River. I was lagging behind, my gait slowed by my one-heeled shoe situation. I clutched Mr. Kane's case folder tightly.

When Carter and John looked back at me in unison, I was listing to the right. I felt the need to explain. "A subway grate and my heel came to blows this morning, and the heel lost."

John frowned and looked troubled, as if it were not within his ken as a senior partner to deal with such problems. Carter Kane glanced down at my shoe and laughed. "Yeah, I hate it when that happens." He leaned forward and lowered his voice. "Lean on me; or better yet, take the damned thing off."

He shook his head and held the door open for me. I felt a flush of gratitude as I moved to the glossy mahogany table with its vase of fresh wildflowers and pitcher of water alongside crystal glasses. I sat and opened my folder, pulling out a few sheets of paper. Once the men were seated, I licked my lips, poured some water.

"Well, Mr. Kane—"

"Carter. Call me Carter." He sat back, pulled a cigar from his inner pocket, and cut it. "Is this a problem for you, Finn? I smoke rarely, but once in a while, it's relaxing."

I looked up from my file. "Oh no, sir. I'm used to cigars. My father and his friends are always puffing away. Thank you for asking though."

He put a match to his cigar and took a few puffs.

I started, picking my words carefully. "Carter, without proof, or without faking your own affair, we can't get you a divorce in New York. Adultery is the only basis in this state.

We can hire people who could set up the trappings of a supposed affair in order to provide the judge with a basis to grant a divorce based on adultery. We know the hotels and photographers who facilitate the choreography of this pretense." Carter was frowning. I rushed on. "I know. And that's just one option some people have chosen. Such actions would constitute lying in court, and we can't advise this as a good course of action, but sometimes people are desperate enough to fake their own infidelity."

Carter tapped his cigar. "Look, Finn, let me put my cards on the table. I need out of this. I've done a lot wrong, but I haven't been unfaithful to Johanna, and I'm not going to trump up a fake adultery charge so I can get a divorce and she can end up with way more of my money than she's entitled to after a five-year marriage. She's unbalanced. Last week, she cut up every suit I have except this one, because I was wearing it at the time. I've found her drunk several times when driving with our son—on those rare occasions she's with him at all. And, frankly, I just don't like her."

John handed Carter a scotch. Carter sipped it and puffed on his cigar.

"She's rude to my friends. At Christmas, she showed up two hours late for a dinner with the prime minister of England. She has no interest in doing anything with me. My first love is photography—modern stuff—but she won't attend any events there, even though my name is on one wing of the New York Museum of Photography.

I nodded. The NYMP was one of my favorite places to wander around on a rainy Saturday afternoon.

"My second love is theater. I back a show every few years, just for fun. She thinks it's boring. Actually, everything I do is boring to her. Her narrow niche interest appears to be shopping, and more specifically, shopping for diamond jewelry. *That*, she's excited about." He stopped and looked at me expectantly. His powerful persona was gone and he became just someone who needed help.

"Well," I began, looking at him squarely, "you have a house in Greenwich, Connecticut, where you spend a few months each year. If you could spend seven months a year there and make it your primary residence, you could file for divorce in Connecticut on the basis of intolerable cruelty. You'd need to prove bad behavior on Johanna's part, and that you sought medical help for the distress. John tells me your doctor prescribed sleeping medications and had real concerns for your health. He also said you had your son seen by a psychologist for some problem behavior."

Carter looked at me appraisingly. "Some nights, I can't sleep at all. Even lost some weight." He was a pretty trim man already. "I'll be honest with you, Finn, I'm a little old to be the father of a four-year-old—I have two grown sons from my first marriage—but I love the little guy. Mickey, we call him."

Carter smiled. It was sweet and a little sad. He reached into his inner jacket pocket, pulled out his wallet, and slid out a photo. He handed it to me. I looked at a grinning, gap-toothed blond boy. It made me smile too, and it made me like Carter Kane. He was no longer just a folder, or a rich guy trying to save a few bucks on a messy breakup.

"Mickey spends ninety-five percent of his time with our Spanish housekeeper and Nicaraguan driver. Kid's starting to speak English as his second language."

I chuckled.

He sighed. "Hey, it's my fault too. I should be there more. But I hate being with Johanna, and I'm trying to run six international businesses, so, no excuse, I know, but maybe an explanation. I'd love to know what the staff has seen. I don't think they are fans of Johanna, but we don't have a lot of communication. Paycheck is about it. I could bring in an interpreter to interview them, but I don't think they'd trust an outsider."

"Can John and I talk to them?" I asked.

Carter seemed dubious. "Sure—if you speak fluent Spanish."

"I do," I said. Carter looked surprised, and John raised an eyebrow. I shrugged. "I spend a lot of time in Cuba."

Carter crossed his legs and nodded with a very nice smile. "Ah, yes, Hemingway." He tapped on the table. "So, Finn, what will all this get us?"

I glanced at John. "First of all, it will get you divorced. In New York, you can't be divorced under your facts. In Connecticut, we can point out that Johanna is barely with you, neglects your son, drinks too much, and has caused you pain, anxiety, and weight loss, and you can get a divorce based on intolerable cruelty. We need two witnesses."

Carter took another sip of scotch. "No problem there. I can get witnesses."

"Second, it is hard to win custody from the mother of a young child—tender years doctrine says children under five should be with the mother, absent extraordinary circumstances. It's possible you could win, but you travel a great deal and would have to delegate most day-to-day tasks to a nanny. The court doesn't like that."

Carter frowned but nodded.

"However, we can request that Mickey stays in this area, spends significant time with you, and you'd have a say in hiring the nanny. You would pay some child support, but you could control your son's trust funds. I'd suggest that, as to alimony, we offer one lump sum."

Carter's eyes narrowed. He nodded again, still puffing on the cigar. "Yes, I'd like one payment and being done with it. And she insists she's moving Mickey to Italy. I can't have that."

"If we can't negotiate a deal, we can fight in court. I've reviewed all of the cases that have come down in the past ten years, and I think we can accomplish that. Do you want to try?"

Carter Kane took a sip of his scotch. "Yes, let's try."

I looked at John. He nodded and stood.

39

I may not be as strong as I think, but I know many tricks and I have resolution.

~ Ernest Hemingway, *The Old Man and the Sea*

Once Carter had established genuine residency in Connecticut, CARTER KANE VS JOHANNA KANE moved forward in Connecticut's Superior Court, Fairfield County. Carter wanted me to handle the case both in and out of court, despite being warned by his long-time lawyers it would almost certainly hurt his case, perhaps fatally.

A month before the trial, Carter was escorted into the law firm's conference room. The mood was funereal.

John Hannon opened. "Carter, we value your business and friendship, and as your lawyers, we have to stop this insanity. Finn's a wonderful lawyer. She wouldn't be here if she weren't. But it's foolhardy—even suicidal—not to use Presley Harding for your case. Finn can be second chair. Even that's risky, but we're willing to allow that," he said, gesturing to his two partners. They nodded solemnly.

Carter set his jaw. "I'm sticking with Finn."

"Carter, don't be ridiculous," John Hannon said, shaking the file at him for emphasis. "This is your life and child. You can't play 'flaunt the rules' with that at stake."

Carter sat back and thought for a few seconds. "So let's play 'change the rules.'" The trio of lawyers stared at him with something like pity in their eyes, as they might at a simple child who did not understand reality. "Look, this is not some social experiment for me. I hear you, but Finn is the most qualified. She knows my case inside out."

"That's not the issue, Carter." Now Warren Lind, managing partner of litigation, spoke. "She does, but they won't listen to her. She won't be taken seriously. Let her help, but for heaven's sake, use Pret Harding in court."

Carter walked to the bank of windows overlooking the East River. He shoved his hands into his pockets and stared out, his back to us. Then he turned and looked at me. I'd been sitting silently next to John Hannon like a potted plant.

He said, "Finn, can you do this? You won't get a welcoming committee there, but can you present the evidence needed? Are you ready?"

I swallowed and almost leapt up and yelled, "Carter, for God's sake, use Pret Harding. You can't take a chance on me. It's too big a risk."

Instead, I said, "Yes, I'm ready."

Carter nodded. He slowly pulled a cigar from a vest pocket and lit it. He looked calm, but I detected a tremor in his hand.

John wagged his head, a frown on his face, and shook a finger at Carter. "Don't say I didn't warn you, Carter. Don't come crying to me when you pay millions to Johanna and when your son is moved to Europe." He scowled at me.

I remained silent, praying I was up to this job, and that some judge in Connecticut was fairer than my colleagues assumed he would be. The thought of letting Carter down made my stomach twist and my skin prickle. And I knew my job was on the line.

Carter looked at me, then John. "We'll see," he said as he puffed on his cigar.

***

I met with the housekeeper and driver shortly before the trial. Not only were they overjoyed that I spoke fluent Spanish and was related to Ernesto Hemingway, *el escritor famoso de Cuba*, but it was as if they'd waited for someone to finally ask them about Johanna. Once they started spilling information, they couldn't stop.

And as expected, Johanna Kane dug in her heels and agreed to nothing. The case went forward to a full trial, and I was admitted to appear before the Connecticut Court pro hac vice, meaning I could act as Carter's lawyer even though not a member of the Connecticut bar.

The first day of the trial, I stepped into Center Courtroom 101, shaky but determined, as lead counsel for the plaintiff, Carter Kane, in *Kane v Kane*. The room itself was dark and paneled, all to inspire awe. With its high ceilings and grand paintings of unsmiling jurists, the courtroom seemed to say, "Make no mistake. Justice is serious business."

I set up my eight boxes of exhibits and trial preparation as Carter sat stiffly next to me in his dark-gray suit, hands folded in his lap. The three managing partners from Sloane White were seated in the front row behind us. They made me more nervous than opposing counsel, Jonathan Seabury, did.

When the bailiff intoned, "All rise," my legs weakened, but I managed a stand just as the Honorable Burton Yates strode in, looking grim. He took his place on the bench and said, "Counsel, names for the record."

"If it please the court, Finley Hemingway, appearing for the Plaintiff, Carter Kane." I heard a stir behind me and glanced over my shoulder. The eyes of the lawyers in the courtroom—all men—flew open as if disbelieving what they'd heard. Heads bobbed up and eyeglasses were adjusted to see if a woman was actually about to handle the high-stakes divorce trial of millionaire businessman Carter Kane. The Sloane White lawyers shifted uneasily.

The only other woman in the courtroom aside from Johanna Kane was the judge's clerk. She sat several steps below Judge Yates, ready to hand him whatever he required. When she heard my voice, she jerked her head up and her hand flew to her mouth. Then she sat taller and a smile slowly spread across her face.

By the afternoon, it was standing room only as the news fired through the building that a woman lawyer was litigating a multi-million-dollar case.

On that first morning, Judge Burton Yates, black robe cloaking him in gravitas, peered down at me through thick glasses that slid down his nose. Still, he nodded without emotion at my opening declaration. After Jonathan Seabury announced his appearance for Mrs. Kane, Judge Yates said, "Fine. Are you ready to proceed with your first witness, Attorney Hemingway?"

"Yes, Your Honor. I call Carter Kane to the stand."

Carter looked anxious; he tripped stepping up to the witness chair and sat on the edge of the seat, hands on his knees, leaning forward. My questions were workmanlike and elicited basic facts about the length of the marriage, Mickey's birth, Carter's finances, and marital history.

At the end of the seventh day, after accountants and our numerous character witnesses, the judge rubbed his head as if troubled. "I've heard that Mr. Kane loves his son, and there are concerns about Mrs. Kane's drinking, and innuendo of another man in her life. A child needs a stable base, but there is no evidence yet endorsing your claim that Mrs. Kane has not made the young man in question a top priority or that clearly she has committed adultery, is there?"

Johanna and Jonathan Seabury smiled at each other. I quickly said, "If Your Honor please, we have other witnesses on rebuttal who may address Your Honor's questions. May I continue?"

Judge Yates raised a hand as if to say, "Fine, we'll see what you've got."

When I rested our case, I was not sure if we'd proven what we needed to. However, with cross-examination and rebuttal yet to come, I was hopeful.

On day twelve, Johanna Kane took the stand. She glided forward in a plum wool suit, her champagne-blonde hair in a chignon at the nape of her neck. Tall and almost gaunt, she appeared confident, yet demure. Carter had done well on the stand, but Jonathan Seabury was able to hammer the fact that Carter himself was away many months of the year, and that to compel Johanna to stay in the United States would be punitive to her. Carter had emerged standing, but battered. The judge was starting to look bored and had stopped writing notes, not a good sign.

Johanna was flawless on her direct examination, by turns charming, eloquent, and self-deprecating as she testified about how she met Carter, her care of Mickey, and her wish to return to Italy where she and Mickey, according to her, could live more freely, without publicity. She added that since Carter was in Europe regularly, he and Mickey could maintain their bond without difficulty. When asked about contact with Mickey's half-brothers—Carter's two older sons—Johanna noted that they were so much older that they were not "really" like brothers. Carter growled, and I had to poke him to silence him.

Finally, Jonathan Seabury was done. He tossed his pen onto counsel table and turned to me, smug and close to smirking when he said, "Your witness, Counsel."

I stood at counsel table, notes in hand in case I lost my way. Johanna shifted in her chair to look at me. Despite the fact that we'd shared this space for the past twelve days, she had a wide-eyed look as if she'd never seen me before. I decided to hit her vulnerabilities head-on rather than ease her into the cross-examination.

"Now, Mrs. Kane, you've indicated to this court that you've been faithful to your husband since the date of your marriage, have you not?"

"Yes, that's correct."

"But in fact, Mrs. Kane, there was at least one occasion when you committed adultery, was there not?"

Jonathan Seabury was on his feet. "Objection. Asked and answered, Your Honor."

Judge Yates didn't even look up. "It's cross-examination, Counsel. Plaintiff is allowed to test the answer. Overruled. The witness may answer the question."

Johanna looked agitated. She glanced up at the judge and back to me. "No, in fact, there was not any such occasion, Miss Hemingway."

I walked to counsel table and pulled a photo from a folder. I paused to look at it, walked back to the stand, and handed her the photo. "Ma'am, if that's so, would you please explain to the court the meaning of this photo?"

I handed a copy to Jonathan Seabury, who blanched when he saw it. As Johanna turned her gaze to it, her face reddened and her breathing became heavier. "I . . . where did you get this? I had . . ." She stopped talking and stared at her lawyer. He shrugged as if to say, "I can't help you from here, Johanna. It's your show."

I moved closer to the witness box. "Mrs. Kane, that *is* you in bed with a man who is not your husband, is it not?"

"I . . . I . . ." She stopped. I examined the photo again: Johanna grinning over her naked shoulder—actually, naked everything—in bed with a very undressed and handsome young man. Silence from the witness.

"Would Your Honor please instruct the witness to answer?" I said.

Judge Yates rotated his large head. He no longer looked bored. In fact, he looked energized, leaning forward and writing notes. He pushed up his glasses. "The witness is directed to answer the question."

Johanna let out her breath slowly. "Yes, that's me." She regrouped and added quickly, "But that was taken before my marriage to Carter."

I was ready for that. "Your Honor, I offer this photo as a full exhibit."

"Any objection, Attorney Seabury?" the judge asked.

Seabury stood. "No, Your Honor, with the understanding that my client testified that it pre-dated her marriage." The judge nodded and admitted the photo. He looked at it himself, then set it aside and looked back at me.

I turned to Johanna and feigned puzzlement. "Now you've indicated that this is an old photo. Do you read the *New York Times* daily, Mrs. Kane?"

Her features relaxed, glad to be done with the photo, confident that she'd dealt with it. "No, I don't read it. Carter does. It's delivered daily to the apartment though, yes."

"Ah. But, ma'am, isn't that Mr. Kane's bedroom that the photo was taken in?"

She was squirming again now that we were back to the photo. "Carter and I were friends long before our marriage, and he offered me his apartment whenever I was in town. This must have been taken on one of those occasions—before we were seeing each other."

"Ah," I said, nodding like she'd made a good point. I strolled back to counsel table and stood with my hands on the back of my chair, taking my time. "Ma'am, may I ask you to take another look at the photo, please?"

She tapped her foot. It echoed in the quiet courtroom. The charm was gone, replaced by hostility. "Oh, for heaven's sake."

"Please humor me, Mrs. Kane, and take another look at the photo."

She shifted her eyes from me and made a show of holding the photo close. The judge, following suit, found the photo among the debris of papers in front of him and took off his glasses to study it. I glanced up in time to see his eyes widen; he looked at me and raised an eyebrow. I thought I saw the edge of a smile. I slid my gaze back to Johanna.

"I don't see anything I didn't see the first time." She slapped it on the flat railing.

"Maybe a larger photo would help, ma'am? If I may, Your Honor." The judge nodded. I had copies for him as well as for opposing counsel, blown up twenty-fold. I set a super-sized copy of the naked Johanna and friend on an easel to the left of the witness box where it looked very . . . large. "Mrs. Kane, can you read for the court the headline that covers the top half of the *New York Times* lying on the end of the bed?"

She finally got it. She looked up, her mouth snapping shut, hand fluttering to her neck.

"The headline please, Mrs. Kane," I said.

Quietly, she read, "And He's Out; Truman Fires MacArthur."

"Louder please, Mrs. Kane, for the court record."

She glared. "And He's Out; Truman Fires MacArthur."

"Can we agree that then President Truman fired General MacArthur on April 11, 1951, over a year ago, as shown by the date on the *New York Times*?" Johanna suddenly found her nails all-consuming. Her head was down. "Can you answer the question, Mrs. Kane?"

She jerked her head up and snapped, "Yes, we can agree."

"And you were in fact married to Mr. Kane well before April 1951, were you not, ma'am?"

"Yes," she mumbled.

"And according to his calendar, he was in San Francisco for a week, including April 11, 1951, and while away, you had sexual relations in the New York City apartment with another man, did you not?"

Johanna's composure was rapidly failing. Her lawyer just shook his head when she appealed to him with big eyes to help her.

"He's just a friend," she said, fingering her necklace.

"And your naked friend's name is what, Mrs. Kane?"

"Um . . ." Long pause and much staring into space.

"Let me help you out. Paolo Brunetti, is it not?" She nodded with reluctance. "You have to answer for the court's record, Mrs. Kane."

"Yes, that's his name."

"And who took the photo?"

The courtroom stirred. Johanna paled further.

"Mrs. Kane, can we agree that this picture didn't take itself?" No answer. By this time, the judge was on high alert, pen poised, sitting forward. The spectators were still, and Johanna's own lawyer was on the edge of his seat.

"It was Paolo's brother, Aldo," she said softly. When I went to take the photo from her, I had to pry it from her fingers.

"Aldo Brunetti," I repeated. "And isn't it a fact that you are now having a relationship with Aldo after ending the relationship with Paolo, Mrs. Kane?"

At that, the courtroom was so still that the ticking of the wall clock could be heard.

Johanna exploded, full of indignation. "No! That's absurd. And Carter was away so much . . ."

I interrupted. "That was a yes or no question, Mrs. Kane. No other question is pending. Will Your Honor strike the last portion of that answer as non-responsive to the question?"

Judge Yates, bright-eyed now, said, "Yes, answer may be stricken after 'No.' Next question, Counsel." He was smiling at me now; a small smile, but definitely a smile.

Just then, the heavy door to the courtroom opened. All heads turned. In marched a man with shoulder-length, black hair in a slim, European-cut black suit. The judge stared and looked down at the photo. He sat back, arms crossed on his chest, and looked amused. His head swiveled from the witness to the man. It was the man from the photo, Paolo Brunetti. He was grave-faced today, not jaunty as in the photo, but there was no mistaking that it was him. Johanna looked ill.

I walked close to the witness box. "Are you sure you don't want to change your testimony, Mrs. Kane? My next witness, otherwise, is Mr. Paolo Brunetti."

Johanna, hand at her neck again, was toying with an expensive diamond necklace. "I did—in desperation—become involved with Paolo, but I ended it for Carter's sake. Paolo did not take it well." She glared at Carter, then at me, then at Paolo. Paolo ran a hand through his hair and glared back. The three partners from Sloane White smiled at me for the first time in twelve days.

The judge watched the drama closely, wrote some notes, and nodded to me. "Any other questions, Counsel?"

"Not for this witness, Your Honor."

After a few more days of Johanna's character witnesses—a parade of society women at New York's highest level—Johanna and Jonathan Seabury announced that the defense rested.

Judge Yates said, "Any rebuttal, Attorney Hemingway?"

"Yes, Your Honor. I call Candelaria Garcia-Arroyo."

The Kane's Spanish housekeeper trudged from the spectators' gallery to the stand. Dressed in her long, black skirt and simple white sweater, her long, dark hair pulled back into a low ponytail, Candelaria had a quiet dignity about her. She looked straight ahead, particularly avoiding Johanna Kane's eyes. A Spanish interpreter was sworn in.

After preliminaries about her job and length of employment in the Kane household, I asked, "Now, Señora Garcia-Arroyo, did you have an opportunity to observe Mrs. Kane with her son, Mickey Kane?"

"Yes, but not much, miss."

"Why is that?"

Candelaria played with the fabric of her black skirt. "Because she was not the one who took care of Mickey. The nanny, Elena Albaritas, or Manuel—Mr. Kane's driver—or me—we took care of him. And when she was there, she drank a lot. A lot, miss. And when she drank, she was mean. She would push Mickey. Sometimes she would hit him, and most nights, the señora locked the door to her room to be sure he would not bother her." Candelaria looked pained and twisted to look at the judge. "He is just a little boy, Honorable Judge. Yes, he makes noise, but he is a good boy."

The judge nodded solemnly upon hearing the translation.

"Have you ever seen this man, Mrs. Garcia-Arroyo?"

I handed her the photo of Johanna with Paolo in bed. She'd seen it before but still blanched. Through the translator, she said, "Yes. He stayed with Mrs. Kane often while Mr. Kane was away. Last winter he was at the apartment a lot, while Mr.

Kane was in London. Then the other one, the brother, started staying. They drank all the time, and she never saw Mickey. Sometimes weeks went by without seeing him. He would be in Greenwich, and she stayed in New York City."

The spectators buzzed when that translation was stated. It was enough. It was more than enough. Candelaria had found the naked photo on the floor under the bed while cleaning and turned it over to me when we met. A private detective was able to find Paolo and Aldo. It was not hard to get Paolo to testify, as he was the jilted lover, replaced by his younger brother Aldo. In fact, Paolo was more than eager to tell his side of the love triangle, but it wasn't necessary. His presence in court had been sufficient.

After waiting anxiously for two months, the decision arrived. It was all we'd hoped for, with court orders that kept Carter active in Mickey's life with no move permitted out of New York, Johanna's drinking to be monitored by a counselor, and a lump sum ordered for Carter's financial payment to Johanna.

Amusingly, the three Sloane White partners congratulated themselves on their progressiveness and foresight in allowing me to handle Carter's case. Shaking my hand, Warren Lind crowed, "Finn, I never doubted you could do this. Carter told me he couldn't be happier with the outcome."

"Well done, Finn. Glad we could be there to support you," said John Hannon.

I smiled, knowing it was not quite true, but I still felt lucky. After that, Carter Kane sent more and more business my way.

40

January 5, 1953

    Dear Flea:

    Congratulations on your first court victory! Lo siento mucho, hija mia, about my gift of Taitinger's finest to my AA-attending daughter. (It was a good year though! Do I get any credit for that?) So sorry though, Flea. Glad you gave it to the newlyweds upstairs. Had a bad bout of black ass depression for a few months, and you know how I get when that happens. I delegated everything to my assistant. Told her to send you a celebratory gift, but forgot to add that it needed to be of the non-hooch persuasion. Pulling out of black ass now though as the writing is rolling. Sorry, Flea. I'm a real shit.

    Just sent a check to the stable for Dancing Girl, and she is now a lifetime resident of Claremont Stables. Maybe her stall is rent-controlled? She is your heart, and I want her always to be with you without it being a sacrifice.

    Love, your idiot Papa

I stared at the handwritten note. Just when I despaired of my father truly understanding what mattered to me, he'd rally and grandstand a bit, but he let me know he knew.

41

"Fish," he said. "I love and respect you very much. But I will kill you dead before this day ends."

~ Ernest Hemingway, *The Old Man and the Sea*

A few weeks later, the phone rang at six o'clock in the morning. I'd been up for an hour and had just walked Tess. She'd become my sole roommate since Jeddrah married Robert in June. I'd moved to a smaller apartment in the West Village, one block from where Jedd lived. Each morning, Jedd walked with Tess and me down to the Battery and back, filling me in on the hospital and her marriage and hearing about my life.

As I sipped my second cup of coffee, I grabbed the phone.

"Flea?"

"Papa! What's up with you at this hour?"

"I got it."

"Got what?"

"The Pulitzer Prize for Literature."

I sank onto my saggy couch. I knew what this meant. Validation. "Oh, Papa! I'm so happy for you. What an honor!"

Papa had been so determined to get this new book out, *The Old Man and the Sea*. He'd keenly felt the loss of Charlie

Scribner, Sr., who'd passed away, as well as the absence of Max Perkins's sharp editing. Without the two of them, Papa had been uncertain of the book's worth. He was also sensitive about the fact that it was short.

"Other writers write short books," he complained to me one day. "Sure, that James Jones book, *From Here to Eternity*, was big, but I didn't know that I was being paid by the pound, and I think I can show the soul of a man without needing seven hundred pages to do it."

I understood his fears. Critics and non-fans were salivating for another *Across the River and into the Woods* to put a final nail in the coffin of Ernest Hemingway.

"Guess *this* old man—meaning me—is not as washed up as they thought." Papa took a breath.

"You were never washed up, Papa. Anyone who thought so knew nothing."

He coughed. "I just need time. I still have things to say." His voice dipped low, and I could almost see him leaning down to pet Black Dog and staring out at the Cuban hills.

I looked out my small living room window onto the tree-lined New York block. The sun was just poking above the roofs across the street. I closed my eyes. "I know, Papa. You still have a lot to say. A lot to write."

I wondered if he realized he'd spoken words close to those he'd written for Harry in *The Snows of Kilimanjaro*. Now he would never write the things that he had saved to write until he knew enough to write them well. I said nothing, and in this moment of triumph, I felt a wave of melancholy.

Papa revived. "Nice to win after the shit I had to eat about the last book."

And was it ever vindication. "Best story Hemingway has ever written," *London Sunday Times*. "A tale superbly told," the *New York Times Book Review*. "Mr. Hemingway is once again 'the champ,'" the *Listener*. Even William Faulkner called it "his best." Five million copies of *LIFE* magazine, where *The Old Man and the Sea* was serialized, sold out within forty-eight hours. He received eighty to ninety letters a day, and he was repeatedly approached on the street by readers and fans who burst into tears upon touching him. Papa claimed it was "worse than *Pagliacci*"—an Italian tragic opera—but he was laughing and happy when he said it.

As we talked on the phone that morning, I could picture him pacing the front hall of the Finca, switching the black phone from one hand to the other. I joked, "And hey, I helped. Remember, I said, 'Don't kill off Santiago, whatever you do.'"

At the time, Papa had mumbled that "you never want to kill anyone off, Flea," and that "maybe it was better for Santiago and for the story for him to succumb." I was sad that old Santiago was doomed until a few days later when Papa sent me the last pages in the mail. *Up the road, in his shack, the old man was sleeping again. He was still sleeping on his face and the boy was sitting by him watching him. The old man was dreaming about the lions.* I'd let out a sigh. Papa had let him live.

"Yeah, people always want the hero to live..." Papa's voice drifted off. "But I grant your point. Santiago deserved to live."

"Yes, he did," I said, sipping my coffee and stretching out on the couch.

Papa coughed again. "Have to go, Flea. Doorbell ringing. Black Dog and Negrita going crazy. Mary gardening. I'm working on that book about the woman named Elena. It's puzzling me, but I love it. It's a quiet book. Less action, more thinking than my other books. Ha, probably because a woman is the main character. Also new for me." He paused, then said in a seeming non-sequitur, "I haven't always been the best father, Flea. I know that, and I sure was never a good husband, especially to your mother. I'm sorry for that, too. I always loved you all though." There was a pleading quality to his voice, as if he needed me to understand.

I said without hesitation, "You never need to be sorry, Papa. We knew."

***

For the past year, I'd taken to calling Logan Grant every Sunday night. He seemed happy to hear from me, but didn't reciprocate if I happened to skip a week. When I was out in Idaho, we spent much of our time together; until my last visit. We'd just put the horses away. Logan had lingered in Arc's stall, taking extra care with his cooldown. The night was warm and clear, and after loosening my boots and rolling up my sleeves, I plopped down in an Adirondack chair. Logan handed me a Coca-Cola, and I took a long swig. He sat down in the other chair.

He looked at me and sighed. "It's kind of sad that we can't get into anything—you know, a relationship—because we get along so well, Finn." He stopped, then turned to look at me.

He saw my frown. "Look. I'm sorry if it hurts you, but I can't compete with some dead perfection. When I visited you in New York and saw that damned hoof pick sitting on the table next to your bed, I wanted to smash it. It's not real, Finn, and when I saw it, I knew. It would always be Nick."

My face hardened. I'd made it clear to him that I was interested, and it was he who turned away. If he needed me to turn my back on the past in order to be with me—well, that wasn't possible. There was some truth to what he said, but I resented the hell out of the hoof pick comment. I sat still and stony.

He continued. "And you know what? Since I've already irritated you, I'll say it all. I can't compete with your father, either. I love the guy. I do. He's not what everyone thinks. He's a shy, gentle man when he's not drinking, but he's goddamned bigger than anyone's life."

He took a breath and gently turned my face toward him, making me look at him.

"No one can compete with *that*, either. You push that whole Hemingway thing away. You have your fake name ready if anyone asks, but he dominates everything, and you can't get away from it. I don't understand why you can't just live your own life without wondering how he will react or comment or how other people will see you. You say you're independent, but I know what I see. You can't deal with the reality of a normal relationship, and I'm not going to enter that no-win contest. Too much pain. I want kids, and someone here all the time whose mind isn't on some dead sweetheart or on a father who is attentive when he wants to be and you always scrambling to try to get his notice."

Ouch. Reality Rule #2 and #3, brushing up to #4. I bristled and said sarcastically, "Well, who knew you had all of that hostility to let out, Logan."

He got up and began to pace, then abruptly sat. "You know, Finn, I'm sorry Nicky died, but I can't be him. Just give me some sign that you can leave the past in the past." Logan was leaning forward now, forearms on knees, gaze penetrating.

I hardened. "Anything we start will fail anyway, as these things always do." I shook my head, frustrated that he didn't see where all of this would end. It wasn't because of Nick. It was the nature of love, in my experience. "I don't understand you optimists. Even my father. He keeps trying to find true love over and over, and it always ends badly, with everything broken and everyone mad or disgusted, or both."

Logan sagged. His silence ended in a sharp inhale of breath. Then he slapped his thighs with both hands. "OK, then. That's it. We'll both move on, knowing there was no possibility here."

He got up and turned away. I half-stood and seized his arm. He turned to look at me. "Logan, can't we still be friends?"

He gave a low chuckle. "Yeah, sure, Finn. We can be friends." I dropped his arm and he walked into the barn. There it is: *Love always ends for us Hemingways—even before it begins—and usually, it ends badly.*

42

It's silly not to hope. It's a sin he thought.

~ Ernest Hemingway, *The Old Man and the Sea*

After our falling out, I stopped calling Logan. Mary said he was seeing a local schoolteacher. A few months later, when I spent a week with my father in Cuba, it was still on my mind. While we were out on *Pilar* and Papa was preparing to cast a line, I told him about the rift with Logan. He stopped, turned to look at me, then reeled in his line. He lay down the pole and sat on the rear transom facing me, arms crossed.

He was quiet for a moment, then said, "What happened?"

I shrugged. My bathing suit strap slipped down my shoulder and I shoved it up. "He said I was living with Nicky's ghost and we couldn't consider a romance with that between us. But you know what, Papa? I don't believe in that kind of love, and I am not forgetting Nicky for anyone. If he can't live with that, good riddance. And frankly, from what I see, if you want to stay in love, never get married or never fall in love with someone going to war. It's surefire pain in spades." I turned away.

Papa reached down for a baseball cap from a basket, slapped it on his leg, and put it on to keep the hot Cuban sun out of his eyes. "That's a bit cynical for twenty-eight years old, isn't it, Flea? Is it me? Because you know, not all love ends up like mine. And I keep trying because it's worth it."

I twisted to face him. "How? How is it worth it? Looks like a pile of pain to me, and then you start over again with someone else." I really wanted to know.

Papa pointed at a marlin leaping into the air. Gregorio Fuentes, who was steering the boat, nodded and smiled. He was like family, and we made no effort to disguise our conversation. Papa fiddled with his cap, took it off, adjusted the back sizing, then put it back on. "I'm sorry you feel that way, Flea. Your mother and Paul are happy."

"She still misses you. Anyone else you can think of? Jeddrah feels smothered by Robert. Jack is not spouting poetry. You and Mary are not exactly in bliss, not to mention your other wives. And feel free to expand to our circle of friends. Any delighted couples out there?"

Papa was quiet, clearly having trouble coming up with examples.

"See? No. Love is all fun and games at the beginning, but it never lasts."

He scratched his beard, then shook his head. "Yeah, I know Mary and I scrap, but there's a core of love there. Always will be. Plus, love takes many shapes, Flea, and you don't know what's under the surface of other people's feelings." He leaned forward, holding onto the transom's edge as the boat pitched. "Hell, the one thing that kept me going through the worst of the shit was you; my love for you. That's love too, you know. I started writing *The Sun Also Rises* the day you were born, July 21, 1925, our mutual birthday. Took me just six weeks after years of slogging to get the first draft down. Because of you. Because of love. Never wrote that fast or that well before you."

He paused, then went on. "When your mother handed you to me, I fell hard, and it's still going strong. So think about that, kid. I knew that for all of my little successes up to then, I needed a real hit to be worth a shit, to be able to care for you—Bumby too, and later Gig and Mouse—but that love lasted. And the love I had for Max and Charlie and Pauline and your mother—hell, even for Marty—is still always with me, even though they aren't."

I waved my hand in the air. "That's not lasting love. Those marriages all ended badly, Papa."

He shrugged. "Yeah, sure, but I poured everything I learned from all of them, including the love I feel for you, into the best book I ever wrote, whether the critics thought so or not: *A Single Drop of Red Wine*. Elena was the best of Pauline and Marty, but mostly of you. Especially you. And she was a survivor."

He took a big breath and let it out slowly as he gazed at the horizon. The man of words was grasping for syllables. He reached over and touched my cheek. "There is lasting love, *querida mia*. You just have to beef up your definition of 'lasting,' and take in love in all its forms." He shrugged and picked up his rod again. "But, hell, what do I know? I'm just a simple guy from the backwaters of Michigan and Illinois, but I know that love is all there is. Once you have it, part of that person is always with you. That's real."

I looked out to sea and thought about *A Single Drop of Red Wine*, the book of his that I loved more than any other and that revealed more about him than any other. It was so unlike the others that critics and readers didn't know what to make of it. His heroine, Elena, was heartbreakingly touching in her dignity, her steadfastness, her love for Jonathan, and her shatterproof hope for a happy outcome.

"The real Hemingway finally on display," wrote David Gussman of *The New York Times*. "Hemingway shows what he has hidden in all of his other works: that he has more empathy than a man who writes of war, hunting, and drinking is believed to have and more raw sensitivity in one sentence than most other writers can smash into 400 pages, without getting close to what Hemingway has managed here. Read this one slowly and relish each word like each sip of the symbolic single drop of red wine. What you'll taste is tender first love that lasts a lifetime."

On the other hand: "Hemingway's gone soft. Wine and flowers and hills and wisps of red hair blowing in the breeze? If we wanted to read of small lives and loves, we wouldn't grab Hemingway, now would we? Aberrant, unexpected, and of little moment. Hem, where have you gone?" wrote Samuel Dorance of the *LA Times*.

As for me, I am never without the slim volume detailing a passionate and sensitive ten-month love affair between Elena Cortez and Jonathan Manudos in Key West just before Jonathan was drafted. Elena had so much of me in her—and there was so much of Nicky in Jonathan—that sometimes I had to close the book for a few minutes to re-center. Usually I wept quiet tears of regret, joy, surrender, hope. The book ends without saying definitively if Jonathan comes back from the war, but it ends with faith, expectation, and optimism as Elena stitches a quilt for their bedroom and for his return.

"I want to believe that, Papa. I really do, but I can't. Nicky isn't with me. It has to last here and now to be real." This metaphysical mumbo jumbo was not for me.

Papa knelt down, pulled a knife from his back pocket and began to cut up some fish for bait. "No, it just has to have *existed* to be real. Lasting is a whole other matter. And all I'm saying is that just because I'm a many-time loser in eternal love doesn't mean it doesn't exist. I only regret one marriage, and I don't regret any of the love. Plus, Flea, you aren't me."

He looked at me over his shoulder as he continued to cut. "I need the challenge, the rush. You need the steady coursing. But never doubt that love exists. It damn well better exist, or we're all bitched."

"Exactly, Papa." *As long as there is one of us, there is both of us.* Could that be true?

Papa smiled sadly. "Sweetheart, love will find you if you refuse to find it. That's its mission."

I stared at the horizon, then turned to Papa and said, "What about Mother? You said you put the best of Pauline, Martha, and me into Elena. What about Mother? Is she nowhere?"

My father looked down, then at me, eyes moist. "She's hard to write. My guilt kills the ideas before they're born."

I understood, but I didn't like it. My mother deserved better. Still, my discontent fled for now. I had my father and Cuba and the sun. I had *A Single Drop of Red Wine*. I picked up my rod and changed the subject. "So how are you feeling, Papa?"

Papa took the hint and picked up his fishing pole too. "Pretty good, actually. Taking more walks, less booze, getting more rest. In fact, I feel so good, Mary and I are going to Africa soon."

He sounded as good as I'd heard him in a while. He was wearing his beard full-time now. His mostly gray hair was thinning, and he combed it back. He still looked strong and vigorous. He was drinking so little that we could have a conversation almost any hour of the day. Papa was kinder to Mary, which was a relief, and the only sadness was that Willie, a great favorite cat, had passed away. When Papa told me, he started to cry, and I did, too.

"Papa, I thought you never cried," I said through my own tears. I was sitting on the floor, my head on Papa's knee. His hand was stroking my hair gently. It felt good.

"I cry, Flea. Believe me, when the hurt is bad enough, I cry."

Despite that one sadness, congratulations on the Pulitzer were still rolling in, and Western Union was always at the door. One note that particularly touched Papa was Marlene Dietrich's, saying the book was a "masterpiece and I am acting like a proud wife who always knew her husband had even deeper greatness than was realized by those not privileged to know the real inner man." He handed it to me with a shy laugh.

Papa and Mary were excited about their trip to Africa. Papa had contacted Mouse—now a big game hunter in Kenya—about details. I felt nervous about the trip. It had been twenty years since his last African sojourn. He was now fifty-four and anxious about leaving the Finca, especially Black

Dog and Boise. Both were aged. Black Dog hobbled now but insisted on not being left behind when Papa took his morning stroll around the grounds. Boise chased birds and iguanas less and less, but still joined the garden walks at Papa's heels, a few steps ahead of Black Dog.

43

September 1953

Dear Flea:

Not sure when you'll get this, but we're here. Africa! You remember me talking about Philip Percival? Just left his Kitanga Farm, about 40 miles south of Nairobi. Having a grand time. Africa is changed from when I was here in 1933 with Pauline, but just as inspiring and stunning. I'm using the camera this time more than *las armas*, the guns.

I'm glad you're going to Nick's sister's wedding. Sometimes after a tragedy, the worst fear is that no one remembers. Being remembered and missed is just about sacred. It means you were here and you were loved. That matters more than any words can say.

Sorry we won't have Christmas together this year, but I always carry you with me in my pocket. That compass you gave me when you were ten guarantees I'll find my way back to you. I already miss the Finca and the critters, but it's good to explore. Freshens the viewpoint. Via con Dios, mi hija.

Love, Your crazy Papa

Go with God, my daughter. I smiled. I'd told him just before he left that the Armstrongs had invited me to their daughter's wedding, and I was excited to be included.

"By God, I miss you, Papa. You be careful out there," I prayed silently.

44

No one should be alone in their old age, he thought.

~ Ernest Hemingway, *The Old Man and the Sea*

About six months after Carter Kane's divorce, he stopped by my office and plopped into my client chair. I was delighted to see him. He ran a hand through his hair as he sat.

With no preamble, he said, "Finn, I haven't been able to get you out of my mind since you first said let's change the jurisdiction to Connecticut, and then when you hobbled along with that broken heel and started speaking Spanish like a native, I was a goner. I've waited six months and can't possibly wait one more day to ask you. May I please take you to dinner? You say if, when, and where."

I laughed at the jurisdiction comment but was otherwise speechless. I had enjoyed working with Carter. Over those months, I'd seen that while he was tough in business, he was kind with his son and considerate of his employees. He was also whip-smart and dryly funny in a way that always made me laugh. Still, I hadn't noticed any special fondness for me at the time, and I was caught unawares. I opened my mouth twice to say something, but nothing came out.

"Great. I'll take that as a yes. You amaze me, and that doesn't happen much." He stood and left.

I'd been seeing Carter now for several months. Though I didn't feel the roar I'd felt with Nicky, I enjoyed his company.

With Carter, I felt cared for, but I never felt he needed or wanted more, marriage or children. He'd been married twice, had two grown children plus Mickey, and seemed content with life as it was. Heads turned for him when we walked into restaurants or openings. In New York, Carter was as visible as a billboard. He was a presence in theater, the arts, Belmont Park, his box at Yankee Stadium, and his charities for New York City children.

That Christmas, while Papa and Mary were in Africa and Carter was with his two adult sons—Mickey was with Johanna in Italy—I motored up to New Hampshire to visit my mother. Jack, Puck, and their daughter, Muffett, were there too. Puck was very pregnant, and in February, she had her second daughter, Margot, later known as Margaux.

When the phone rang on Christmas Eve as we sat around the tree having dessert and coffee, Mother dashed to answer it. I turned to see her face light up. "Tatie! Merry Christmas!"

Jack and I sighed in unison. Our parents always talked too long for our taste. When we were kids, we both were always grabbing for the phone, dying to talk to Papa ourselves.

After enduring ten minutes of their talk, Jack said, "Mother! Can we please talk to Papa before the Kenyan phone service cuts out?"

She ignored him, but said, "All right then. The kids are getting impatient. Stay safe, Tatie."

She handed the phone to Jack and I hopped onto an extension. Soon we were all laughing and talking at once. Papa sounded ebullient, and promised regular reports on "Africa: Take Two" as he called this second African trek.

As he described the boat ride from Italy to Mombasa, I suddenly felt a wash of desolation roll over me. All our previous Christmases at Key West and then Cuba flashed through my mind: the laughs, the animals, the stories, the Christmas hats, the silliness, my father at the center of it all. Now Papa was across the world, and I could barely hear his voice through this static-filled phone line that could drop at any moment. I longed for us all to be together again. I felt a flick of foreboding that it all might never be the same again. I knew I was being foolish, but I blurted, "Papa, I don't ever want to miss Christmas with you again. It's awful not to be ending the year together."

"Thanks a lot!" my mother called over.

"Jeez, don't listen to Finn, Papa," Jack interrupted. "Finn! He's just on a vacation, not falling off the end of the world. Have a great time, Papa. Write all about it, then tell us all the stuff you can't put into the book because of the censors."

Papa boomed out a laugh. "Ah, you know my tricks, Bumb! And Flea, I pledge to you that I'll be with you at Christmas from now until *el finito de tiempo, hija mía*; unless, of course, I'm dead. How's that, sweetheart?" *Until the end of time, my daughter.*

I grinned. "Deal! You are an indestructible force, Papa, so we will have endless Christmases together."

45

Up the road, in his shack, the old man was sleeping again. He was still sleeping on his face and the boy was sitting by him watching him. The old man was dreaming about the lions.

~ Ernest Hemingway, *The Old Man and the Sea*

January 23, 1954, started out like a normal day as I tossed on my camel hair coat and hurried to the subway. It was blustery and cold as I grabbed my usual copy of the *New York Times* from my favorite newsstand and tucked it under my arm. As I stopped at a light that had just turned, I quickly unfolded the paper to catch the top stories.

I gasped at the headline that filled the top half of page one.

HEMINGWAY, WIFE KILLED

IN AIR CRASH

NO SIGN OF LIFE AT THE WRECK

I read it again in disbelief, then couldn't breathe. I leaned against a building for support for fear of falling, then whispered, "No, no, oh God, no. This can't be true!" The telegram announcing Nicky's death flashed in front of me. "Not again!"

With a spurt of energy, I ran down Fifth Avenue, my heeled shoes painful until I tore them off and finished the dash to Charles Scribner Jr.'s office in stocking feet. He'd already heard and looked weak, face drained of all color. "Sit, Finn. We're trying to find out details."

His assistant handed me a glass of water, but my hands shook so badly that I spilled water onto the carpet. I needed my mother and Jack, the only two people in the world who knew what he was to us—not to the world, but to us. I refused to imagine a world without my father.

I listened as Charlie made call after call to all of his contacts in Europe, then Nairobi, and finally Johannesburg. I stared anxiously as he first averted his eyes, then looked at me and shook his head.

Hours crept by as I paced Scribner's halls. I called my office, then my mother, then Carter. He had heard, and had been trying frantically to reach me for the past few hours.

"Finn, do you want to go over there? I'll charter a plane and go with you."

My gratitude swelled for this man. "Thank you, Carter. I appreciate that offer more than I can say. Let's wait to see what happens today. Thank you so much."

It was a full day before news began to seep out that Papa might be alive, and that he and Mary had been in not one, but two plane crashes. Mary broke two ribs and Papa had badly damaged his spine, his right arm, and his shoulder in the first crash. The second crash was worse. It had just lifted off when it took a 180-degree plunge. The gas tank ignited and the plane became a death trap. The pilot and Mary crawled out a small window but Papa was too big to fit, and he was trapped inside.

Despite an injured arm, shoulder, and spine, he used his head as a battering ram and forced the door open.

In Entebbe, Papa was asked to speak to the press, as well as the Kenyan aviation board. While in great pain, he gave a full account with details, including defending Roy Marsh, the first pilot. The next day, Papa was in pain but amused by his obituaries, reading headlines and chuckling as we spoke on the phone. The relief I felt when I heard his voice, strong across the wire, was like having a standing rhino finally lumber off of my chest. Whatever his injuries, Papa was alive, and anything else could be fixed, I guessed.

Papa had refused all but the most basic medical care, and we learned soon after that his lower intestine had collapsed, a kidney was damaged, he threw up constantly, and his vertebrae had been jammed so violently in the first crash that any movement caused extreme pain. His wounded head from the second accident was cracked and aching. Papa was in very bad shape, his stoicism masking the physical complications.

"Fleasy, I'm OK," he said when I reached him for the second time. "Was a little dicey there, I'll admit, but anything I have is a hundred percent fixable."

After talking to Patrick, who had flown to the scene of the accident, I did not feel so sanguine. I cleared it with my office and boarded a plane to Venice, Mary and Papa's next destination, to see his condition for myself.

Aaron Hotchner was already in Holland on other business, and after a quick conversation, we agreed to connect in Amsterdam and fly together to Venice. Aaron tried to calm me, regaling me with the funniest and craziest stories he'd heard about the disaster.

"Finn, the first call I got said Papa emerged from the jungle carrying a bunch of bananas and a bottle of gin, exclaiming 'My luck, she is running good.' Of course, that was before the second plane crash." I laughed because I could picture Papa doing that.

On the plane, Aaron kept all newspapers away from me. Every time I read another account, I became too nervous to sit, and paced the aisles like a border collie along a fence line.

46

"Fish," he said softly, aloud, "I'll stay with you until I am dead."

~ Ernest Hemingway, *The Old Man and the Sea*

When we arrived at the Gritti Palace Hotel in Venice, Papa was sitting by the window reading, a white tennis visor on his head. My hand flew to my mouth to stifle a cry. He looked a decade older and had to be twenty pounds lighter. His hair was mostly burned off and what was left was white. His beard looked even whiter, and he seemed unwell. But when Papa saw us, his face split into a wide grin. I pasted on a smile that must have looked cartoonish.

"Hotch, Flea! You're here. Flea! You didn't say you were coming, Daughter. And Hotch. Damn! You're a sight. Help me up." Aaron gripped Papa's arm and Papa struggled to his feet. He moved slowly and winced, clearly in pain. "I feel like the Creature from the Black Lagoon." He turned to Aaron. "I hope I didn't pull you away from your work."

Aaron smiled and said, "You probably saved me from a miserable fate in The Hague."

"Jaysus, The Hague. Even the name sounds dull. Thanks for coming, both of you. Welcome to *The Old Man and the Crash Landings*, my next short story; very short story." Papa reached for the back of a chair to steady himself and smiled as if to reassure us.

"Papa," Aaron said, "I'm sure as hell glad to see you on your feet. When I saw those obits blaring from the front page of every paper, I lost a little confidence in the viability of our future projects."

Papa chuckled and gestured to a table in the corner where a small Italian man was clipping articles. He looked up and waved. "Over there we have Obituary Central. Great morning reading. Krauts apparently think the crash was death wish fulfillment on my part. They apparently know something I don't about my wishes."

Papa lifted his shirt to show us his burns, cuts, and horrid scars. My eyes welled up and I moved in to give him the gentlest hug I could muster. His large paw dropped around my shoulder. "It's OK, Flea, my girl. I'm still here. I'm a hard man to kill, sweetheart. This was close, but no Cuban cigar yet."

He rested his head on my shoulder. He was still two inches taller than me. That used to feel like a lot with his massive upper body. Now it felt less significant. I swallowed my tears and stepped back.

"Not near your time yet, Papa." He got a funny look—a shadow catcher—then it cleared.

"Yup. But how are you, niña? How is Carter? Sorry to pull you away from your work. Gee, no one is Hemhating this week, figuring I need a break. I'm even back in Mary's good graces. Plus, when you almost die—twice—everything gets a new *punto de vista, verdad, hija!*" (Point of view, right, Daughter!)

"Sí, es verdad, Papito!" I replied. (Yes, that's true, Daddy!)

He pointed a finger at me and winked. My heart flooded with love. He turned to Aaron. "You know, I never wanted to get married. Once I did, I never wanted to be without a wife. And with kids, same thing. Never wanted any till I had one, and then never wanted to be without 'em. And when I had that one there," he was now shaking his finger at me, "I never wanted her to ever be far from me. Couldn't go on without my daughter."

Papa's eyes became misty, and he wiped them.

"Papa, sit down. Save your strength," I said, and he sat carefully in his large armchair. He filled his champagne glass, rested his head back on the chair, and closed his eyes.

I had to leave Europe sooner than I wanted to start a trial in New York. I was worried that Papa was continuing his trip to Spain, but he wouldn't hear of cutting it short.

Aaron gave me a full report over lunch when he was back in New York. "Papa was subdued. I think he hurts more than he wants us to know. The rest of the trip was a bit of a letdown except for seeing Ava Gardner in her hospital bed. Gallstone or something." He paused, brow furrowed, recalling it all. Then, he brightened. "Oh you'll like this, Finn. When she told him about her analyst and asked Papa how he'd survived without one all these years, he said, 'Portable Corona number three is my analyst.'"

I smiled at that. It was so typical of my father to view his writing as the best cure for depression or whatever ailed him. It had always been that way. When the work was going well, so was he. And despite his fame and infamy, he sometimes said things that made me think part of him was still that eighteen-year-old kid from Oak Park, Illinois, who had so much to say that he needed to start early to get it right and to say all of it.

47

Work could cure almost anything.

~ Ernest Hemingway, *A Moveable Feast*

Back in New York, Tess and I were delighted to spy signs of summer. I'd recently received a letter from Marty—my former stepmother, Martha Gellhorn—who was about to remarry an English journalist. It felt good to hear from her, especially since she sounded happy.

As for me, I'd just finished trying a wrongful death case in which the money awarded to my client was less than we hoped for but more than the offer, so I called it a win. Jeddrah just had her second child, a boy this time, named James—her maiden name—and I'd ridden in my first horse show in almost ten years.

For the past year, I'd ridden three times a week to get in shape, and Dancing Girl had evolved into a lovely hunter. I felt complete joy in saddling her up—Nicky's favorite—in picking out her feet, grooming her, and cooling her down. I didn't care if I got a ribbon or not. I was happy just to be there.

And I savored the deepening of my relationship with Carter. Intimacy and I were not always comfortable with each other, but I had begun to trust this new feeling of closeness with him. What I valued most was what a superb listener he was. He'd cock his head, ear moving closer, as if to fully hear me. If he were buttering a piece of bread, he'd lay the knife down and lean forward. If he were reading a newspaper he'd fold it, place it in his lap, and look at me. He'd absorb it all, then reframe it so everything became clearer.

One Friday morning in my apartment when I'd taken the morning off, we lingered in my little living room. I was painting my toenails. Carter was reading his paper before heading to his office. I began my questions.

"Carter, where do you think Jack should stay when he visits with his family?"

"Just put them up at the Ritz. Tell them it's on my tab in my favorite room."

"Carter, I need a dress for the Barrister's Ball. Where's the best place to look?"

"See Jonelle at Saks. She'll help you get the right thing."

"Carter, I feel burned out from work. Any ideas?"

He thought for a second. "Sure, kid. First, get a massage and get the kinks out. I'd try Jennifer at Elizabeth Arden on Fifth. Then take Tess and book a room at the Green Mountain Inn in Stowe, Vermont. I'll ship your horse up. Stay two weeks. Walk in the mountains. Eat good meals. Ride the trails. Forget the law firm. Forget the clients. Even—if you can—forget me." He smiled. "Read good books, but not your father's. Too sad. Too meaningful. Read about love and happy endings. I can suggest a few. You'll come back a new woman." Carter sat back on the sofa and looked at me quizzically. "You don't have to put up with this, you know, Finley."

I looked up from applying a supercharged vamp red to my left big toe. I stopped, admired the toe, and said, "Huh? Put up with what?"

"Me taking over. You throw out a question, and I take over." He shrugged. "It's what I do. I'm a vacuum-filler. I do it in business, and I can't help doing it whenever someone leaves the tiniest gap. You hesitate, and I swoop in to fix things."

He was sitting across from me in my tiny living room. While he lived in a fourteen-room apartment at the Dakota on Central Park, he liked my little place, too. He set down the paper and crossed his legs. "You don't have to let me do that, Finn. You don't need my help, although I'm always happy to give it. Just so you know, I know that you know that I know that you choose to *let* me step in and take over."

A wash of appreciation engulfed me. I walked over, red toes winking, and sank down on his lap, mussing his custom suit and Hermes tie. I wrapped my arms around his neck and gave him a deep kiss. "I know that you know that I know that you know I can make all of those choices. But sometimes, after a loaded week of endless decisions, I kind of like letting you take over. I like letting you fill the vacuum, Chick." Chick was my nickname for Carter because his initials were CK, and Carter was a really formal name.

When I'd first called him that, he'd said, "Finley, my mother picked a name that no one could shorten. She didn't want me to be Tommy, Jimmy, or Johnny. No one can shorten Carter. Now I'm Chick, huh? She'll be turning over in her grave." I knew he liked it though, because he always laughed and preened just a little when I used it.

I kissed him again. I started to get up, but Carter put both hands on my hips and held me for a minute. "Hey, I like you here. Just let me savor the moment."

I settled back down. In a minute, he loosened his grip. I kissed him a third time. Then I hopped up, grabbed myself another cup of coffee, and lay down on the sofa, reading an issue of *TIME*.

After a few minutes, without looking at him, I said, "So you think some country air is what I need to fix me up?"

"Finley, Finley." He lowered his newspaper, raising an eyebrow. "You don't need any fixing up. Just some relaxation with your own company. That's never a bad thing."

I smiled, went back to the magazine, and lowered it to my lap. "Hey, do you hate my hoof pick, Carter?"

"What hoof pick?" he asked.

"The one on my night table."

"The Nicky engagement hoof pick?"

"Yeah, that one," I said.

He paused, looked blank, then shook his head. "No, I don't mind it. Should I?"

"No, but does it bother you? You know, that I kept it all these years?"

Carter thought, then said, "Nope. It's part of your history. It's part of what made you . . . well, made you, you."

"Really?" I asked, sitting up straight, happy.

"Yeah, really." He stood up, straightened his tie, and looked at his watch. "I have a meeting in an hour, so I'd better get to my office. See you tonight, sweetheart."

When I waved, he turned and actually blew me a kiss. As he walked out the door, I sighed and had to admit I'd begun feeling a big blaze of that "in love" thing for Carter Kane.

"OK, Chick," I whispered after him.

***

The night after I returned from the Vermont trip, we had an early dinner before attending the opening of a musical called *Jazz Angels*. We ate our preshow dinner in a booth at Sardi's in the heart of the Theater District. I was still humming from the emotional high of my trip.

I didn't know how to tell Carter about the stillness of walking in woods so quiet that all I could hear were birds singing. Or of the freedom of galloping down dirt paths on Dancing Girl with no one else around. Or of the tang of fresh asparagus on top of salmon with just a squeeze of lemon. It was so simple. It was enough to build a life around.

Just as our drinks arrived, I noticed a group of four sliding into the booth behind us. The two women had on cocktail dresses, and the men wore blazers and slacks.

"Carter, it was amazing," I said. "You were right. I wasn't sure about going alone with just Tess, but each day, I felt clearer. We should go together sometime. Don't you want to go?" I asked, seizing a slice of bread and buttering it generously.

"I've been, and sure, I'd like to go again. But you needed it."

"Hmm, that makes me sound needy."

"Not at all. It's not needy to grow and learn. It's smart." He sipped his Manhattan.

"How come you're so smart, Chick?" I asked, tenting my arms on the table, chin resting on my hands.

Carter wiped his mouth with his white napkin. "I'm not. I just observe everything, and it's the difference between me being forty-six and you being twenty-nine. That's all. More life under my belt."

"Is it that simple?" I asked, sipping my glass of ginger ale.

"Yep, it's that simple, Miss Hemingway."

"What's your favorite meal—your all-time favorite?" I suddenly wondered.

Carter thought for a moment. "My mother's meatloaf. Simple and loaded with love."

In some ways, Carter Kane was a mystery to me. After all this time, I realized how little I knew about his childhood. I knew all about his businesses, his marriages, his children, but not much about his earlier years. It just hadn't seemed important.

"So, Carter, were you born with a silver spoon, or did you just acquire a taste for it as you climbed the ladder?"

As Carter cracked a lobster claw, he began laughing. He laughed so hard that he dropped the nutcracker. The claw flew across the table and landed on my plate next to my chicken parmigiana.

"I thought you might want to try my lobster, so there you go," he joked, wiping his fingers on a napkin. "Silver spoon. That's too funny, Finley. Did I not just say that my mother's meatloaf was my favorite meal? You don't eat meatloaf unless the meal has to stretch into three dinners and two lunches, sweetheart. No, I was born in New Haven, Connecticut. My mother, Kathleen, was single, and my father was gone before I was born. My grandmother generally referred to me as 'Carter, Kathleen's little bastard.' Thought it was part of my name until I was five. Then she'd go on about my name. 'You couldn't name him Bill, like a normal person. Always have to be different. What the hell kind of name is Carter? Fine mess you've made of it all, Kathleen, you and your little bastard.'"

I was horrified. "That's terrible!"

Carter shrugged. "Mom didn't care, so I didn't either. She sewed in a factory, making ties to support us. A silver spoon never saw my lips, kid. We had nothing. But she made that meatloaf once a month—that's all we could afford—and she would mix it with so much care, adding breadcrumbs to stretch it. I didn't think of us as poor because she and I had such a good time together that she never made it seem like we were."

"If I could cook, I'd make it for you." I could scramble eggs, and that was about it.

He laughed. "Now *that* I would view as a sign of undying love—you in the kitchen making a meal just because I love it. Be still my heart!"

In that moment, I vowed to learn how to cook. "So how did you get to Yale and Columbia Business School?" I asked between bites of caprese salad. I handed his claw back to him, then cut a piece of my chicken, speared it with a fork, and held it up for him to try.

He leaned forward and ate it. "Good. That's good." He continued his story. "I happen to have been blessed with a decent brain, a funny bone, and good reflexes, so I became a triple threat. I had top grades. Kids liked me because I made them laugh. And I played football like I'd been born with a pigskin in my hands coming out the chute."

"Graphic. I like it." Now I was laughing.

"I got into Yale, right in my backyard, except it was on the right side of the tracks. I'd always lived on the wrong side. We couldn't afford Yale, but I got a scholarship for tuition and lived at home, saving us room and board. Worked at a men's clothing store for books and spending money. I did learn how to buy a good suit, however; always select quality over quantity. Remember that, Finley. Still, I could barely afford to get a lunch in Mory's, the Yale men's club. One drunken October night after a big football victory, one of my well-heeled buddies treated me to dinner there, so I did manage to carve my initials in a table. It's a tradition at Mory's. You're supposed to do that. Check it out next time you're in New Haven. It's still there. First table on the left as you go in. Take a look."

"I will next time I'm in New Haven," I said.

He continued. "So by my third year, I got a full scholarship. The football coach thought my job was interfering with our Saturday games, and Yale does so hate to lose to Harvard, or worse yet, to Army. I lettered in football and graduated magna cum laude. My roommate's father headed a division of Sikorsky Aircraft. He liked me. Thought I had a head for business. He knew I also made side money making book on college sports, except any games I was in. He said, 'We could use someone like you, Carter.'"

I laughed and grabbed more bread.

"I applied to his alma mater, Columbia Business School, and the rest is history. Started when I was twenty-seven with one little company that I turned around, then another, then I did my first merger, and then another." Carter sipped his wine.

"Did it feel good to do that, to make all that money?" I asked.

Carter cocked his head. "Money was the least of it. I was independently wealthy by the time I was thirty-five, but what felt good was providing jobs. My mother died five years ago. With all my money, I couldn't save her from the cancer that killed her. She always told me she was proudest of the fact that I gave people work, and that I hired women for jobs women never had before. Women never did more than type in these companies, but if I saw talent, that woman went somewhere, and for equal pay, too."

I put my fork down and rested my head on my hand, elbow on the table. "And that's one of the reasons I love you so much."

Carter's eyes opened wide. "You never said that to me before, Finn."

"What?"

"That you love me."

"I thought you knew."

"Maybe, but it's nice to hear."

I smiled. "Then I'll have to say it more often."

As I finished my chicken and Carter his lobster, we chatted about the musical. Rodgers and Hammerstein, so successful with *Oklahoma!* ten years earlier, had collaborated on this one too, hoping to duplicate its success. Carter glanced at his watch.

"We'd better get going, Finn. The show starts soon."

As we waited for the check, I couldn't help overhearing the conversation behind us.

One of the men said, "He may still be alive, but he's done. Everything after *For Whom the Bell Tolls* was a disaster."

"And my God, his women are awful. They're either pandering doormats or sleazy sluts. He couldn't write a woman if his career depended on it. His daughter is probably a pathetic tramp if she's anything like his heroines," added one of the women. Laughter bubbled from the four.

"Now wait a second," said the other woman. "Elena—the woman in that 'drop of wine' book, was really good. She felt... oh, I don't know... like someone we'd know. Someone full of dreams, kicked by life but still willing to keep trying. I loved that book and the woman. I think he can write women when he lets go of that he-man stuff."

"I think his wife must have written that one. It was so different. I loved it too," joked the other woman, and everyone laughed.

"Kids actually are all messed up. One son a queer, or worse. The other some big game animal killer. Who knows about the other two? Probably more messes, especially the girl."

Carter's jaw had set and he wadded his napkin into a clump. He was about to go over to the table. I held up my hand. "Let me."

He thought a second, then nodded. I stood slowly, my red, wavy hair hanging loosely to my shoulders and my long, golden gown falling into pleats as I slid out of the booth. I turned to the other table and just stood, five foot ten, plus two-inch heels. The foursome looked up.

"Excuse me. I couldn't help overhearing your conversation. You may think you know Hemingway, but you're wrong. He's shy, kind, and writing every day. You don't have to like his work, of course. But please, it's a bit unfair to assassinate him and his family personally when you don't really know them."

The bigger guy puffed up. "Young lady, I've read a lot about him and his family, and it seems to me that he's a drunken, self-centered has-been, and the family's a bunch of misfits."

I stood taller. "I don't know what you've read, sir, but I doubt that you've spent days with him or his friends and family. It feels like you're just slandering based on innuendo you saw in some gossip column. And to talk about his kids? It seems kind of mean, sir."

The smaller of the two men lifted his chin. "Jesus, lady, who *are* you? The free speech police?"

I flipped the end of my turquoise shawl over my shoulder and looked down at him. "Here's who I am. I'm a lawyer at Sloane White. I graduated magna cum laude from Smith College. I play a solid game of polo on my own horse. I pay taxes and am *not* a mess, nor a pathetic tramp," I said, looking at one of the women. I turned away, then pivoted back, "Oh, and I'm Hemingway's daughter."

All four jaws dropped, and one of the women started to sputter. "We didn't know . . . didn't mean to suggest . . ."

The big guy started, "I'm sorry. I was just having some fun."

I held up my hand to stop them. "I understand. No need to apologize. I just thought you should know."

I spun around and strode out, dress billowing behind me, head high. Carter tossed some bills on our table, tipped his fedora to them and smiled. He followed me out in the wake of my Fracas perfume.

48

I've seen you, beauty, and you belong to me now, whoever you are waiting for and if I never see you again, I thought. You belong to me and all Paris belongs to me and I belong to this notebook and this pencil.

~ Ernest Hemingway, *A Moveable Feast*

I spent two weeks at the end of that summer in Cuba. Carter came down for a week on his way to Argentina for business. He and Papa had sized each other up like two alpha dogs circling and sniffing, then sat on the terrace with cigars, a bottle of whiskey between them, telling each other war stories—in their case, literal war stories—and laughing like madmen.

When he left, Carter said to me, "Big shadow, but not a smothering one. It still permits growth. You just have to wiggle around a bit to find your own light." He smiled. "I love you, kid. See you in two weeks."

We kissed on the Finca steps. "I love you, too, Chick," I said. He ran for his taxi, and I walked back to the pool.

Papa was sitting in a beach chair, legs crossed, sipping his coffee as he read the newspaper. Without looking up, he said, "Hmm. So, my potential son-in-law is going to be like the brother I never had?" He looked up and laughed. "Oh wait, I do have a brother, now that I think of it, but like I said . . ." He was not close to his brother, Leicester. His voice trailed off, but he was smiling.

I stared, expectant. "So? What do you think?"

Papa took off his glasses. "Just seven years younger than I am, but I like him, Flea. I like him because you are his top priority. I'd still be married to an earlier wife if I'd done that."

I beamed, feeling warm and happy. "But would there have been *The Sun, Farewell, Bell Tolls,* and *Old Man*, Papa? And especially *A Single Drop?* If one thing is changed, all of the rest might change too."

Papa chuckled. "You sure know how to give a guy perspective, Flea."

"It can't be easy being a good father and husband as well as a world-class observer of the human condition."

That made him laugh hard. "That sounds so grand and elitist, Flea. All I do is put words together. Some days I succeed, and some days it's like drilling rock and trying to blast the good stuff out." He was silent for a moment. "And as you know, I was very far from a perfect father, and I was a downright lousy husband except in some rare flashes of decency. It's like there is only so much . . ." He paused, trying to grasp a word. "Only so much *chispa* . . . spark, juice, you know, to draw on, and whatever I had went into my work, not my wives." He shrugged, then laughed to lighten the air around us. "Poor excuse, but true."

Papa and Mary had been back from Europe for only a few weeks and were thrilled that Negrita and Boise had survived their absence. Black Dog had made it too, but all three seemed wobbly, as if they were held together by thread, like they'd hung on just long enough to see the master one more time.

Sometimes, I'd see my father stretch to pick up Boise and flinch as sweat broke out on his face. He'd say nothing, but would take a moment to cope. The pain was intense.

"Papa, can't the doctors do anything?" I'd asked in frustration.

"Not really, honey. A drink helps the head and the back, but I can't take a drink every time it hurts, or I couldn't write. Writing is the only thing that makes me feel like I'm not wasting my time, not just taking up space."

Then the Nobel Prize rushed in like a late prom date—so darned pretty, you overlooked her lateness. After all of the negative critics, Papa was really pleased. He couldn't make it to Stockholm due to his lingering injuries. He'd always been shy and eschewed public speeches and tuxedos, so I think he may have been glad to have an excuse to stay home.

"Wearing underwear is as formal as I get," he said. "Don't want to fly to Sweden and put on the whole getup."

Of the scores of telegrams from well-wishers, he was especially touched by two that he always kept in his top desk drawer. Each was creased from folding and unfolding. Ingrid Bergman wrote, "THE SWEDES AREN'T SO DUMB AFTER ALL," and Jackson Armstrong wrote, "Congratulations, Mr. Hemingway. I must say that of all your fine works, *A Single Drop of Red Wine*—Elena and Jonathan—are in my heart and my wife's heart always because . . . well, you know why. Thank you for that." I knew Papa was honored by all of it, but he never felt he'd done enough. To him, time was always the prize eluding him.

***

In the fall of 1955, Carter Kane asked me to marry him. We were walking in Central Park, the trees various hues of red, orange, and yellow. Paths were teeming with people walking dogs and riding bikes as vendors hawked chestnuts on corners. Carter and I shuffled through colorful leaves in the crisp air.

Carter sat me on a bench, then abruptly went down on a knee in his custom-tailored gray suit. He said, "Finn, I'm not the most romantic guy in the world, and I didn't get your father's permission, because I think that's bullshit. You're thirty years old, and you know what you want. Marry me, Finn. I love you to hell and back."

I stared, shocked. I thought Carter was content with our unconventional but committed relationship of best friends and lovers with no next step. I loved his son, Mickey, and we all spent time together with no expectations—or so I thought.

"I've got some wear, but I'm durable. I will never hurt you, and I will always back you on what's important to you." He spoke deliberately. "You're the only one for me, Finn."

People were casting backward glances at us as they passed. Most smiled and nodded, clear that an engagement was in progress. Carter went on. His voice now had an urgency. "Say yes, Finn. Please say yes, for God's sake."

I paused, then said slowly, "I don't want to marry anyone, Carter. If I did, I would marry you in a split second and only you, but I just don't want to belong to someone else."

Carter's face clouded. He lurched up and collapsed on the bench next to me. He studied his hands and was quiet for a minute. "So I guess I shouldn't pull out the five-karat diamond I picked up at Tiffany's? We're not going to end this with a kiss and plans for our honeymoon?"

I smiled a little. "Guess not." I gave him a light kiss on the cheek but he was turned away. "Carter, I love you, but marriage—I don't think it's for me; the Hemingway jinx and all."

Carter shook his head. "It only has the power you give it. And by the way, I'd never see you as belonging to me. Slavery was abolished about a hundred years ago, as I recall." Carter sighed. "And, by the way, I would be very happy belonging to you, Finley." He shook his head again and his eyes looked sad. We sat for a few minutes and then Carter stood. "I think I could use a walk by myself, Finn. Would you excuse me, please?"

***

"So tell me again why you said no to marrying one of the most wonderful men on earth?" Jeddrah said. "I know you love him."

Just before Christmas—a couple of months after Carter's marriage proposal—Jeddrah and I were ice skating in Rockefeller Center. Ellen and James were with a sitter, and we glided around in our full wool skirts, tights, and bright berets, feeling like two college girls again.

I slipped, and Jedd grabbed for me. We both went down, laughing. Children whisked by us. We got up, wobbly, and continued.

"I do love him, but I just know I'll ruin it. I'd rather remember it this way as long as possible rather than risk a bad end."

Jeddrah thought for a second. "You're just afraid. Look, Robert isn't perfect, but he said just before his trip that he understands my work is as important to me as his is to him. He's trying. You're afraid to try because it might not work out."

I spun around and began to skate backward, facing her. "Darned right I am. Fear's what's kept the human race alive. Survival of the scaredest!"

"Cynic."

"Cockeyed optimist." We laughed, then I quieted as my eyes slid to a skater picking up her little girl who'd just fallen. Our eyes met. It was Prill Lamont. Jedd saw her exactly when I did. "Let's go, Finn. I'm suddenly cold."

I nodded but stared, haunted by the last time I'd seen her. I was still at Getty, Chatsworth, and Humph Reed assigned me to AJ Packer for a few days while he was away. AJ in turn had ordered me to help his wife—Prill—one morning. I hated the idea, but needed my job. When I arrived at their tidy brownstone—but not a grand one—on the Upper East Side, I plastered on a neutral look and rapped the brass lion doorknocker.

The brownstone's door opened slowly and standing there, one hand on the doorknob and one holding a cigarette, was Prill Lamont Packer with a smirk on her still pretty face. She was not a waif anymore, having put on about twenty-five pounds, but she was wearing a look of triumph.

"Well, if it isn't my old friend, Finn Hemingway, or should I say Lee. And to think you're working for my husband after all of your education and airs. Even Daddy couldn't get you a job? Or a husband?"

I stood silent. She turned and strolled to the kitchen where a little girl of about three, a mini-Prill, stood peeking out. I could see a little boy about nine months old propped in a high chair, chewing and dribbling carrot baby food on his white bib, which was speckled with remnants.

I followed Prill like a monstrous geisha. The dread I felt was so reminiscent of the awkward girl I was at Ellsworth that I shivered involuntarily. In the kitchen, Prill leaned against the sink, studying me openly. "Still the strong, silent type, are you, Finn?" She paused, then said, "Just watch the children and make the dinner menu for Inez, the cook. Tell her not so much bread." She added under her breath, "God knows, AJ hates this added weight on me."

She eyed the wall clock. "It's already ten o'clock?" She reached up to grab a hat, and her short sweater rose on one side to expose a black-and-blue bruise the size of a baseball. She saw my gaze and quickly lowered her arm and tugged on the hem but in so doing her hair swung out, exposing a fading purple shiner high on her cheek. She quickly pulled it forward again. Self-consciously, she said, "Fell in the park playing with Evie. Let's go." Prill yanked the girl's arm and Evie began to scream.

Prill pulled a chocolate from her purse, tore the paper off, and held it out. Evie popped it into her mouth, quieting immediately. Prill turned to me as she dashed out. "Get Henry and his bag. All the good ones will be gone!"

We went to Harlem, where Negro women milled about hoping to be hired for day work. It was a sad spectacle, and Prill hired a young woman very cheaply for the day to assist with her housework. When we returned to her brownstone, the young woman showed up and Prill turned to me. "I'm leaving for lunch. Put the children down for naps and Cook will take over from there. My husband said you're needed back by two." She pulled on long gloves. "And don't get any ideas about him. I know how you use your wiles to get what you want from men."

I was too startled to speak. The thought of me as some sort of femme fatale was laughable enough, but the thought of AJ Packer as an object of my desire was so repulsive that I grimaced involuntarily.

Prill noticed and screeched, nostrils flaring like a dragon, "Don't give me that look, you... you hussy! As if you wouldn't try! You forget, I know you! Just stay away from him."

I caught my breath, then exploded. "I wouldn't touch your lecher of a husband if he were the only man left in New York City, so sleep very well at night knowing he's all yours. Oh, a little suggestion; be careful of that left hook of his. Hate to mess up that pretty face of yours."

A stricken look darted across Prill's face as quick as the flick of a hummingbird's wings. I was pained knowing I'd gone too far. Prill turned away. I looked down and wrapped my arms around myself. "I'm sorry."

Then Prill said softly, her back still to me, "Please leave. I'm sorry I tormented you at Ellsworth. Jeddrah too." She made a half-turn toward me, still looking down, her hands trembling. She shoved them into the pockets of her coat. She continued, as if talking to herself now. "If I'd only had half your confidence and that . . . core of steel that you had . . . *You had everything.* A mother always sending packages; a famous father; a best friend who would give her life for you; the respect of all of the other girls; a look all your own, like no one else . . . and Nicholas." She turned and walked to the front door, then turned back as she opened it. This time, she did look at me. "I can't stand the sight of you. You remind me of how it all could have been different—for me. Goodbye, Tess. I pray I never see you again." She stepped out and closed the door behind her.

I was so stunned that I leaned against the wall, fearing my knees might not hold me. I moved to the sofa and sat motionless until Evie came in and offered me a bite of her sandwich. *An apology from Prill. Jealous of me at prep school?* She called me Tess, like Nicky. She'd heard him that day at the polo match in Newport. I was unnerved by her words and never forgot them.

That day in Rockefeller Center, I hesitated, then gave her a small wave. She nodded and returned a similarly small acknowledgement of what once had seemed so full of importance.

***

Christmas at the Finca was quiet, with just me there that year. Patrick was in Africa, and Gig was distant. He'd started living life as a woman, which was viewed as very deviant and not something my father could deal with easily. Jack was planning a move to Havana to work for Merrill Lynch there.

I told Papa about Carter's proposal as we strolled around the property. "I never guessed he wanted more."

"Everyone wants more, Flea, but I trust your judgment. Still, Carter is a good man, and I'd love to see you settled with a good man. What did Jeddrah say?"

"She said if not Carter, then there will never be anyone. She thinks he understands me, and if I can't marry him, I can't marry anyone."

Papa nodded. "She may be right. But just remember, don't give up on someone you can't go a day without thinking of. Do you think of him every day?"

"Gosh, Papa, I think of him dozens of times a day." *And I think of you scores of times a day.*

He nodded as if satisfied. As we walked, I keenly felt the loss of Negrita. We all did. She'd been buried near the pool under a giant ficus tree where she'd frolicked for years with Black Dog. Papa had rescued her from the slums of Havana, and she had repaid him by becoming a confidante and the Finca court jester, as needed, breaking tense moments with her funny tail chasings and tricks. Papa erected a headstone that just said NEGRITA.

There was a touch of melancholy during that trip as Papa held Boise, now frail. Loyal Blackie was resting at Papa's feet.

Anytime Papa spoke, the spaniel's tail wagged and he'd lift his head to be sure he didn't miss anything Papa did.

After dinner, Papa and I sat in the living room after Mary had gone to bed. He was in his usual shorts. I'd kicked off my loafers and slouched all five feet ten of me in a club chair, legs slung across an arm. I sipped my coffee, blowing on it to cool it. "So do you think I should have said yes to Carter, Papa?"

"Flea, you're asking the opinion of someone who's had every one of his love stories end in death or disaster. You're asking someone who's been married to four women and who got it right the first time but had to ruin that single-handedly. And you're asking someone who still needs fresh love to feel alive. In short, you're asking the wrong man. Use your judgment, sweetheart, and stand by it."

I sat silent for a few minutes, just enjoying his proximity. Then I spoke up. "I think you got it right in *A Single Drop of Red Wine,* Papa. I think Elena and Jonathan lived happily ever after too. I mean, didn't they?" He just smiled. I persevered, now with some urgency. "Didn't they, Papa? I have to know." I really did, as if the answer would explain so much.

"Now why do you think I know how it turned out, *hija mia?*" he asked, eyebrow raised, amused.

I gave him a sidelong look. "Well, you wrote it. It's in your head. *Only* you know."

"Ah, but once written, I let my creations go and you, the reader, add to the story and you decide."

"Oh come on, Papa. How do you think it ends? Tell me."

"I'm a hopeful guy, Flea. So take that for what it's worth." He laughed hard, and I joined in, since he wrote some of the most tragic endings of all time.

I sighed. "Oh for gosh sakes! Thanks a lot! You can be maddening, Papa." He smiled like a male Mona Lisa.

"Well, won't you at least say something about me and Carter? You know me better than anyone else. Do you think he'd be good for me?"

"Never mistake motion for action, kid. If you want to stay still, then stay still until it feels right. Only you know if he's good for you. From what I see, he's not bad for you."

"What about Logan? Should I have done all I could to have made it work with him?" Logan and I actually did become friends after his marriage. He still had Arc and Sara's Silence. His little daughter loved riding Sara, who was now as gentle as a sweet beagle.

"Maybe. Maybe not, although I do love an Idaho man, and it'd be nice to have a doctor in the family. I'm falling apart, and Mary's not far behind. Now we just need a family vet and we'll be self-sufficient. Any vets ask you to marry them last year? Or this year? I'm flexible on timing."

I clucked my tongue in exasperation but laughed at how good he was at the dodge, duck, and weave. "You're not going to answer, are you?"

Papa took a sip of his drink. He smiled at me, a beautiful, loving smile. "I trust you, Daughter, to manage your own fate. I would trust you with mine, but would never burden you with that one."

He winked and refilled his glass with champagne. We talked about Cuba's deteriorating political situation. So far, both sides—Castro and Batista—had left Papa alone. Rumors were spreading though that Castro intended to seize all land if he came to power. I saw signs everywhere blaring, "Cuba Sí, Yanqui No." We toasted in the New Year, 1956.

49

Never go on trips with anyone you do not love.

~ Ernest Hemingway, *A Moveable Feast*

"Finn, I need to go to Paris for a year. I'm consolidating three of my European companies, and I can't do it from here."

Carter announced this news over dinner at The Manhattan Brasserie. I felt a tremor of alarm. He'd never mentioned the possibility. My eyes shifted, and my gaze locked with his.

"I tried to send my top man to manage things, but there are decisions daily that only I can make. So, it just has to be done. Mickey is coming for the year, which will be good for him, I think." Carter studied his hands and, for the first time since I'd known him, he seemed evasive.

I nodded, stifling a cry of despair. "Yes, yes, of course. Good plan. I'm sure he'll get a lot out of it."

Carter's face looked strained, his jaw tight. I studied it to see if there was a joke here, a spark that said, *Just kidding! I'd never leave you, kid.* There was none, just a lifeless numbness.

After my decision a year ago not to marry him, the discomfort of the moment receded. We continued to be together daily, to travel together, and to make plans together. I didn't see this coming, but should have. Despite pretending all was the same after the marriage proposal, it wasn't. My rejection was always there under the surface. Carter had enough self-esteem to not be wounded mortally, but he felt it.

And I knew absence would not make the heart grow fonder. It created a chasm that made it easy for someone new and glittery to swoop in and be all I was not. I felt abandoned, but knew it was my own doing.

I eyed him, filet of sole abandoned, voice dripping with torment. "Oh, Chick."

He tilted his head, eyes sad. "I'd ask you to come with me, but I know you wouldn't."

He was right, but I wished he weren't. I wished I had the optimism to just throw in my lot with him. "I . . . I want to, but my work . . ."

"You don't have to justify it. And maybe it's a good time to evaluate the future. Gives us both some room. I don't need promises, Finn, or guarantees. But I . . ." He shrugged. "I guess I just need more. This will give both of us space to think."

I dropped my fork and it clattered to the floor. I bent to grab it, my hand shaking, but Carter put a hand on my wrist.

"Just leave it, sweetheart. Look at me."

I straightened and looked into his eyes; a little tired, very kind. I relaxed just looking at him, and my shoulders lowered.

I whispered, "Is this the end, Chick?"

Carter gently brushed back my hair and touched my cheek. "I don't know." He took a sip of water. "You know, I was thinking the other night that when I die, I don't want my obituary to say he left behind his good friend, Finley

Hemingway. I'm not afraid of being alone, but I'd rather have someone trotting down this crazy path of life with me. I guess I do want a wife, not to complete me or any of that bullshit, but to say to the world, 'We are in this together to the end, whatever happens. We have the conviction about the rightness of us to make that declaration to the world.'"

I nodded, but my face crumbled into pieces, starting with my mouth twisting and eyes blinking fast. "I understand, but it hurts like hell, Chick."

Carter took both of my hands. "Don't cry, sweetheart. Time is just time. We'll see after a year."

But I knew that a man like Carter Kane in European business circles on his own would be wooed by lovely, quality women more than eager to make that declaration to the world that I seemed incapable of. *Why couldn't I just tell him yes?* I didn't know, but I couldn't.

I held onto his hands tightly. "Promise me you'll never forget me because, if I thought you would, I'd never let you leave."

Carter lifted one hand and kissed it. Then he smoothed my hair. "For sure, Christopher Robin. I'll never forget you, not for a second."

I couldn't bear any more of this goodbye. I knew as surely as I knew that Nicky was my first love that Carter was my last love. "I have to go," I said, stumbling as I shoved my chair back. It toppled. I bent to right it and grabbed my jacket from the floor. I held the table edge to steady myself.

Carter rose, but didn't try to stop me. "Cab?"

I shook my head. "Thank you, but I'd like to walk." I stepped out into the street alone.

***

I filled my time with work, generally litigation. The firm was adding new lawyers to the litigation department at a rapid pace, and I was in charge of training. The new associates shadowed me and then were given cases to co-counsel with me. There were no women out of the four trainees. My "big" case that year was defending my father against a libel lawsuit. A woman, claiming she was the model for Lady Brett Ashley, sued Papa for defamation and libel.

"What the hell! That was Duff all the way! Jeesus! Duff never complained. She was proud of it. Dammit to hell, I don't have time to deal with this shit. Flea, fix it, would you?"

Flea, fix it? "Papa, I'm not a consigliere. Everyone has a right to file claims, even weak ones." I wasn't keen on Papa's legal defense being, "It wasn't you, madam. I lifted the character of Brett totally from someone else and defamed *her*, not you."

Lady Duff Twysden, the actual model for Lady Brett Ashley, had died many years earlier, and this suit was as stale as they come. However, the woman in question was in the Paris social set of the time, and there were parallels. When I finally got the suit dismissed a year later, after Papa was forced to take a two-day deposition and attend court for a week in Manhattan, he was so thrilled that he took all partners at Sloane White to Toots Shor's and crowed, "That's my daughter! The one over there. Brilliant and beautiful! Spared me the gallows. Isn't she something? Drink up!" He bought rounds of drinks and held his own court in the bar into the wee hours, with the Sloane White partners reveling in Papa's stories.

Jeddrah, too, was working long hours as more and more young children showed up with symptoms of polio. Parents were panicked, and many kept their children at home for fear of its spread. Even at that, the number of cases grew exponentially.

Carter wrote sporadically and called occasionally. I tried not to think about how he spent his free time, but the nights were hard. Since Mickey was with him, he chose not to return to New York for Christmas. His grown children visited him in Paris in the fall, and it was almost a year that he'd been gone now. I contemplated a trip there myself but felt that we had nothing to say until we had a plan. But I wondered recently if I had it backwards; maybe we needed to talk to hatch a plan.

As for my father, I'd become worried about him, too. After he returned to Cuba following our legal victory, he sometimes seemed confused when I phoned. He had always fretted about the IRS, although he was in solid financial shape. Now he seemed to fear the tax collectors obsessively and, per Mary, was starting more and more days with a tumbler of vodka. He'd also become paranoid about talking on the phone.

"Flea," he'd say, "we shouldn't discuss this over the phone. When you come down, we'll talk about it."

It was odd and disturbing. He was now doing almost all of his writing standing up due to the back pain that lingered from the plane crashes. He found it harder and harder to do his own first-cut editing as he'd always done in the past. Adding to

Papa's disorientation and darkening moods were the deaths of his two stalwart companions, Boise and Black Dog.

He told me, "I miss Boise like hell. Always on my lap, took a walk like a dog. Damned if getting old isn't overrated. I'd give my Ignoble Prize to have him back."

Even worse, though, was the sudden death of Black Dog. When Batista's soldiers initiated a weapons search and Black Dog acted protectively they'd killed him, which sent Papa into a deep despair. The beloved dog was buried beside Negrita with a matching headstone that just said BLACK. Usually resilient despite "black ass," Papa was unable to shake this one. When I visited that summer, he tried to pretend he was OK, but couldn't pull it off.

As we sat around the dinner table, he was remote, and in the middle of a discussion about Mouse/Patrick in Africa, he looked away and said, "Me, I'd trade all the honors in the world for two good bottles of Claret a day and to have my Black Dog back again. I miss Black as much as I've ever missed any friend."

Tears were rolling down his face and I started to cry too. Mary looked stricken and helpless. I went over to hug my father as we both broke down.

Then, just a few months later, Papa called, sounding tired when he told me he and Mary were thinking of leaving the Finca, his sanctuary of almost twenty years. He'd sighed heavily. "I love Cuba, Flea. And maybe Castro will leave us alone because I'm good publicity. But I'm an American, and I can't stay when other Americans are forced out. It's the end of something, Flea."

Papa sounded defeated, and I wondered if he purposely quoted the title of one of his grimmest and most realistic short stories, "The End of Something." For the first time, I felt frightened for Papa and what was ahead.

I felt the loss of all of it and dreamed of Carter Kane coming home to me, because I missed him like a pole-vaulter misses a leg. The gusto of life was extinguished.

50

If you are lucky enough to have lived in Paris as a young man, then wherever you go for the rest of your life, it stays with you, for Paris is a moveable feast.

~ Ernest Hemingway, *A Moveable Feast*

The plane landed at Orly Airport on the outskirts of Paris with a jolt, then a jab, and then a thud. I seized my bag and, violating airline protocol, shot down the aisle to deplane before anyone else was even on their feet, a slip of paper in my pocket with Carter's home and office information.

I was weary after the overnight flight, but adrenalin raced through me. Three nights before, I'd dreamed I was in some unnamed country, but it felt like Ireland. Something about the green, rocky hills and rough sea felt like the photos I'd seen of County Kerry. Everywhere I wandered, I smelled sweet pipe tobacco and spied piles of jagged teapot pieces and tweedy woolen sweaters, even in the middle of fields.

At first I heard the strains of cheerful stringed music and I began to dance, grabbing a maypole ribbon, where I went around until I was dizzy. Then it all shifted to a dirge of droning uillean pipes and wheezing accordions. I collapsed in a heap and saw Carter's face come into view. I reached out, exclaiming, but he sidestepped behind a curtain. I laughed and chased him, but as I got close and pushed aside veils of fabric attached to nothing, he was nowhere.

I kept separating layers of gauze to find nothing behind them except more veils. Then Carter's face sharpened out of a fog. I smiled and arched forward to embrace him, but he disappeared again. Finally, I saw my father's face. He turned to wink at me as he always did when we shared a prank, and then he too faded as I ran toward him.

I woke in a sweat, just knowing: love and goodness offered up to you generously with no expectation of payment was a miracle, a golden gift. It was a sin to spurn it, a crying shame to squander it. I had to fix this, if it wasn't already too late. In ten minutes, I had a one-way ticket to Paris.

I emerged through double glass doors at Orly at 8:00 a.m. and hailed a cab, leaning out almost into the road to be sure I snagged one. I'd already tried Carter's home phone, and there was no answer. I tried his office and spoke to his secretary, using my rusty but still decent French.

"Ah, Mademoiselle Hemingway. Monsieur Kane est occupé maintenant." *Mr. Kane is busy now.*

"Ah bien. Merci," I said, spirits plummeting. I tried again at noon, with the same answer. I spent the day in my hotel room, then tried his home phone again at six. Again, no answer. I hadn't left my hotel name or number, so he couldn't call me even if he wanted to.

Impatience growing by the minute, I threw on my coat and walked briskly to his home address. I glanced at my watch—7:00 p.m.—and decided I'd sit on his doorstep until he returned if I had to. As I approached, I halted in my tracks and ducked like a fugitive into a doorway, peering around its corner. There was Carter, walking with a lovely brunette woman, their heads bent together, whispering, then laughing, as if sharing a private joke. They went into his apartment building together, and I stepped out into the raw wind.

***

The next morning, I got up at 4:00 a.m., sandy-eyed and unrested. I called the airport for a flight back to New York on Saturday, two days from now. I sat at the desk in my hotel room, chewing the end of a pen. I started a sentence ten times only to crumple the page, toss it in the vicinity of a wastebasket, and begin again. I wondered how my father did it; put his deepest beliefs down on paper, using the simplest words possible, all to maximum impact and optimal comprehension, day after day. Clearly, I did not inherit his talent.

I paced, and when it was light enough, I opened the French doors and collapsed onto the balcony lounge, a blanket wrapped around me. I stared at the dawn Paris skyline, its rooftops and its soaring spires. I wanted the city to swallow me. What I thought was here, wasn't. I thought about what I truly needed Carter to know, no matter the outcome. It took hours. I wrote—and rewrote. Finally, it was as good as I could make it.

> *Darling:*
>
> *My father once told me not to give up on someone I can't go a day without thinking of. Since the day you told me you loved me, I haven't gone an hour, much less a day, without thinking of you. You are the last person I want to talk to as the sun sets, and the first one I want*

to talk to when it comes up again. When you are away, I long for your return, and the only thing that makes it tolerable is that I know—well, I used to know—for certain you would be back.

I am so adrift now, Chick, I don't know how to find my mooring. My father was 100 percent reliable—60 percent of the time. And I hated that, and thought that's what love was: something to keep you off-balance, perpetually longing, never satisfied, always unfulfilled—and I never wanted that. But then you shoveled all of that thinking into a ditch and covered it for good. Your love was constant, without conditions, and it was my armor, my cloak in a chilly world. You are the riskiest, most certain thing I've ever known, darling. Choose me again. Please choose me again. You and me. It's that simple. The rest is details.

With immeasurable love, Finn

I folded it and placed it in an envelope. I tucked it into my purse, then whipped out the door. In ten minutes, at precisely 7:30 a.m., I was at Carter's office, ready to wait until he arrived.

To my surprise, his office was already buzzing. Phones were ringing. Secretaries were typing. Workers were striding through the halls with files. I stepped up to the receptionist's desk. She looked up at me with soft, brown eyes. I said, "Monsieur Kane, s'il vous plait. Je suis son amie des Etats-Unis. Je m'appelle Finley Hemingway."

"Ah, mademoiselle, may I practice my English?" I nodded. "Monsieur Kane is in a meeting. I do not expect it to end for a few hours. I am so sorry, Mademoiselle Hemingway." She pointed to a closed door.

My frustration was at a fever pitch. I had to know now. I gave a little cry and rushed toward the door, grabbing the handle and flinging it open. I stopped. Carter was standing in the front of the room, his back to me as he wrote some numbers on a blackboard. Twelve sets of eyes turned to stare at me. The set closest to him were those of the woman I'd seen him with last night. Her hazel eyes stared from a perfect, oval face. Her dark hair was in a low chignon.

My eyes moved down the table. Some eyes looked curious, others startled, others amused. I turned to look at Carter, who still had his back to us. Hearing the door, he turned and saw me, chalk poised in midair. He stared, his face blank. I'd envisioned a huge smile and, in my wilder dreams, something like, "At last, you've come for me, Finn. About time, sweetheart."

Instead, he stood paralyzed, a look of shock on his face. Then his face relaxed a bit and his arm dropped to his side. He raised both eyebrows in question, and said, "Well, everyone, this is a friend from the States, Finley Hemingway. Finn, this is . . . everybody."

He gestured around the table, then rubbed his forehead. "Um, Finn. I have some business here to finish. May I help you?" *Carter, ever the gentleman.*

The man closest to me smiled warmly and said, "Ah, it is not enough that you Americans have meetings at seven a.m.—

a desperately uncivilized time of the day, I must say—but now, Carter, you are turning away the most interesting thing to happen in this room in years. Bonjour, mademoiselle." He pronounced "Carter" as "Cartère." He looked questioningly at Carter. "Shall I pull up a chair for mademoiselle?"

I now froze like a statue in the Rodin sculpture garden. I stammered, "Oh, I didn't think this would be such a big meeting. I just . . ." I was deflating after my initial burst of swagger.

Carter cleared his throat and cut in. "No, Francois, she won't be joining us. Finn, I'm trying to conduct business here. Perhaps we can meet later."

I reddened, seeing how badly I had miscalculated. I was embarrassed and unwelcome. Still, I had to know. I hadn't come all this way to leave without answers. I marshalled my courage. "*We* have business, Carter, unfinished business. I need you . . . your time. You said one year. One year. It's been a year and three months. We have business to finish too."

Carter's mouth opened as if he were going to reply and he looked at the faces swiveling from me back to him. He rubbed his forehead again and ran his fingers through his hair, a sign of nervousness.

He looked around the table. "Gentlemen, and Gabrielle, would you please excuse me for a minute?" The woman seated to the left of his head of the table position nodded and sat back, looking at me, pen tapping.

Carter walked the length of the table and took me by the arm, shepherding me to the door. "Let's step out, shall we, Finley?"

His voice was strained. In the old days, he would have laughed if I'd stumbled into a meeting, and said something like, "Well, gentlemen, I can see that my talents are needed elsewhere more pressingly than they are needed here. The fate of this multi-million-dollar transaction apparently can wait. May I excuse myself for a few minutes, please?"

Instead, he walked me silently to his office, face grim. Once there, he let me go and shut the door. The room was French elegant; light oriental rug, cherry desk, brass sconces, clean lines, French doors leading to a patio, lots of full sun.

"Sit," he said, gesturing to a loveseat as he lowered himself heavily into his office chair across from me. Through the window behind him, I could see the sky and a red roof with gables.

"What was *that*?" he asked, giving me a look drenched in pain. He folded his hands then unfolded them, then said with quiet intensity, "And why in the hell didn't you tell me you were coming to Paris, Finn? Good grief, you shook me. To see you here, in Paris, in this office, after a year, no visits, few calls." Now there was something like anguish in his voice.

"You never invited me to visit here, and you never called me. I thought you wanted to be left alone." I knew I sounded defensive.

"Like you need an invitation? What are we? Neighbors who exchanged pleasantries? I've loved you for seven years. I never wanted to be left alone. What on earth would lead you to think that? Aren't we just great communicators." There was a knock on the door. "Come in."

Carter's assistant poked her head in. "Excusez-moi, Monsieur Kane. The Japanese ambassador has only a half-hour more. Just a reminder, monsieur."

Carter nodded. "Thank you, Marie Claire."

She bowed out of the doorway, closing the door with her.

I was unnerved. This was not what I envisioned. "You said when you left that a break would be good, give us time to think. I didn't want to push myself on you. Carter, I need more than five minutes with you. I need more."

The irony of my statement was not lost on me. He looked so distressed that I felt weak and wrong. He said, "Finn, I honestly don't know what you want. *Push yourself on me?* In my wildest dreams, I could only hope for that. I've spent a year trying to get over you. Now, here you are and I just . . . I can't go forward. I can't go backward. What do you want from me?"

I sat mute. Just sharing the space with him felt like I was in the right place, despite him being far from welcoming.

He twisted his arm to glance at his watch. "Look, I need to finish this meeting. Three of the men are in from Japan and have to leave tonight. The ambassador has to leave now. Just pick a place for dinner, and we'll talk tonight. Leave the time and place with Marie Claire, my secretary." He stood, but before leaving, he said, "You look just plain beautiful, Finn. You take my breath away."

He looked at his shoes, shook his head and strode out, leaving the office door open. I wrote a message for Marie Claire and set to work, my note to Carter still in my purse.

***

At 9:00 p.m., I sat at a table in Mon Petit Chou in front of a stone fireplace that dominated one end, a fire glowing in the grate. The restaurant was a tiny jewel in the Marais that accommodated only ten tables set in a glass conservatory with vines that reached high, twining across the ceiling. Each table had a starched, white tablecloth and chocolate-brown, cushy suede chairs. Golden sconces and tiny, white lights on the trees gave the room the feel of a fairyland.

After exiting Carter's building, I stopped in to see the owner/chef of Mon Petit Chou, Julien Malraux, who was a friend of Julia Child, who was a dear friend of my mother's. Being a true romantic, and it being a quiet, mid-week evening, Julien was excited to lease out the restaurant for the evening for my rendezvous. While he prepared the appetizer and dessert, I cooked the main course.

At 9:03 p.m., Carter, always on time, opened the heavy door of Mon Petit Chou and stepped in cautiously. I was easy to spot in the small, empty dining room. He looked puzzled, but came over and kissed me on each cheek. I wanted to melt into him, but the mood was not right.

"No one else likes this place?" He looked at the empty space.

"It's ours for tonight."

He cocked his head. I poured champagne for him, ginger ale for me. On the record player, Frank Sinatra was warbling as Carter took a sip, but I just watched him. He looked tired, but the same; thinning, light-brown hair, bright-blue eyes, dignified.

"I may need something stronger than champagne, sweetheart. Seeing you was a real shock. Are you trying to kill me?" He smiled though when he said it and gazed around the restaurant. "You mean they closed down for us?"

I wondered if the "sweetheart" was more than a generic term or meant something. "Kind of. And we won't need menus. Julien and I decided on the meal."

Carter looked more puzzled than anything else. "Are you wooing me, Miss. Hemingway?"

"Maybe."

He shook his head. "Never a straight answer." He took another sip of the champagne. "Seriously though, I was really thrown for a loop seeing you this morning, Finley. It was like seeing something so out of context, like a mirage from wishing for it for so long, but one that you'd stopped hoping for. Then the next second, I felt guilty for not letting you know what's gone on in my life, what I've been doing to try to move forward without you."

I sank deeper into my seat, fearing the words that usually follow "move forward without you." I put up a hand, hoping to delay bad news. "Let's just enjoy dinner, then talk."

He nodded as Julien and company marched in with shrimp cocktails and fresh bread. We dug in, although my appetite was almost gone. I picked at a corner of bread.

"What have you been doing for the past year? And you not eating bread? You must be suffering extreme jet lag." He tore a corner of crust off and began to butter it.

I thought of the past year, but it all seemed unimportant in this stunning setting. *Tess had surgery for a tumor but was OK; Jedd was studying to become a surgeon; I was making a name as a civil rights litigator and I'd be assisting on the brief for my first case in front of the U.S. Supreme Court.* Still, I made a feeble stab at it.

"I'm getting more responsibility at the office. Spent some time in Cuba at Christmas."

"How is your father?"

I shrugged. "He's been better. Some health things since the plane crashes never cleared up. He's estranged from Gig and says he doesn't care, but he does. He's working on some new books—one he won't talk about—but I think he's struggling."

"Sorry to hear that, Finn. I like your father."

"What about you?" I asked, faking joviality. "Did you show the French how it's done?"

He nodded. "The business is in much better shape than I found it a year ago. Sales have picked up, and we're rebuilding the credibility. However, everything is so international that we need distribution in Asia, and that's our next task."

Our appetizer plates were removed and the main course was paraded in. Martine, Julien's assistant, placed a handsome meatloaf with a single candle on it in the center of the table. She laid a knife next to it. Julien himself presented the scalloped potatoes and slim French green beans with almonds.

Carter chuckled. "This classic French bistro made meatloaf with ketchup on top? With a candle! But I do love meatloaf."

"I know. You said it was your all-time favorite meal, and you gave me the recipe six years ago. The candle is to commemorate that one year apart is too much."

Carter looked surprised. "Last thing I knew, you didn't cook. And is that you, Finley Hemingway, saying that 'one year apart is too much'? What have you done with my former girlfriend?"

Former girlfriend did not sound good. I tried to stay the course and lifted my chin a little higher. "It's not so hard, actually. They have these things called cookbooks; you read the recipe and then you follow it, more or less."

Carter laughed. "I like the more or less part."

I laughed too. "I hope it's something like hers—your mother's."

Julien popped around the corner. "She did very well. Très bien! I did nothing. Perfection. Her white sauce for the potatoes was brilliant! Très difficile, but done very nicely by mademoiselle, Monsieur Kane. She will make a wonderful wife, sans aucun doute!" *Without any doubt.* He popped back into the kitchen.

I groaned. Carter cut each of us a slice of the loaf, laughing, "Was that a paid political advertisement?"

"Had I known Julien was going to ad lib on my behalf, I would have given him a more detailed script to follow." I grimaced.

Carter took a bite. I waited anxiously. He chewed and was silent for a moment, his eyes closed. When he opened them, they were wet. In almost a whisper, he said, "Just like my mother's. Really, Finn, it's just like my mother's. Takes me back to our little apartment above the pizza parlor in New Haven. We had to make it last, but we were happy." He put his fork down, wiped his mouth, and reached for my hand. "Thank you, Finn. I couldn't think of a better gift if I tried. She would have loved you."

I breathed out, relieved. "You said her secret ingredients were a touch of Dijon mustard and a dash of nutmeg. So it's OK?"

"It's so much more than OK. It's a memory brought to life. A fantastic culinary memory."

Carter had seconds of everything. After Martine brought coffee, Carter said, "We made a mistake being so out of touch this past year, Finn. I'm not sure why we did that, but we've lost those little moments that make up the pace of life. We have no idea how the other managed or what mattered to each of us as the time passed. We lost that and can't ever make it up."

"I know. I thought you wanted time alone. My pride didn't want to have you reject me so I stayed away." I pointed through the lights and branches. "Look, Chick. The stars."

He looked up. "This is so beautiful." He turned to me. "Look, Finn, it's been quite a year of adjustment for me here. I've met so many people, great people, and have grown close to many of them. I wish I'd told you." He looked pained. He turned his chair and crossed his legs.

"Ah, excusez-moi!" Martine scurried in, slipped a plate of sweets on the table, and tossed another log on the fire. I was glad to have a diversion, and smiled as she passed.

My stomach started to hurt though as Carter mentioned the year and his new direction. I clutched my skirt to steady my hands. I rushed in to jump the gun. "Please, Carter. I know you're involved with someone else, and that you are done with me."

Carter had taken a slice of a napoleon but stopped. He put it down. "What are you talking about, Finn?"

"I saw you. Last night walking home. I wasn't spying, but I tried to meet you at your apartment and waited. Then I saw you with another woman—the one in the meeting today." I swayed a little. Just hearing myself say those words made it real. "I wrote you a note, and I've made plans to go back to New York on Saturday."

"Saturday! That's the day after tomorrow! I thought you would be here for longer than that."

"I don't want to be a burden. You know, the 'former girlfriend' and all that."

He paused and stared off as if running a movie in reverse in his head. Then his face brightened. "Oh, last night, that was

Gabrielle. She's become a close friend. She knows all about you."

"That's great. How come I don't know all about her? And are you with her now?" My heart sped up and was pounding. We'd circled this all night.

"You don't know about her because, as we just noted, we didn't talk. And, well, yes. I am with her now. As a business partner. She's smart, and knows the markets over here."

I studied his face. I didn't want to ask. To suspect is bad. To know is worse. I had to know. "Are you in love?"

Carter looked down, then nodded. "I am. I truly am in love. And it is all that every poet ever said it would be."

My face colored. I felt hot, then chilled. I slowly put my hands over my face and leaned onto the table to stay upright so he couldn't see me crumble, piece by piece. I knew I could never get further into this evening, not now.

I saw our future, the one that had propelled me to fly to Paris—finishing raising Mickey together, running around our home in the morning as we raced to our jobs, working together on causes we love, maybe even having our own children, putting up the Christmas tree, visiting my father and mother as often as we could—all of it disappeared. None of that would happen now, ever—and I'd condemned it to death by my refusal to accept that love could last, and that it could change you, and that it was how *you* shaped it, not how your father shaped it or how Nicky and I might have shaped it, but how after all of the events of your own life crashed over you—you and this one unique other person would shape it together in all of its flawed perfection. I breathed in slowly and took my hands away from my face.

"I don't know what to say, Carter. I . . . my own fault, I know—I'm so sorry, but I need a moment. Please excuse me." I bolted toward the ladies' room. Carter jumped up more quickly than I did and seized my hand to stop me.

"Wait, Finn." He pulled me to him and wrapped me in a tight hug. I could feel his breath on my neck. He pulled my head into him, just like my father used to when he was reassuring me. Carter was trying to soften the blow, weaken the sting of what he had to know was a bitter rejection, a sad end for me, a joyful beginning for him.

Then he stepped back. "Please sit, Finn." I lowered myself slowly into my dining chair and watched the fire flicker and the lights around us twinkle. Such a happy setting and beautiful evening, but not for me; not for us.

Carter reached across the table, swiping away a tear. He said softly, "Finn, I'm in love with *you*, not Gabrielle. God knows, I've tried not to be. But I am in love with you, completely and irrevocably. I always will be. You are the wildest woman it has ever been my honor to know and love, and you are wild in the stillest, most intriguing way, a way all your own. Gabrielle is an extraordinary businesswoman and friend, but nothing at all that attracts me. And it just so happens she is happily involved with Marie Claire, my secretary."

I hadn't realized that I was holding my breath until I let out a gust of air. I looked up, my eyes full with the relief of knowing there was a chance.

"Thank God," I said as I clasped both of his hands. "And I am in love with you, and only breathe right when you're with me. Marry me, Carter. I want to belong to you and for you to belong to me."

Carter began to laugh. "Oh boy. We're back to that slavery thing, are we?"

He reached into his jacket pocket and placed a small, blue box in the middle of the table. "I've carried this with me since I bought it, when you told me you wouldn't marry me. I had it engraved after that because I knew I would never give it to anyone but you. And if you never would have me, it would remind me in my dotage that I once loved hard and without holding anything back." He pushed it toward me. "And I wrote a poem. It's . . . it's in the box. Not a good poem—you deserve much better—but a poem nevertheless."

I looked into his eyes, then at the box, and burst into laughter, head back, savoring the moment. *I had inspired poetry after all. So, dammit to hell, take that, Zelda Fitzgerald!*

I opened the box. A sparkling, emerald-cut diamond ring sat bright and clean. I lifted it out and twisted it to read the engraving. It said, *To Finley, The One, forever.* I leaned over to kiss Carter, then dug deeper and drew out a blue paper. Slowly, I unfolded the square and read Carter's cramped script, written from his heart. I mouthed the last two lines:

I am yours forever and always

If you will have me, my wild girl, my gleaming selkie, my true north.

My hands dropped to my lap, my grasp on the note slipping. I was touched to the core by this glorious effort by my steady businessman/lover. I silently rejoiced, looking forward to learning the layers of this man, layers that I had a lifetime to discover.

"Oh, Chick. Forever is just right."

"That's the idea, sweetheart." He took my hand and slid the ring on my fourth finger.

Carter said softly, "It's perfect. Hey! Where's that letter you wrote to me? Maybe we can actually start to communicate." He held my hand tighter. "I'd like to try. What do you think?"

I handed him the letter.

51

But Paris was a very old city and we were young and nothing was simple there, not even poverty, nor sudden money, nor the moonlight, nor right and wrong nor the breathing of someone who lay beside you in the moonlight.

~ Ernest Hemingway, *A Moveable Feast*

I went up to see Mother for Thanksgiving that year. Carter and Mickey came with me. Carter was back and forth from Paris with more and more time spent in New York. Mother had made a good life for herself up in New Hampshire. She enjoyed cooking, drinking a fair amount, and reading. Mother's old Irish pine table groaned under the weight of a glazed stuffed turkey, mashed potatoes, and sweet potatoes with marshmallows.

As we dug into the pies for dessert, talk turned to my father. Mother and I both heard updates from Jack, who was living in Havana full-time. Papa's depression did not seem to be improving, and no one knew what to do.

"Mother, what did you do when he got like that?"

She thought for a minute. "Well, it didn't happen much in those days. If it did, we'd drink some, go out for a great, cheap dinner, dance a little, and he'd be fine by morning. He doesn't get that way if he's working well."

"Well, he gets that way a lot now, and it's scaring me to death."

Mother's face clouded. She shook her head as if clearing a haze. She turned to Carter and said brightly, "Carter, did I ever tell you about the last time I saw Finn's father?"

"No, Hadley. Please tell me." Carter smiled and held my hand under the table. I had heard the story many times, and of course I was there, but I never tired of hearing her tell it.

Mother could still be coquettish, and that evening, she leaned toward Carter, head tilted as if letting him in on a secret to be shared only by the two of them. To me, she looked like a twenty-eight-year-old flapper flirt. Her still-red hair was piled on her head, and her light-blue eyes glittered in the light of the candles.

She tented her arms on the table. "It was September 1, 1939. I was in Wyoming with Paul, Bumby, and Finn. Finn would have been about fourteen then, and Bumby about sixteen. That day was sparkling, and the river was so clear you could see all of the rocks lining the bottom. We were heading back to the ranch where we were staying after a day of fishing, and for the first time, Finn caught more fish than Bumby. She was needling him, and he took it in good spirits."

Mother tucked my hair behind my ear and slid her glance back to Carter. "Well, who should come trotting down the path toward us but Ernest Hemingway, looking like a burly mountain man with his dark mustache and wire glasses. A little heavier than when I'd last seen him, but still very handsome. He'd heard from Jack that we were there, so he set out to find us."

Mother paused to take a breath and looked away as if seeing it all again.

"Well! He cuffed Jack and swung Finn around so her feet were off the ground. The kids never could get enough of him. Well, he was bursting with news that Germany had just invaded Poland earlier that day. Jack and Finn were thrilled to see all of us jabbering like capuchin monkeys. And Tatie—that's what I called him—was so relieved and pleased to find that Paul was such a fine man."

Mother glanced at Paul and took his hand. "Ernest constantly worried about whether I was getting along. He was a very sweet man. Yes, at times he could be rough, but any man of any value at all can be rough." She pronounced "at all" like "a tall."

Mother took a sip of her wine and inhaled deeply. "It was such a fitting end to a wonderful day—seeing Tatie like that, the children prancing." Mother stopped and dropped her hands into her lap. "It was the first time since Paris—before he left me—that we'd all been in the same place at the same time—me, Tatie, Bumby, and Finn." Mother's voice was wistful. "As it turned out, it was the last time—at least so far—that we saw each other. But maybe we'll see each other again at Finn's wedding." Mother smiled at me.

Carter smiled. "Great memory, Hadley. And yes, there will be a wedding soon, I hope." He kissed my hand.

For me, listening to Mother was like a film I'd watched many times but that never lost its magic. I could still see them—Mother and Papa, with Paul off to the side—strolling down the dirt road back to the ranch, Jack and I bringing up the rear. Papa had a spark in his dark eyes as Mother gazed at him fondly, striding beside him, sometimes grasping his hand in excitement. It was as if all of it were flashing by her now—

Windermere House on Walloon Lake, where they'd honeymooned; Paris in the twenties, when Papa was no one and they were young and madly in love; Pamplona, where it all began for Papa and where Mother was left behind; the Fitzgeralds, with their wild nights and road trips; the Murphys with their generous, rich people's ways; Gertrude, with her salon of intellectuals and artists; and always, my father. I like to remember him from those early wedding photos when he was young, handsome, just starting out, and in love with my mother.

After their divorce in 1927, my parents were in touch by phone and letters, but they never saw each other again after that bright Wyoming day in 1939, a time when just catching fish made all of us giddy. I leaned over and kissed my mother on the cheek. "Thank you, Mommy."

Mother's eyes opened wide. I had stopped calling her Mommy when I was about seven. "For what, darling?"

"For being my memory about Papa back then. I don't ever want to lose how I felt that day."

Mother smiled a wobbly grin. "I don't ever want to lose that either. We are each other's memory, Finn. When I'm feeble in some corner of this house, you'll tell me the story. You'll be my memory?"

"I will."

I too wish I'd known way back then that it would be the last time I would ever see my parents together. But then, maybe it was easier not to know.

52

By then I knew that everything good and bad left an emptiness when it stopped. But if it was bad, the emptiness filled up by itself. If it was good you could only fill it by finding something better.

~ Ernest Hemingway, *A Moveable Feast*

Dr. Seuss, that great philosopher of love, once said you know you're in love when you can't fall asleep because reality is finally better than your dreams. On that basis, I was in love and thrilled to have Carter back in New York full-time.

Still, there were other problems. Papa and Mary rented a small Manhattan apartment on East Sixty-Second Street, and I finally saw more of Papa, although he was not fully himself. He was distrustful of everything, and his phone fears had resurfaced. He would regularly pause a conversation, listening for phone taps. He claimed the IRS was after him. Repeatedly, he begged me to be sure there was money in the tax account.

I tried to calm him. When I joked that he'd always looked good in stripes, in case he was ever jailed for tax fraud, he exploded at me.

"Jaysus, Flea; that's not funny! You don't know what it's like to have them at you day and night. I feel like a prisoner in my own house."

I reeled. "Sorry, Papa," I said meekly. Just a year before, he'd have laughed and said, "Yes, I do, but jail stripes are horizontal, Flea. I prefer vertical stripes. So much more slimming."

At a dinner at Tavern on the Green in Central Park, Papa kept glancing around and insisted two men in suits who'd arrived after us were staring at him and were from the government. He refused to stay for dessert.

In desperation, Mary decided they should spend a few weeks in Ketchum, where Papa usually rallied. He didn't, and Logan Grant called me the day after they arrived. "Not good, Finn. Your father has kidney and liver disease. He has diabetes. His blood pressure is two fifty over one twenty-five, which is bad. He won't stop drinking, and his depression is seriously worrisome. There are paranoid overtones to it. He should be in a hospital."

Carter suggested the Institute of Living in Hartford, Connecticut, known for discretion regarding famous patients and conservative treatment of emotional issues. Mary had the final say and registered him at the Mayo Clinic in Minnesota under a fake name.

There was no joyous Christmas for any of us that year. They let me in for a visit on Christmas day. I tried to keep my face neutral, but when I saw him, I was stunned. He'd lost about fifty pounds and looked painfully thin.

"So, Papa, how goes the battle here?" I said as cheerfully as I could muster.

"It's OK, Flea. But they watch me all the time. I can't live in a cage. I want to go home."

We talked about Jack, the grandchildren, my work, Carter. Then he asked to speak to Aaron Hotchner on the phone. I brightened, thinking he wanted to work—always a good sign. I hustled to the front desk to arrange it, and a half-hour later, Papa hurried to the phone on his floor.

"Come along, Flea. I want you to listen so when you see Hotch in New York, you can remind him of all this."

I only heard Papa's side of the conversation, but he sounded normal, if you didn't know how irrational he'd been just a few days ago.

"Hotch? I'm reading the galleys of Plimpton's book, *Out of my League*. Like it, but hard to enjoy much in a place where you're frisked and locked in."

He laughed at whatever Aaron said and talked about the edits on *The Dangerous Summer*. "Please, Hotch, get your ass out here. I'm dying of boredom. Flea is the only bright spot, and she has to get back to some damned trial. Says I'm not her only client." He winked at me and went silent as he listened. "Yeah, that's a good idea." The hospital operator cut in to end the call. Papa rushed to finish his thoughts, then hung up.

When we returned to his room, Mary, who was reading in the corner, looked up and smiled at us. She'd brought Papa books and fresh clothes. He started out thanking her, but within minutes was attacking her for putting him there. She slipped out of the room, and when I went to check on her, she was heading back, eyes red. When we reentered Papa's room, he was smiling as if nothing had happened.

"Flea, look at this." He handed me a telegram. "From the president. Inviting us to be his personal guests at the inaugural." His face clouded. "I wish I could go, but . . ." His gaze traveled the perimeter of the room. "That's not going to happen. I want to write a good answer though."

For almost two hours, we labored to pen a gracious and appreciative answer to the new president, John F. Kennedy. The effort was painful. This man, whose life was writing, struggled to compose a simple thank you note. I finished it that night and sent it off.

At the Mayo Clinic, unbeknownst to me until afterward, Papa suffered a series of disastrous electroshock treatments. Papa no longer could recall events or find the right word. A man who lived to write no longer had access to vast portions of his memory. He missed his kids and his pets, and the future being presented to him by his doctors was one without the foods he loved, the booze he craved, and the writing that was as necessary to him as air.

When Papa was finally released, Mary and I accompanied him to Ketchum. I headed back to New York thinking he was improved. However, a month later, my father became despondent again. I flew back out to Idaho. Carter came with me on that trip.

Aaron Hotchner and I were the only ones who knew that part of his despondency was his inability to finish a book he'd started, the secret book he refused to talk about.

"Well, Papa, then next year. It can come out next year, can't it?" I asked as we sat on the porch of the Ketchum house.

Papa's eyes dulled. He picked up Big Boy Peterson, his new cat, and sat back down. "No, Flea, it can't come out next year. I can't finish it. This fantastic book I've started, and I can't finish it."

He said it flat and dead. *I can't finish it.* Not, *I'm having trouble finishing it,* but, *I can't.*

For the next few days, he just sat in the house and stared out the window. I looked at Mary, who avoided my eyes. I wrung my hands raw in those few days, feeling helpless. I sat by Papa, got him food and drink, but he touched little of it.

"Flea, I can't write anymore," he said in tears the day I was leaving for New York. "I am dead, good as dead."

I stilled with fear at those words, then wrapped him in a hug. "You'll feel better soon. You just need rest." Papa had always been so resilient, but I was scared now that his well of reserves had evaporated.

"No, it's gone." He took his glasses off and rubbed his eyes.

"You can retire, Papa. You've done plenty. There is no shame in retiring." I was grabbing at any lifeline.

He scoffed and took a long swallow of a drink. "A writer can't retire. Everyone keeps asking, 'So what are you working on now? When's the next book coming out?'"

"Can't you just say you're not writing anymore? That you're retired?"

"Maybe some people can, Flea, but I *am* my writing. It's my reason for sticking around."

Dread swept in. I knelt in front of him. "But, Papa, you have us kids. We love you. Isn't that enough for sticking around?"

Papa reached out and stroked my head. He smiled a little smile, but didn't answer.

A day later while Papa was napping, Logan stopped over with his little girl, Emma, now eight, and just shook his head. He gave Carter the once-over but directed all his conversation to me. "How could they use electroshock on a thinker, a man who lives by his memories? He'd rather be dead than lose that."

"That's what he said," I replied. Logan stared at me grimly, and I stared back.

***

My father's residency in Cuba ended suddenly and unexpectedly. The FBI told Papa while he was in New York that he could not go back. Just like that. He'd left everything there.

On April 21, 1961, Papa attempted to kill himself with a gun. Mary did not tell us; she told Aaron, who told me. Then he apparently tried to walk into the propellers of an airplane. Jack and I were beside ourselves. I delegated all of my active cases to one of my partners, advising that I didn't know when I'd be back. I flew out to Rochester, Minnesota, where Papa was readmitted to the Mayo Clinic.

I sat with him and read to him, but there was no cheer. When Mary said it appeared Papa would be released soon—much to our shock, given his condition—I flew back to New York and waited for word on his progress.

Papa was released a few days later. Always an actor, he had conned the doctors into thinking that being at home was just the inspiration he needed to get well. Mary protested, as did Jack and I, all to no avail. Patrick, still in Africa, felt we had to leave it to Mary.

53

When I saw my wife again standing by the tracks as the train came in by the piled logs at the station, I wished I had died before I ever loved anyone but her.

~ Ernest Hemingway, *A Moveable Feast*

I have come full circle, back to the last letter I received from Papa about finishing the book for my mother—the place where this story began.

He sounded so good in that last letter because he was creating again. For him, writing was like practicing law was for me: a force energizing everything you did. Your life might be formless and in shambles, but while you were spawning that perfect sentence or clinching that singularly on-point legal precedent, in that moment and space, nothing else mattered and all slid into place for that instant.

In our last phone call a few days after I received his note, I actually thought that maybe everything would turn out alright. Maybe Papa was bouncing back. That call felt like every good conversation we'd ever had, like the best of times. His voice was strong and sure, but thinking of him in a hospital with bars on the windows made me think of a wild animal that couldn't survive under those conditions for long. On the phone, he repeated some of what he'd written in that last letter.

He chuckled. "Did I tell you, Flea? The dedication to the new book will read, 'To Finley Hemingway, my Daughter and my Muse.'"

I remembered, but it still affected me like nothing else in my life ever had. For thirty-six years, I'd waited to hear those words—that I mattered, that I made a difference to what was at his core, his writing, the place where he tunneled down and exposed his soul. I had trouble replying. Finally, I said softly, "You mentioned it in your letter but . . . really?"

Papa laughed, and the sound was like rolling thunder. "You made me want to try for something no one else had done, kid. That's what love is, after all the rest clears: knowing there's one rare jewel out there you'd move the pyramids for just to see her smile, to make her proud of you, and you'd throw away everything you thought mattered to know she thinks you're the true gen. Whether it lasts seven seconds or ninety years, you had it. It's that simple. And us—you and me, kid—we have it." The "true gen" was Papa's shorthand for the genuine article, the real thing.

My voice caught. "I . . . I never knew you thought that."

He laughed. "Hell, because of you, I gave Catherine Barkley a career so she could take care of herself, not be a victim; I made Maria a survivor who was loved forever no matter what came after. In the first draft of *For Whom the Bell Tolls*, Maria and Robert die together—but I couldn't. She was you. She had to live." There was a catch in his voice when he said that.

I stilled. I was nothing like Maria, the abused and rabbit-sweet love of Robert Jordan's life. As if he'd read my mind through the phone line, he said, "No, I don't mean in the details of her life, but in her innocence and in the purity of her love for Robert. I couldn't kill her. She had to live, or it was like killing you. She had to go on, and in that way, so did he."

He wasn't done. "Then when Nick died, it felt like I'd foreshadowed all of it, and that more than ever, it had to be true what I'd written: that as long as there was one of them, there was both of them. It had to be true, because I was so afraid of losing you after Nick died." He took a breath, and I remained still. "And I let the old man endure. Because of you. They all were bitched to hell in my first drafts. I chose life."

Papa paused, and I was flooded with gratitude and an overpowering sense of peace, the kind of peace that swamps you after an emotional reckoning has finally ended. I pictured him leaning against a wall, phone in hand, shaking his head, thinking about the hours that went into each of those books, from first draft to scores of redrafts to publication.

He went on. "Then I thought about you reading them, maybe thinking that life is just one big dead end. I wanted you to believe in hope, and in surviving, and in love lasting forever. Those women and the old man all had to be strong—stronger than I'd first written them. For you. They had to endure. And even though Catherine died, Frederic never got over her. She endured. And, hell, I wrote *A Single Drop of Red Wine* for you. Sinker and all. For you. And it was the best book I ever wrote. All I believe in is there. Because of you, my Daughter." He paused a second, then added, "You do know that only yours has a capital *D*, right?"

I'd been standing. At his words, I lowered myself to the couch to slow my breathing. I'd accepted that he was "Papa" to the world, but I'd always resented his use of "daughter" for all of his favorite women. It was an inner raw spot, picked at whenever another woman was greeted with my identity. Now, I couldn't find words adequate to tell him that maybe he'd just saved me.

He coughed a few times, then was back on the phone, voice robust. "You there, Flea?"

I swallowed hard. "Yes, Papa, I'm here."

"Good. Jaysus, Flea, you're the one. You've turned into one hell of a great lawyer and an unequaled woman, *hija mia*. I love you to hell and back. I'd say to heaven and back, but who are we kidding!"

I laughed with tears mixed in, then sank back onto the pillows, humbled and sated at last. "Thank you, Papa," I whispered.

Now I knew. I knew that I mattered to his work, the place that defined him, and after all of my agonizing and railing against the family fate, I realized the Hemingway love jinx only had the power I'd given it, just as Carter had said. Papa had made his choices and lived with them for his reasons. I'd done the same, with nothing predetermined. I'd made the decisions that worked out and those that didn't. Papa had given me the key long ago that day we were on the boat, but I'd chosen not to use it. If you had one person for whom you'd move any obstacle just to see them happy, and they'd do the same for you, you had it. You had true love. It might be a flash or enduring, but it was real either way, and it didn't end because of death or growing apart. In that moment, when that person turned and smiled at you over his shoulder, you locked it. What came after couldn't change that tamper-proof moment. I knew for sure that Jonathan returned to Elena in *A Single Drop of Red Wine*. In a soundless prayer of gratitude, I knew with certainty born of a private religion that if there is one of us, there *is* both of us. I'd had three people for whom

I'd move those pyramids, and they'd move them back for me, no questions asked. *Nicky, Carter, Papa.*

I smiled as I sat on the edge of my sofa, the raw place inside of me closing finally and forever. We were quiet, then I said, "The title is beautiful. She'll love it."

"*A Moveable Feast*," he said. "Paris is a moveable feast. Yes, she will."

I nodded in my empty room. "Perfect, just perfect." And I now knew that his "stronger in the broken places" and "your first job in life is to survive it" had penetrated my bones and become part of me. I'd survived the un-survivable—Nicky's death. I'd lived through Michael Jenner's betrayal, and I'd triumphed over the insistence of all around me that I would never set foot in a courtroom as a trial lawyer. And I'd found the truest of love with Carter. It was my father who'd taught me all of that—to parry what life shoves at you, deal with it, and shape it in your way.

I couldn't see him, but I kind of could, as he would be if he were lounging at the Finca instead of in the hospital. Cigar in the ashtray, legs stretched out, a cat next to him, drink within reach, Black Dog at his feet, and a firm nod of the head. He said, "Yeah, that's what I'm callin' it."

"Thank you, Papa. And you *will* make her immortal with this book, you know."

"Yeah, I think I will. Love can do that. Don't doubt it. And I love you too, kid. Times ten. No way around it."

***

Papa and Mary drove back to Idaho. Papa's show of sanity and improved health had fooled the doctors. He was hiding deeper depression and paranoia than before. When Papa and Mary went out to dinner that evening, he was quiet. Mary recalled singing a little Italian song just before turning in for the night, and Papa joined her in the refrain. Then he said, "Good night, my kitten."

The next morning, July 2, 1961, Papa tiptoed down the basement steps and pulled out his favorite double-barreled Boss shotgun. The cabinet was locked, but the key was in plain sight on a windowsill in the kitchen. Papa killed himself twelve days after our last call.

I learned of it from Aaron, who got the frantic call from Mary. Mary never called me. I sobbed in my apartment alone, then called Mother, and we cried together. Carter was my third call, then Jack, who had already heard from Aaron. The only solace was, it was what he wanted. Papa had always been clear that living was more than taking in air. It was living on your terms and doing what you were put on Earth to do.

The headline this time was real, and it was international front-page news.

HEMINGWAY DEAD OF A GUNSHOT WOUND

For several years, Mary insisted it was an accidental shooting while Papa was cleaning his gun. It wasn't. Patrick was furious with Mary for not locking up the guns, but I suspected Papa would have figured a way to do himself in even if it hadn't been that day. His mission in leaving the Mayo Clinic was to end it once and for all.

When I spoke to Mother, she told me she'd received a call from Papa several months earlier. He'd asked about some details of their life in Paris that had escaped him. Their conversation had been pleasant, with Papa sounding outwardly cheerful. "But, Finn, when we hung up, I just started crying. I felt this sadness in your father, in his voice."

Many months later, Mary returned to Mother a large packet of love letters Mother had sent to Papa. He had kept them all of those years. A sheet of edits on *A Moveable Feast* was found in his Smith Corona the day Papa died. It couldn't have been uplifting for Mary to know her husband's last work was a love poem in prose to his first wife. For me, it was a small happiness that his last thoughts were of my mother.

When Aaron gave me the news, I bit down on my wrist to change the direction of the pain and to stop the wail perched at the top of my throat. I swigged my last bottle of scotch ever and tried to drown a loss I never got over. The day Papa died was the last time I took a drink. I needed anything to lessen a pain that felt impossible to bear. Papa had nursed me through Nicky's death, and now, despite the love of Carter, Mother, Jeddrah, and Jack, I felt completely alone. I sobbed into the furry head of my black dog, Big, the Bouvier I bought after Tess passed away.

I drank, and when the glass was empty, I drank more, toasting Papa in my sloppy stupor. I had to vanish to make it through that night, to flatten the torment of facing life without my father. I would be level tomorrow. I would force myself to face it tomorrow, but not tonight. As I sat keening on the floor of my apartment, I dreamed of the way it used to be and never would be again.

In the morning, Carter let himself in with his key and lifted me from the heap of tangled sheets and bottles. He cleaned me up and made me eat something, then made the arrangements to get both of us out to Idaho.

54

There is never any ending to Paris, and the memory of each person who has lived in it differs from that of any other.

~ Ernest Hemingway, *A Moveable Feast*

Papa was buried in Ketchum. The funeral was private—only family, per Mary's edict—but had to be delayed until July 5, as Patrick was flying in from East Africa. At the gravesite, we all stood on one side—Mary, Patrick, Jack, Gregory, and me, while my aunts and uncle stood across from us. Carter stood next to me, never leaving my side. Mary didn't dare to bar him, even though he was "not family." Aaron held his own private ceremony—party of one. He was heartbroken.

There were legions of press lurking on the perimeter, hoping for photos. Mary barred Marlene Dietrich from the funeral as "non-family." Papa would have welcomed her there. Her daughter, Maria Riva, said in *Marlene Dietrich* that Marlene "played widow, wearing black and locking herself in her room reading Ernest's letters over and over. She never really came to terms with her friend's death nor ever forgave him for deserting her. She secretly blamed his wife." The last time I had dinner with Marlene in New York, she said, tears falling, "If I had been there with him, Finn, he never would have done it. Nie! Never. Mein liebling."

Papa left his estate to Mary. He'd written his last will and testament by hand, but noted in the will that he trusted Mary to provide for his children. Alfred Rice, Papa's lawyer, suggested trusts be set up for the boys and me and that royalties be deposited into the trusts. Mary agreed.

A few days after Papa's death, Mary was approached by the Cuban government. They claimed they wanted to negotiate for the Finca to be a memorial dedicated to Papa's memory.

Mary, with the intervention of President John F. Kennedy's administration, finally was able to return to Cuba to pack up their things. Mary was permitted to take paintings and papers out of the country, and in return, she gave the Finca Vigía and its remaining contents to the Cuban people.

Papa was a pack rat, and Mary rescued many boxes of materials. Papa had asked that his personal letters and correspondence never be published, but Mary did it anyway. They were edited by Papa's biographer, Carlos Baker, of Princeton University.

The Finca Vigía lay abandoned and received little care for years. Books were left open, shoes were left out, a Glenn Miller record was on the phonograph. The departure had been forced, with Mary and Papa never to return. At the time of Papa's death, relations with Cuba could not have been much worse. The Bay of Pigs invasion had occurred in April of 1961, just three months prior.

There were many suitors for Papa's papers, letters, notes, and photos. Mary maintained her connection with the White House after traveling to Cuba to retrieve her things, and she was the guest of President and Mrs. Kennedy at the White House dinner for the Nobel Prize winners in April 1962.

In 1964, Mary contacted Jacqueline Kennedy and offered Papa's entire collection to the John F. Kennedy Presidential Library and Museum, which was still in the planning stage, with the intent that it be a national memorial to John F. Kennedy. Jackie remembered me, asked how I was, and whether I was still riding.

Mary told me, "That Mrs. Kennedy is so gracious. I met her in 1962 when her husband was still alive. Handsomest man I ever saw except for Papa when I first met him. She—Mrs. Kennedy—she said she knew you. Something to do with horses and your riding days."

My riding days. Indeed. So long ago.

The collection included drafts of various Hemingway novels, rewrites, and a sense of how he wrote and revised. In 1972, Mary deeded the collection to the Kennedy Presidential Library and began depositing papers in its archives. On July 18, 1980, Patrick and I, along with Jacqueline Kennedy Onassis, dedicated the Hemingway Room in the JFK Library. Mary was still alive then, but she was not well.

Mary never consulted any of us, but maybe that's as it should be. Her fierce protection of Papa's legacy was solid, but we always felt a lack of warmth toward us. It took Mary years before she would admit that Papa's death was a suicide, not an accident, and she viewed Aaron Hotchner as a traitor for making it all public. On this, she was wrong.

We all drifted a bit in the years after Papa's death. The glue was gone. Jack and I were closest, as Mother kept us bonded. Mary moved back to Ketchum, where she spent most of her time. She did little to stay in touch with us, and once when I tried to reach her, she left a message saying to call her lawyer, Alfred Rice. He handled all things involving the estate.

Key West remained open as a museum, and I visit once a year. For me, it was a beautiful place, but the homes that bring back the most memories are the Finca in Cuba and the plain house in Ketchum.

Strangely, now that some classified documents are no longer classified, it appears that Papa's paranoia regarding the FBI was not delusional. J. Edgar Hoover had in fact been keeping tabs on Papa since as early as the 1940s, apparently suspicious of his "ties to Cuba." At times, Papa was followed, and his phones were tapped. I don't believe the surveillance drove him over the brink, but it didn't help him, given how fragile he became after the electroshock treatments.

A Moveable Feast, the book written for my mother, was published in 1964, three years after Papa's death. There was no dedication. Mother wept quietly when she read it. She felt honored and humbled. I read it in one night into the wee hours, crying. The writer John Dos Passos, a close friend of my father's in the Paris years, once told me, "When they first came to Paris, I was so jealous of them. They were poor as peasants, but so attractive, and happy, and full of fire, and they had eyes only for each other." That's how I want to remember him—young, strong, handsome, and in love with my mother. That is the story his last book told.

It was like Papa was sitting at the kitchen table in Cuba, with Boise to his left and Black Dog on his right, just telling me these stories in his own way. It was edited by Mary, and later re-edited by my nephew, Sean, one of Gig's sons. Neither version had a dedication. At first, I thought that it should not be published, as Papa hadn't had the final say. He'd always edited extensively and vigorously, and he'd died before his efforts were complete. However, after reading it, I changed my mind. Aaron said the bulk had been in decent shape before Papa died. I'm glad it's out there. He made my mother immortal after all.

55

Paris was always worth it and you received return for whatever you brought to it. But this is how Paris was in the early days when we were very poor and very happy.

~ Ernest Hemingway, *A Moveable Feast*

Key West: July 21, 1934

My ninth birthday epitomized the blessing and the curse of being Hemingway's Daughter. It was the day I first sprinted smack into my father's feet of clay. It was our mutual birthday. He was turning thirty-five to my nine. Dispatched by Pauline to see what kind of cake he wanted for our joint birthday dinner, I went on a hunt for him. Not finding him in the main house, I slipped out the kitchen door and skipped toward his writing studio, where I assumed he was hard at work.

It was equator-hot for me in Key West compared to Paris, where I'd lived until recently. I loved the heat, the gigantic flowers, the tall, curved windows of the house, the grand balcony surrounding the second floor, the batch of dogs and cats always roaming the property perimeter, and Papa looming large around every corner.

As I approached the small, shingled studio, I slowed, hoping to surprise him. I tiptoed, closing in on the front door of the building, left ajar.

I crept forward and soon heard two voices. One was Papa's and the other was . . . I stopped and listened more closely. It was Jane Mason. I smiled. Jane was loads of fun, and we got along famously. I picked up my pace. At the studio door I stopped to regroup, with the intent of bounding in like a Labrador retriever puppy. In that pause, I heard them speak.

Papa said, "So are you coming to the party tonight?"

"Oh, sure. I'll have to bring Grant though, since he's in town," Jane said.

"Ah, yes, the husband." Papa sounded amused.

"So before the hordes move in, darling, let me wish you a very personal happy birthday." Jane drawled out the words "very personal."

Hearing movement, I peered through a window in time to catch my father kissing Jane, her arms around his neck, him bending to meet her lips, his arms tightening behind her back as he pulled her close. My stomach skidded, and heat rose to my face. I silently pivoted and scurried back through the house to the front path where Pauline and the boys were waiting.

Pauline looked at me, dark eyes wide, expectant. Her short, brown hair lay neatly on her head like a cap, and her white linen dress fell a few inches above her ankles. The three boys were now rolling on the front lawn, all tangled legs and flailing arms.

"So, chocolate or vanilla?"

I stared at Pauline dumbly. "Pardon?"

"Finn, where is your head today? Did your father want chocolate or vanilla?"

I snapped to. "Oh. Devil's food. He said it's more decadent."

"Hmm, yes, he would. OK, let's go. Boys, stop wrestling."

I never said a word about what I saw or felt, but the next day I awoke disgruntled and feeling small. It had been my birthday too, after all, and seeing my father with Jane was a lousy surprise. I wasn't mad at Jane, but I was confused. She was married, and so was my father. And, I was a little jealous that she had to do so little to attract his focused attention. As I rolled over, still stewing, I spied the note, white and folded in half on my bedside table, no envelope, fluttering from the window's breeze. That note is now creased and thin, but I read it every year on our birthday. I open it gently these days for fear of tearing its old seams. It read:

July 22, 1934

Dear Flea:

Happy birthday yesterday, hija mia. It's now or never, kid. As soon as you get your now nine-year-old ass out of bed, meet me at the dock. I'll have the drinks chilling. (Just kidding. Your mother would kill me.) Time for you to learn to hook a marlin, or failing that, gracefully plummet overboard in shame. Don't worry. We'll never forget you if you don't make it back on board, and we'll toast your fine memory every July 21.

Seriously, Flea, I want today to be special, like you. Yesterday got away from me, and I am really sorry. Lo siento mucho. But I have a surprise planned for tonight, so it's going to be a sunny day all day, and we'll celebrate your post-birthday day. And yup, I'm yours all day, so your incomprehensible birthday wish is granted. See you soon. Breadies and cheeses await your arrival. Never forget I love you, even though I can be desconsiderato (Webster: inconsiderate, thoughtless) as a father—at times.

Con completo amor para siempre, mi hija hermosa,

Your demented Papa

With total love forever, my beautiful daughter.

That morning, some eighty-two years ago, I read the note three times, then began to breathe easier, the agitation of the day before melting. I folded it into thirds and tucked it into a corner of my jewelry box, where it's been ever since, moving with each replacement box. Whenever I read it, I'm flooded with the same sense I had then—that all was right with the world despite the day before being a sorry mess, and tomorrow possibly being a disaster. The day before, Papa had been confusing and distracted, and I felt diminished in every way, but today... well, today he was here and dazzling. Today would be magic, and that was enough.

The year of the note was just after Papa's first African safari, and just before his rising celebrity. And I knew even then that I would always have to scrap with the world for my share of him, not to mention vying with his dream creations—

Lady Brett Ashley, Catherine Barkley, and later, Maria, the heroines of his novels—for his devotion.

Still, I smiled fully that bright Key West morning and hopped out of bed, eager to tear off to the dock to join my father. Yes, I always could forgive him anything. He was that good.

Epilogue

One generation passeth away, and another generation cometh; but the earth abideth forever. The sun also riseth and the sun goeth down, and hastesth to his place where he arose.

~Ecclesiastes. The Bible, King James Version.

If the reader prefers, this book may be regarded as fiction. But there is always the chance that such a book of fiction may throw some light on what has been written as fact.

~ Ernest Hemingway, *A Moveable Feast*

On a blue, frigid January day in 1962, I married Carter Kane at city hall. I wore a white wool peplum suit and my hair was down. Carter dressed in his best navy suit. He was nervously pacing the icy sidewalk when Jeddrah and I pulled up in a cab, five minutes late. I swung out of the backseat wearing a gray wool cape and pumps, and Jeddrah slid out behind me, carrying my bouquet of red and yellow roses—passion and friendship.

Just Mother and Paul, Mary, and Jack with his family, were there for me. Mickey and Carter's two older children from his first marriage were there for him. After the ceremony, we took cabs up to the Café des Artistes, where a back room was reserved for our little group. Mary stared off. Though she was cordial with Mother, there was little interaction. She had been very kind in returning to Mother my father's letters saved from their youth. We all knew that she, in a way, was the most adrift of all of us. I had Carter and my work. Mother had Paul.

Jack had his family, and so did Gig and Patrick. She alone had built her identity around Papa, and without him, she was bewildered.

***

My ninety-first birthday was last week. I am an old woman now with a face full of pleats and white hair, still thick, falling straight to my shoulders. I could tell you about my marriage to Carter Kane, which was not just good but spectacular. I could tell you of the death of our only child of Sudden Infant Death Syndrome or about my appointment to the New York State Bench as one of its first female judges. I could tell you about the day I was sentencing a murderer to two life terms for raping and killing two Barnard students, and how just after the sentencing, the crowd parted—or so I recollect—and there was Logan Grant, standing tall in the back of my courtroom. He waved tentatively, and I returned a smile full of question. Those are stories for another day. This book is about Papa and me, and our story is over.

I live now exactly as Nicky and I had planned—by the sea in a cottage full of twists, turns, fireplaces, and lots of light. The cottage is on my ten-acre farm near Mystic, Connecticut. I still keep two horses, and I have a fence to keep in my two shaggy dogs. My house cat is named Boise Too. And I have a library with many Hemingway first editions.

I live alone, but I still drive and have many friends. Jedd is a widow now and lives near her daughter, Ellen, in North Salem, New York. We see each other once a month, usually meeting in Westport, Connecticut, for lunch. In the summer, she spends a month with me and at Christmas, I spend a month with her. We spend much of the time laughing and taking walks with my dogs. My stepsons, especially Mickey, visit regularly. I belong to a women's club called The Red Tent, where we talk about courage and honor and living free. I also love my book club, where we sometimes read my father's work. On occasion, I'm still called upon to talk about life with Papa. I like to think my memory is good but my legs get a little weak, so they always have an armchair for me to sit in.

Some nights, when I'm between sleep and almost sleep, I dream, as old people do, of crazy things. More and more often, I dream of my wedding to Nicky. I see a big field with a canopy of trees, and it's the Finca in its heyday. All of our friends are there, and it's illogical in the way dreams are. Friends I met after Nicky died are there, as if they knew him. Carter is one of our guests, and Jeddrah stands up front, smiling, a sprig of lily of the valley in her blonde hair, her aging stopped at twenty-three. My mother is young again, her red hair piled up on her head, face tilted up to the sun, and so beautiful. Papa, standing beside me, looks to be forty or so, and is so handsome and straight, wearing a dark suit with a tie.

That's when I know it's clearly a dream, since Papa never wore ties, but I don't want to let go of my dream just yet, so I go on with the fiction, drifting in cloud-like suspension. Papa says, "Flea, this time, I'm the costar. You're the star. Are you ready to go?" I smile and nod, now calm as the flat sea after a storm.

A string quartet starts to play Pachelbel's "Canon" and I take a tentative step toward Nicky. He stands there by the makeshift altar, smiling just like the day I met him. My arm is linked in Papa's, and he steadies me. The sky is navy blue with streaks of pink, and soon it will be night. When I am halfway up the aisle, the music smoothly morphs into a modern ballad that has been in my head since I first heard it, playing on a loop. It is so beautiful and poignant that I can't let it go. It's called "All of Me," by young rhythm and blues singer John Legend. After its unexpected quick first two beats, the music evens, and the lyrics pop up and are so right. *You're my downfall, you're my muse; my worst distraction, my rhythm and blues. But you have all of me.* I wonder if they are for Nicky and me or for Papa and me.

I am carrying my hoof pick instead of flowers, and in this dream, it seems perfectly normal. I get closer and closer to Nicky as I float down the path. When I reach the trellis covered with roses and vines, Papa lets go of me, kisses my forehead, and steps back. Behind him, I can see the headstones, NEGRITA and BLACK. As if choreographed, Nicky and I turn and walk forward together. I say, "You see, I never forgot you. I am here now, forever." He nods, smiles, and takes my hand. Then the music gets softer, the picture fades, and I drift off into peaceful slumber.

Almost all of my men are gone now. Patrick, Aaron, and I are the only ones left who were there, who know. Soon, there will be no one, but the books will speak for him.

All of Papa's women are gone too. Duff died in 1938 of tuberculosis. Pauline died of a stomach infection back in 1952. Mother died in 1979 in Lakeland, Florida, of old age, at the age of eighty-seven. Jane Mason died in 1980 of complications from throat cancer, at the age of seventy. Adriana married, had two sons, and wrote an autobiography about her time with Papa called *The White Tower.* She ultimately committed suicide by hanging herself in 1983 at the age of fifty-three. Mary died in 1986 at the age of seventy-eight of old age problems. Marlene Dietrich died of renal failure in 1992 at the age of ninety. Martha Gellhorn committed suicide in London in 1998 due to ill health at the age of ninety.

Jack has passed on, too. Gig died in a women's prison—he lived his life as a woman for many years—but he left eight children. Patrick is well and lives out in Montana now. He is a stalwart supporter of Papa's memory. I don't see him as much as I'd like to, but we talk often. He is a true gentleman and I love him dearly.

I am on the board of the Hemingway Foundation in Oak Park, and work closely with the Hemingway collection at the JFK library to enhance the collection, as does Patrick. It is my passion. I travel to Boston on the train from Mystic once every month to attend meetings and make suggestions for as much authenticity as possible, but I am a small player on the Hemingway stage.

We were all in his shadow. Every one of us. It was just too big not to be. We kids were always yearning to be number one with him, to matter. He gave all of us nicknames that made clear we were smaller. It was not conscious; it was just him. Jack was Bumby, a baby name; Patrick was Mouse, a tiny presence by definition; Gregory was Gigi, a cute, almost girly name; and I was Flea—enough said there. He couldn't help it. It was his blessing and his torment to be that large, and it was ours, too.

Mouse became a great white hunter in part to not be a mouse; Gig became a woman perhaps in part so as not to compete with his father; Jack was often searching for his place to succeed; and I yearned for my father's love as I envisioned it should be. Even when he gave the best he had, I pined for a perfect love, never realizing that the imperfect is the most honest and true, just as he told me so long ago that the symmetrical loveliness of a pretty face never matched the power of the imperfect face with its captivating, one-of-a-kind beauty.

And it wasn't just us who were yearning. The theme of every one of Papa's books is yearning. Jake knew he could never have Brett; Frederic wanted a life with Catherine that was never to be; Robert Jordan hoped that he and Maria would escape the war and live happily forever, but it was never to happen; Elena pined for the return of Jonathan and the fulfillment of all her hopes; and the old man dreamed of his former glory and his big fish. Papa yearned for his youth and his powers of putting on paper what is beyond capture for most of us. He yearned for Pauline when he had Mother, for Martha when he had Pauline, for Mary when he had Martha, for Adriana when he had Mary, for Mother and Paris again at the end, but it was always just out of grasp. That yearning keeps all of us reaching.

When I am at my loneliest, I pick up one of Papa's books—usually it's *A Single Drop of Red Wine*—and open it to any page. I start reading the words I know so well, and it's like he's here with me because he is. I immediately feel less alone, hearing him in every page. I see him standing at his desk at the Finca, writing each word, leaning down to pet Black Dog, or wave to me, then editing to make it the best he could, to choose not just the right word, but the only word.

Patrick once gave Papa a story of his to edit. Patrick was surprised that Papa only modified one word.

Patrick was chagrinned, and his scowl showed it. "Papa, you only changed one word."

Papa said, "If it's the right word, Mouse, then that's a lot."

Those words that he wrote in his isolation, whether in Paris, or Key West, or Cuba, or Idaho, when the fame and the publicity receded into irrelevance, were what justified his existence. And contrary to the life lessons I thought Papa was teaching by his own example of inconstant connections with the loves in his life, I now know I missed his point. I know that true love *can* last a lifetime. I had it twice—three times, if you count Papa. Just because Nicky and Carter died, the love and memories didn't.

And yes, events can twist on you like a black mamba, but no matter what disaster shatters a life, man can never be destroyed. I forgot that he put all he had and all he believed into his words. I just had to read them to know what he believed at his core. Those are what will stand forever.

I miss him every day. I miss Nicky and Carter and Jack and Mother, but I miss him the most. For me, his failings melded with his kindnesses and his love of life. As Papa said in *For Whom the Bell Tolls*, no one thing is true; it is all true. He was flawed and fabulous, mean-spirited bully and most gracious of men, driven wordsmith and drunken raconteur, braggart and humble man, international icon and Midwestern boy, all of it. It was all true.

Archibald MacLeish once told me he'd only known two men in his life who could empty the air from a room simply by entering it—Franklin Delano Roosevelt and Ernest Hemingway. He added, "Hemingway simply could not stop people from talking about him."

Papa loved us, but his legacy was never us kids. For him, it was the words. Always the words.

Memory is the partner I dance with now. I hold her gently but firmly, afraid that if I loosen my hold, she will not return. I now know that love doesn't always end, and it doesn't usually end badly. It's the best, the worst, the highest and the lowest of all human experience, but love in any form is the only true antidote against loneliness. I recite my father's words every night as I rest alone in bed: *If there is one of us, there is both of us.* I know it is true, and I'm not afraid.

Finley R. Hemingway

Mystic, Connecticut 2016

Author's Note

Hemingway had three sons and always wanted a daughter. I hope he'd have loved Finn as much as she loved all of him: the good, the bad, and the ugly.

I have taken some liberties in this reimagining for the sake of the story. For example, *A Moveable Feast* was untitled when Hemingway died. It was published in 1964, posthumously, and Aaron Hotchner proposed the title at that time. And please do read the wonderful *Papa Hemingway* by A.E. Hotchner, the book that launched my interest and obsession with all things Hemingway.

The timeframes and events involving Hemingway in this novel are all as accurate as possible although conversations are of course my imaginings.

Heartfelt thanks for reading and having an interest in Hemingway and Finn more than sixty years after Hemingway's death.

www.ingramcontent.com/pod-product-compliance
Lightning Source LLC
Chambersburg PA
CBHW042043280426